TEACHERS' EXPERIENCES WITH THE TEACHING PROFICIENCY

THROUGH READING AND STORYTELLING (TPRS) METHOD

OF LANGUAGE INSTRUCTION: A QUALITATIVE STUDY

USING A QUASI-PHENOMENOLOGICAL APPROACH

A Dissertation

Presented to the Faculty of the

Division of Education and Human Services

of Neumann University

Aston, Pennsylvania

In Partial Fulfillment of

the Requirements for the Degree of

Doctor of Education

by

Richard J. Baker

July 2017

ProQuest Number: 10646025

All rights reserved

INFORMATION TO ALL USERS
The quality of this reproduction is dependent upon the quality of the copy submitted.

In the unlikely event that the author did not send a complete manuscript
and there are missing pages, these will be noted. Also, if material had to be removed,
a note will indicate the deletion.

ProQuest 10646025

Published by ProQuest LLC (2017). Copyright of the Dissertation is held by the Author.

All rights reserved.
This work is protected against unauthorized copying under Title 17, United States Code
Microform Edition © ProQuest LLC.

ProQuest LLC.
789 East Eisenhower Parkway
P.O. Box 1346
Ann Arbor, MI 48106 – 1346

NEUMANN UNIVERSITY
Division of Education and Human Services
Dissertation Signatory Page

Teachers' Experiences with the Teaching Proficiency Through Reading and Storytelling (TPRS) Method of Language Instruction: A Qualitative Study Using a Quasi-Phenomenological Approach

Richard Baker

The dissertation cited above is approved by the undersigned dissertation committee chairperson and members:

_____ 7/12/17
James A. Houck, Ph.D.   Date of Signature
Chair

_____ 7/12/17
Aideen Murphy, Ph.D.   Date of Signature
Committee Member

_____ 7/12/17
Karen Lichtman, Ph.D.   Date of Signature
Committee Member

_____ 7/12/17
Cynthia Speace, Ed.D.   Date of Signature
Program Director

Accepted by the Faculty of the Division of Education and Human Services of Neumann University in partial fulfillment of the requirements for the degree of Doctor of Education.

_____ 7/12/17
Barbara Mongelli Hanes, Ed.D. Date of Signature
Dean, Division of Education and Human Services

COPYRIGHT BY

Richard J. Baker

2017

All Rights Reserved

ABSTRACT

TEACHERS' EXPERIENCES WITH THE TEACHING PROFICIENCY THROUGH READING AND STORYTELLING (TPRS) METHOD OF LANGUAGE INSTRUCTION: A QUALITATIVE STUDY USING A QUASI-PHENOMENOLOGICAL APPROACH

Richard J. Baker

Dr. James A. Houck, Ph.D., Committee Chair

This quasi-phenomenological study identified the common lived classroom experiences of high school (grades 9-12) teachers who used the Teaching Proficiency through Reading and Storytelling (TPRS) method of world language instruction. The study also explained why some teachers who were trained in and had some experience using TPRS abandoned the method, and what they perceived as obstacles to its use. Additionally, the study identified the techniques perceived as effective by traditional teachers for promoting student success in producing and comprehending the target language with the goal of bridging the gap between TPRS and non-TPRS teachers.

The central phenomenon studied was teachers' lived experiences using TPRS, a method of world language teaching for providing a near-immersion classroom learning experience. The TPRS method required no textbook or grammar syllabus and focused on providing students with interesting, repetitive, and comprehensible input of commonly used verb structures and high-frequency vocabulary within the context of a story. For this study, a non-TPRS traditional approach included using a textbook, a grammatical syllabus, and production-based communicative classroom learning activities.

A purposeful sample of study participants included three groups of ten teachers each. The first two groups constituted the phenomenological part of the study because they had training and experience with TPRS. In the first group, ten participants used TPRS and considered themselves primarily as TPRS teachers. In a second group, ten teachers were selected because they were trained in TPRS and had some experience using the method but discontinued or limited its use when they encountered obstacles and resistance. A third group, not part of the phenomenological portion of the study, consisted of ten teachers who were not trained in TPRS, used a traditional approach, and had no experience using the method. That group provided a perspective outside of TPRS training and experience to discover which teaching techniques they perceived as effective. That input was included in the study to inform the researcher of potential improvements to recommend for the continuously developing TPRS method.

Data were collected through in depth, face-to-face, in-person, open-ended, semi-structured interviews. The results of the data analysis identified sixteen common lived experiences of TPRS teachers, twelve obstacles encountered by teachers when using or trying out TPRS, and four recommendations to consider incorporating into this changing and evolving method of world language instruction.

ACKNOWLEDGEMENTS

This paper is dedicated to the Baker family, especially Jeannette, Stan, Janice, Brian, Darryl, as well as my growing TPRS family and the Tri-State TCI/TPRS PLC.

The researcher acknowledges the helpful guidance from his dissertation committee, especially the Chair Dr. James Houck, methodologist and committee member Dr. Aideen Murphy, TPRS researcher and committee member Dr. Karen Lichtman, and the Ed.D. program director Dr. Cynthia Speace.

Special thanks go to several professors who were helpful and inspirational along the way, to include Drs. Lorraine Cavalier, Terry Waltz, James Capolupo, Kathleen Conn, Cheri Micheau, Cate Crosby, Ellen Skilton-Sylvester, Aneta Pavlenko, Rod Ellis, Bill VanPatten, Maria Traub, and especially Fr. Philip Lowe and Sr. Pat Hutchison.

I acknowledge the Neumann Cohort 6 members, especially Paul Hanson, Jamar Alston, Mary Chisholm, Kenneth Waters, Matthew Lammons, Maysoon Mohamad Park, and Kristin Borda, plus honorary members Devearl Royster and Frank McKnight.

The university support staff was very helpful during my studies at Neumann, especially Guillermo Gomez and Ginger Daddona. Many friends were supportive and encouraging during my doctoral studies, especially Leslee Kahler and Michelle Gemma.

Among my TPRS trainers were Blaine and Von Ray, Donna Tatum-Johns, Scott Benedict, Michelle Kindt, Susie Gross, Todd McKay, Karen Rowan, Bryce Hedstrom, Ben Slavic, Laurie Clarcq, Annie Ewing, Mike Coxon, Craig Sheehy, and Contee Seely.

A special, heart-felt, "thank you" goes to the many anonymous teachers who allowed me to interview them for this study, but whose names must remain confidential.

TABLE OF CONTENTS

SIGNATORY PAGE ii

COPYRIGHT PAGE iii

ABSTRACT iv

ACKNOWLEDGEMENTS vi

TABLE OF CONTENTS vii

CHAPTER I: INTRODUCTION 1

    What is TPRS? 1

    Introduction 3

    Background of the Study 5

    Problem Statement 9

    Purpose of the Study 11

    Research Questions 12

    Significance of the Study 12

    Rationale for Methodology 14

    Nature of the Research Design for the Study 16

    Definition of Terms 18

    Assumptions, Limitations, Delimitations 23

    Summary and Organization of the Study 25

CHAPTER II: LITERATURE REVIEW 27

    Introduction and Background to the Problem 27

    Theoretical Foundations and Conceptual Frameworks 28

    Review of the Literature 32

Beginnings of TPRS 32

Early Student Achievement Data 34

Development of Method and Skills 37

Empirical Research 53

    Comparing TPRS with Other Methods 56

    On TPRS Alone Without Comparison Groups 109

Teacher Experiences and Method Descriptions 133

Obstacles and Resistance to TPRS 163

ACTFL and Room for Growth in the TPRS Method 167

Changes and Evolution of the TPRS Method 180

Summary 180

CHAPTER III: METHODOLOGY 183

Introduction 183

Statement of the Problem 184

Research Questions 185

Research Methodology 185

Research Design 187

    Population and Sample Selection 188

    Study Participant Demographics and Selection Criteria 188

    Instrumentation 190

    Validity and Reliability 192

    Data Collection and Management 194

    Data Analysis Procedure 196

    Ethical Considerations 198

    Limitations and Delimitations 199

    Summary 200

CHAPTER IV: DATA ANALYSIS AND RESULTS 201

    Group A Interview Results 203

    Group B Interview Results 215

    Comparisons of Group A and B 223

    Group C Interview Results 230

    Summary and Organization of the Study 237

CHAPTER V: SUMMARY, CONCLUSIONS, AND RECOMMENDATIONS 239

    Discussion of the Findings 239

    Research Question 1 240

    Research Question 2 252

    Research Question 3 260

    Summary and Organization of the Study 267

    Implications for Practice 268

    Recommendations for Further Research 271

    Conclusions 272

REFERENCES 274

LIST OF TABLES 301

    Table 4.A.1. Common Lived TPRS Teacher Experiences, part 1 203

    Table 4.A.2. Common Lived TPRS Teacher Experiences, part 2 206

    Table 4.B.1. Obstacles, part 1 216

Table 4.B.2. Obstacles, part 2 217

Table 4.B.3. Obstacles, part 3 217

Table 4.B.4. Obstacles, part 4 218

Table 4.B.5. Obstacles, part 5 221

Table 4.AB.1. Comparing Groups A and B, part 1 224

Table 4.AB.2. Comparing Groups A and B, part 2 225

Table 4.AB.3. Comparing Groups A and B, part 3 225

LIST OF APPENDICES 302

Appendix A – Interview Questions for Group A 303

Appendix B – Interview Questions for Group B 304

Appendix C – Interview Questions for Group C 305

CHAPTER I

INTRODUCTION

What is TPRS?

In his introductory workshop handout, Blaine Ray, the inventor of Teaching Proficiency through Reading and Storytelling® (TPRS), explained that "TPRS® is a method of second-language teaching that uses highly-interactive stories to provide comprehensible input and create near immersion in the classroom" (Ray, 2016, p. 1). Drawing from Krashen's (1981, 1982, 2013, 2015) theoretical hypotheses of second language acquisition, Ray (2016) explained that the goal of TPRS was to develop fluency by focusing on the message content of story details, not language form, and that students could acquire the language subconsciously in a classroom. Ray (2016) listed three keys to fluency which were for the teacher to make the messages comprehensible, repetitive, and interesting to the students. TPRS differed from traditional textbook teaching by mixing verb tenses from the beginning and limiting the number of vocabulary words taught in a lesson, which Ray called sheltering vocabulary but not grammar. Ray (2016) explained that the TPRS practice of teaching fewer vocabulary words for retention (going deep) rather than briefly covering (going shallow) a larger number found in textbooks was informed by Davies' (2006) finding that the top high-frequency 1000 words make up 85% of the language used regularly in daily conversation and by Medina's (2014) finding that people usually forget 90% of what they learn in class within 30 days. Ray (2016) was interested in teaching for long-term retention and to develop language proficiency.

In the workshop, Ray (2016) gave a demonstration lesson using TPRS to teach a story in beginning-level German, a language most of the teachers who attended were completely unfamiliar with so they could remember what it was like to learn a new language, as a student, and to demonstrate some of the principles and practices of the TPRS method. These practices included going slowly enough for everyone to understand everything that was said by the teacher in the target language, as he employed techniques for making the input comprehensible, repetitive, interesting, and interactive. Ray (2016) personalized the lesson, made it engaging through humor and fun, and he asked many questions which the students (teachers-in-training) responded to as the trainer elicited story details from them so that the story created was co-constructed by both the teacher and students. Ray mixed the tenses, speaking both in past and present tenses from the beginning. While he spoke well over 90% of the time in German, he did use some English to establish the meaning of vocabulary words, clear up any confusion, and to check for comprehension. The teacher established a low-stress classroom environment.

Ray (2016) limited the number of vocabulary words and verb phrases used, but they were repeated often in context in non-boring ways by adding surprise details, new locations, additional characters, and by acting out some story scenes using student actors. The teacher-trainer checked for student comprehension of story details often, taught only one sentence at a time, and did not move on until all students who were trying to learn mastered that sentence. After the lesson, many of those in attendance were surprised that they could, in a five-minute timed writing, produce up to, or more than, one hundred words in complete sentences retelling the story using grammatically correct connected discourse in German, a language they had not known before the demonstration lesson. They were introduced to the TPRS method by experiencing success in the student's role. In the afternoon, they began learning and practicing a few of the myriad of TPRS teacher skills. The teachers in attendance taught each other in small groups, with coaching and encouragement from the trainer, and some experienced more languages new to them.

What would a typical TPRS class look like? To explain that, Ray (2016) reported a research study comparing a textbook teacher with a TPRS teacher. Watson (2009) found from her classroom observations that the textbook teacher did not ask the students many questions at all, but the TPRS teacher asked about four questions per minute. Ray (2016) explained that TPRS teachers typically ask four to eight questions per minute or about 400 questions per hour to provide for the repetition of targeted vocabulary and high-frequency (often used) verb structures, to assess comprehension, to engage student interest through personalization, and to co-construct the story with the students. Ray (2016) explained that TPRS drew from brain research findings. Among those were the brain's need for novel or interesting stimuli to gain people's attention, the importance of repetition and emotions to promote long-term memory, and the effectiveness of multisensory input, especially the visual component (Medina, 2014). This peek into a workshop and brief description of TPRS set the scene for the study and may have raised some questions about what teachers using or trying out the method might experience.

Introduction

This qualitative study using a quasi-phenomenological approach identified the common lived classroom experiences of high school (grades 9-12) teachers who used, or tried out, the TPRS method of world language instruction. The study also explained why some teachers who were trained in and had some experience using TPRS abandoned the method by identifying what they perceived as obstacles to its use. In addition, the study identified the techniques, approaches, goals, activities, applications, goals, and strategies perceived as effective by traditional teachers with no experience or training in the TPRS method for promoting student success in producing and comprehending the target language so that recommendations for improving the method might be identified. By including one group of study participants from outside the TPRS community, the researcher attempted to identify potential growth areas for the TPRS method and for its practitioners. However, the primary goals were to identify what teachers experienced when using TPRS and what obstacles to its use that they may have encountered.

The central phenomenon studied was teachers' lived experiences using TPRS, a method of world language teaching for providing a near immersion classroom learning experience. The TPRS method required no textbook or grammar syllabus and focused on providing students with comprehensible, repetitive, and interesting oral and written input of commonly used verb structures and high-frequency vocabulary within the context of a story or interpersonal communicative exchange in the classroom. For this study, a non-TPRS traditional approach included using a textbook, a grammatical syllabus, and production-based communicative classroom learning activities.

A purposeful sample included three groups of ten teachers each. The first two groups constituted the phenomenological part of the study. In the first group, ten participants used TPRS and considered themselves primarily as TPRS teachers. In a second group, ten teachers were selected because they were trained in TPRS and had some experience using the method but discontinued or limited its use when they encountered obstacles and resistance. A third group, not part of the phenomenological portion of the study, consisted of ten teachers who were not trained in TPRS, used a traditional approach, and had no experience using the method. That group provided a perspective outside of TPRS training and experience on which teaching techniques they perceived as effective. That input was included in the study to inform the researcher of potential improvements to recommend for the continuously developing TPRS method.

Background of the Study

Several authors agreed that it was generally more effective to have students use the target language as a tool for classroom communication (Lightbown & Spada, 2013; Met, 1991, 2004; Mitchell, Myles, & Marsden, 2013; Omaggio-Hadley, 2000; Rojas, 2001), while thinking critically about other topics (Lantolf, 2007, 2009), rather than study about the language by analyzing its linguistic features (Ellis, 2009, 2012; Krashen, 1993, 2015). Using the language to learn it has resulted in greater gains than merely talking about how the language works (Ellis, 2008, 2012; Garczynski, 2003; Krashen, 2004; Varguez, 2009; Watson, 2009).

World language programs have not proven to be highly successful in this country, and most students generally have not reached high levels of proficiency. Robinson, Shore, and Enerson (2007) estimated that only 3% of students who studied a foreign language in schools, K-12, were found to achieve at least an Intermediate Low level of proficiency on the American Council on the Teaching of Foreign Languages (ACTFL, 2012) scale, with most secondary school students remaining at the Novice level. Asher (2011) reported that only 4% succeed in learning a second language in the public schools of the United States, while 90% of students who took a foreign language dropped out after three years or less. Schulz (1999) previously had reported that less than 4% taught foreign languages in classrooms reached even minimal levels of fluency. Gross (2012) pointed out that these low percentages of student success in their language classrooms may have reflected the shortcomings and ineffectiveness of the pedagogical methods that were used nationwide in this country. Pufahl and Rhodes (2011) found it difficult to find exact, valid, and reliable numbers on the proficiency levels that students in American schools nationwide have attained through classroom study, partly because of the wide range of assessment measures. They did discover that teachers' reported use of the target language fell substantially below the 90% goal set by ACTFL (2012). If students did not hear the foreign language being spoken with plentiful amounts of comprehensible input, it would have been difficult for them to acquire it in a classroom.

Pufahl and Rhodes' (2011) survey research revealed several other problems with language teaching and they concluded that "overall foreign language instruction has decreased over the past decade and the achievement gap has widened" (p. 258) nationwide, meaning that "schools with a lower SES [socio-economic status] were less likely to offer languages" (p. 262) than more affluent schools. That finding reflected "unequal access to foreign language instruction" (p.272). Pufahl and Rhodes (2011) called the quality of that instruction into question as well, writing that immersion was the "only model that consistently provides instruction that allows students to attain a high level of proficiency [and] was offered by only 6% of public schools with language programs" (p. 274). While those researchers did not include TPRS, a near immersion method, in their survey, Pufahl and Rhodes did recommend that schools provide more options in program offerings, to include content-based language teaching "In which selected academic subjects are taught in the foreign language" (p. 274). Cartford, Kittock, and Lichtman (2015) found positive results in improving writing fluency through content-based storytelling, a type of content-based instruction that emphasized the comprehension of meaningful messages in the target language.

Other research has reported that using the target language to communicate meaningful messages in class resulted in greater gains in speaking and writing than did explicit grammar study alone (e.g., Dziedzic, 2012; Ellis, 2012; Lightbown & Spada, 2013). That knowledge and experience supported the Communicative Language Teaching (CLT) movement that has dominated the thinking in the field of foreign and second language instruction in recent years (Ellis, 2008, 2012; Lightbown & Spada, 2013; Omaggio-Hadley, 2000). Among others, Foster (2011) argued that a place remained for explicit grammar instruction, but within the context of today's communicative, proficiency-based, and interactive classrooms.

Some researchers (e.g., Kaufmann, 2005; Oliver, 2013) argued that TPRS was among the most effective methods for promoting communicative competence and language acquisition in classrooms. Research studies were conducted that provided empirical evidence that the TPRS method was more effective for developing fluency in the secondary school classroom (Spangler, 2009; Varguez, 2009; Watson, 2009). In addition to promoting fluency, Beyer (2008) found that students acquired an accurate use of the past tense, an indication of grammatical accuracy, through TPRS. Braunstein (2006) found positive attitudes for the method among adult students. The TPRS method was described in Ray and Seely's (2015) book on TPRS, *Fluency Through TPR Storytelling: Achieving Real Language Acquisition in School*, yet some researchers have misunderstood and employed the construct inaccurately in their research studies, making their conclusions suspect. For example, Perna (2007) indicated that TPRS was similar to the grammar-based translation method, claiming that TPRS separated out vocabulary and grammar teaching from the context of stories. However, the TPRS method did not incorporate that approach. Rather, vocabulary and grammar were integrated into the story lessons (Ray, 2013; Ray & Seely, 2015).

While some researchers may have not understood, or misrepresented the method, other researchers and teachers simply have not kept up with the 'changes' that have been made to TPRS over time, as reflected in Ray (2013). Instead, those researchers have curiously cited earlier snapshots of the developing method rather than the most-current version at the time of their studies. For example, when Alley and Overfield (2008) analyzed, critiqued, and compared TPRS with other methods, they cited an early second edition of Ray and Seely's (1998) book, *Fluency through TPR Storytelling*, even though three editions had since been published, to include a third edition in 2002, a fourth in 2004, and the fifth edition in 2008. As another example, the TPRS method used to incorporate more actions and gestures that Asher (2009) had found to be effective in promoting long-term memory, but Blaine Ray, Von Ray, and Donna Tatum-Johns had stopped including much TPR in their workshops in 2011. After that, there was much less pre-teaching of vocabulary than before; instead they began to establish meaning of new vocabulary during the oral storytelling (Ray, 2013). Since some teachers continued to use TPR, while others did not, and since the method was constantly evolving, it became increasingly important for each researcher to describe which variation of TPRS was being employed in each individual research study.

On the other hand, what did not change was that the TPRS method always placed primary focus on providing the comprehensible input (CI) advocated by language-learning theorist Krashen (1985, 2015) because CI always has been considered the one most essential element required for acquisition to take place. Krashen (1985) stressed that people acquired languages in only one way: by understanding messages in them. To clarify, only messages received and comprehended in the target language were thought to trigger acquisition, not those given in the first language. For Krashen (1981, 1985, 2002, 2013), acquiring, or picking up the new language naturally, through communicative interaction focused on meaning, rather than on grammatical form, was considered different from merely learning facts about the language. The TPRS method accepted those theoretical foundations (Ray & Seely, 1997, 2015) and has also incorporated the educational applications informed by brain research (Asher, 2012; Medina, 2014; Sousa, 2017; Tate, 2016; Zadina, 2014) that emphasized how the brain was drawn to interesting, or even compelling, details that Ray (2013) and others added into their TPRS stories. Oliver (2013), who reviewed several decades of changing methods and paradigms in language teaching pedagogy, stressed that being able to communicate in world languages today was now more important than ever before. From her own teaching experience, after trying out more than seven methods over time looking for the most effective one, Oliver (2013) concluded that TPRS was the best method for promoting speaking proficiency.

Problem Statement

A growing body of research documented the effectiveness of the TPRS method in a variety of classroom contexts (Beyer, 2008; Braunstein, 2006; Bustamante, 2009; Castro, 2010; Davidheiser, 2001, 2002; Dziedzic, 2012; Garczynski, 2003; Jennings, 2009; Kaufmann, 2005; Miller, 2011; Oliver, 2012, 2013; Roberts & Thomas, 2014,

2015; Spangler, 2009; Varguez, 2009; Watson, 2009; Wenck, 2010). Those studies, among other benefits, showed that students taught using the TPRS method did learn to speak and write in the target language. After training in a language that they did not know at a TPRS workshop, many teachers have learned from first-hand experience that the method could work (Ray & Seely, 2012, 2015). Despite knowing that the method could be effective, many teachers newly trained in TPRS were either reluctant to use the method, or have abandoned its use in their classrooms. Despite the research that documented the effectiveness of the method, some TPRS teachers have encountered resistance to using it from students, non-TPRS instructor colleagues, parents, and administrators (Black, 2012; Espinoza, 2015; Oliver, 2013; Neubauer, 2015; Taulbee, 2008; Whaley, 2009).

A possible contributing reason for that resistance could have been the way information on the relatively new TPRS method was disseminated. The method was developed by a high school classroom Spanish teacher, not a research professor, so many language professionals and administrators may have been --and may remain-- unaware of TPRS or the research on its effectiveness. Another reason teachers may have faced resistance was that there have been different variations of TPRS, as noted by Ray and Seely (1998), with teachers putting their individual marks on the method, and TPRS continued to change and evolve (Ray, 2013). Much of the growing body of research conducted on TPRS has been conducted by language teachers writing theses or dissertations (Lichtman, 2014, 2015) while working on graduate degrees, rather than by the academic writing of seasoned second language acquisition researchers. Since Ray and Seely's (1997) seminal book on TPRS was published by its authors, knowledge of the existence and development of the TPRS method has spread primarily through books and workshops that were written, conducted, and led by classroom teachers. TPRS has been more of a grassroots teachers' movement rather than a top-down initiative endorsed by state departments of education, professional associations, or administrator initiatives.

There has been little quasi-phenomenological research that identified, described, or interpreted the common lived experiences of teachers using TPRS method. Therefore, some educators had little knowledge of how the problems, challenges, obstacles, and resistance that they experienced were addressed, coped with, dealt with, or handled by other TPRS teachers. This study was designed to fill that gap in the research.

Purpose of the Study

The purpose of this qualitative study using a quasi-phenomenological approach was to describe the common classroom experiences lived by TPRS teachers, to identify the obstacles to the method's use, and to discover possibilities for improving the method. That information helped the researcher uncover the essence of teachers' experiences using TPRS and provide data for the subsequent interpretations of those experiences. Exploring those common lived experiences provided insight into the phenomenon of using TPRS. The study focused on discovering why some teachers used TPRS, why others did not, and made recommendations for possible additions to the method.

One group of study participants included teachers who used the TPRS method predominantly in their teaching and considered themselves TPRS teachers. A second group was trained in the method, but decided either not to use TPRS or limit its use in their classrooms. Uncovering their reasons for that choice and what they perceived as obstacles to using the method had potential for gaining a deeper understanding not only about the method, but what their experiences were in fitting the TPRS method into their own educational contexts. In addition to TPRS users and rejecters, a third group was interviewed who had no experience or training in the method to provide, not so much a baseline, but rather an outsider perspective of what good world language instruction {control group} included as they experienced it in their classrooms. The outsider perspective contributed to the study because since the TPRS method has continually evolved over time, and has been open to new developments in the past, recommendations were made on which effective techniques or other potential growth areas might be incorporated into the method to improve it.

Research Questions

The following research questions guided this qualitative dissertation study.

1. What were high school teachers' common lived experiences using the Teaching Proficiency through Reading and Storytelling (TPRS) method to teach modern world languages?
2. What did high school teachers trained in TPRS, who decided not to use the TPRS method in their language classrooms, perceive as obstacles to its use?
3. What techniques did high school language teachers using a traditional approach perceive as effective for promoting student success in learning to comprehend and speak the language being taught?

Significance of the Study

This study was (and is) significant because it filled a gap. There was little or no research that identified, described, or interpreted the common classroom experiences lived by language teachers who used the TPRS method. Little research existed that identified the obstacles to using the method or how those obstacles were coped with by some teachers. A growing body of research was beginning to provide evidence of the method's overall effectiveness through different types of research, but not much was done to study teacher experiences using TPRS. Knowledge gained through their experience was significant in the potential for informing decisions about world language instruction.

The growing body of research on TPRS appeared in various types of studies that appeared as articles in peer-reviewed journals. There were empirical studies which compared the effects of TPRS teaching with other methods; studies on TPRS alone which focused on the method's effects without making comparisons with a control group; and descriptive articles published in journals that described its use in a variety of different school contexts, as well as analyses of the method (Lichtman, 2012a, 2015). There were books and book chapters about the method, doctoral dissertations, master's degree theses, and action research projects that explored TPRS. Studies appeared where the TPRS method was used in elementary, secondary, university, and adult level programs. However, in those studies there was limited attention given to understanding teacher's common experiences with the phenomenon of using TPRS or they obstacles they faced.

This study filled a gap. In no previous study were ten interviews conducted to identify the common lived experiences of TPRS users. No previous study had collected interview data from ten TPRS rejecters to identify what they perceived the obstacles were to using TPRS. No other study elicited input from both insiders and outsiders to TPRS to determine whether effective techniques were missing or should be added to the method.

This study was significant because it discovered, identified, and described what TPRS teachers experienced, the obstacles and resistance they faced, and how they coped with those challenges. By filling that gap in the research, this study extended that new knowledge into the field of world language teaching and informed decision making.

Rationale for Methodology

Since the primary purpose of the study was to discover, uncover, identify, and describe the common lived experiences of teachers who used the TPRS method of instruction, a research methodology designed to elicit and analyze interview data was appropriate. Merriam (2009), Moustakas (1994), and van Manen (1990) all discussed phenomenological studies as an appropriate way to analyze that type of experiential data. By directly asking teachers to reflect upon their own experiences of using TPRS and how they felt about those experiences, their perceptions became identifiable from the data.

A quasi-phenomenological approach was used to explore the essence of the phenomenon of using TPRS, an experience shared by multiple language teachers to understand what it was like to use TPRS. Using TPRS was the central phenomenon being studied. In the phenomenological portion of the study, two groups of teacher participants who had both training and experience using the TPRS method were interviewed to identify the common lived experiences of TPRS teachers and what teachers who used or tried out the method but abandoned it perceived as the obstacles to using TPRS.

A third group was interviewed who had no training or experience with using TPRS to obtain a perspective outside of TPRS of what traditional non-TPRS teachers perceived to be effective techniques, activities, strategies, and practices for promoting student success in comprehending and producing the target language. Adding the perspective of that third group was useful for this particular study because that third group of participants provided information that the researcher could use for making recommendations with the potential of improving the TPRS method. However, by adding that third group with no experience using TPRS, the study was no longer a pure phenomenological study, but rather a qualitative study using a quasi-phenomenological approach.

The semi-structured interviews used for this study (see Appendices A, B, C) provided structure and consistency in the design, but asking probing questions helped uncover the interpretations that the study's teacher participants placed on their experiences. Hycner (1985) provided not only step-by-step guidance for collecting interview data and analyzing it using a phenomenological approach, but he also discussed the conceptual framework behind that approach which was useful in designing this study.

Corbin and Strauss (2015) discussed conducting research studies for the purpose of developing theories, which were grounded in the data from particular studies. A question was raised as to whether a grounded theory approach might have been more appropriate than a phenomenological or quasi-phenomenological approach for this study. A grounded theory approach was considered but rejected because from the outset of the study and for its duration there was never an intention or purpose of developing a theory.

Instead, among the initial goals of this research study were to explore the lived experiences of people using TPRS to teach world language classes and to discover what experiences teachers using the method shared. Those included what they perceived the obstacles to its use were as they had experienced them. Among the questions this researcher was asking throughout the study were: What was the experience of using TPRS like for them? What were the common experiences lived by those who used the method? What were the obstacles to its use as perceived by those who had experienced the phenomenon of using TPRS? A question added later was: How might the method be improved? The driving motivation for this researcher in conducting the study was to describe what experiences the participants shared when they used TPRS.

Nature of the Research Design for the Study

A qualitative quasi-phenomenological design was appropriate and most effective for this study because it provided the informational data necessary to answer this study's three research questions listed above. They involved identifying and describing the common lived experiences of TPRS teachers and the perceptions of teachers who had experience using TPRS, discussing obstacles to its use they perceived and encountered, and identifying effective techniques with the potential of improving the method. The decision on choice of design was informed by Vogt, Gardner, and Haeffele's (2012) descriptions on when to use specific research designs, Richards' (2011) discussion on how to handle qualitative data, and Richards and Morse's (2013) guidance on selecting a methodological design. However, Hycner's (1985) article on collecting and conducting a phenomenological analysis of interview data directly addressed each of this researcher's concerns for the first two research questions.

Both Hycner's (1985) concerns and those of this researcher included the need to bracket out, or separate, the researcher's experience with the phenomenon of using TPRS so that the participants' experiences were obtained. The data were analyzed in a rigorous, consistent, and systematic fashion, which included identifying units of general meaning, and then reducing those to units of meaning relevant to answering the research questions. Steps were taken to address issues of the credibility, trustworthiness, and dependability of the data and the confidence of the data analysis, using member checking and peer review. Hycner (1985) pointed out the differences in participant selection between qualitative and quantitative research designs, plus the limits on generalizing the results, the absence of control groups, random selection practices, hypothesis testing, and prediction in his approach to phenomenological research. Based on reading the above sources and Merriam (2009), a quantitative approach was rejected and a qualitative study was designed.

Hycner (1985) explained that interpretations should be delayed, or even eliminated, to ensure that each informant's experiences were fully described, with as little bias as possible. Hycner (1985) stressed the "fact that the phenomenological researcher's primary thrust is to understand, and as much as possible not to interpret according to some already developed theory" (p. 300). To address those concerns, in this study, face to face, in-person, semi-structured interviews (see Appendices A, B, C) enabled the researcher to discover and describe the teachers' common experiences from rich, deep, personal accounts of the phenomenon of using TPRS and to identify TPRS obstacles.

After interviewing the third group of participants and identifying their perceptions of what techniques, strategies, approaches, and activities were effective, the researcher organized each into three categories of questions. They included: Was the technique already part of the method? Did the technique fall within, or outside of, the principles of the TPRS paradigm? Techniques outside the paradigm and those already part of the method were rejected. All others would be considered for possible method integration.

Definition of Terms

There were three primary sources of meaning for the terms used in this study. One source was the professional literature, another reflected the researcher's views, but the most important source was the meanings that study participants attached to the terms, which sometimes varied according to their differing perceptions or situated educational contexts. The rationale behind this approach reflected Hycner's (1985) insistence that the researcher "stay quite true to the literal statements and meanings given by the participant" (p. 301). Therefore, for this dissertation, the following definitions defined the terms.

Acquisition: a natural, subconscious, process of "picking up elements of a language so that they remain in long-term memory and are easily understood when heard and are readily produced by a speaker" (Ray & Seely, 2012, p. 283). "Acquisition is the result of understanding messages" (Krashen, 2015, p. 168) and comprehensible input.

ACTFL: The American Council on the Teaching of Foreign Languages (ACTFL) is an "organization of more than 12,500 language educators and administrators from elementary through graduate education" and its mission statement is "providing vision, leadership and support for quality teaching and learning of languages" (www.actfl.org). ACTFL (1999, 2012) published the proficiency guidelines and the national standards.

Authentic Text: anything written for a native speaker by a native speaker.

Circling: "asking several questions about a statement and then completing the circle by repeating the original statement" (Ray & Seely, 2015, p. 338).

Cold Character Reading (CCR): "a technique in which students begin to read texts directly without prior instruction in Chinese characters" (Waltz, 2015, p. 174).

Communication: the expression, interpretation, and purposeful negotiation of meaning in any given context, to include classrooms (Savignon, 1998; VanPatten, 2017).

Comprehensible Input (CI): "Language in the target language which students hear or read that is understandable to them" (Ray & Seely, 2015, p. 339).

Comprehension Check: "A quick assessment of whether one or more students comprehend certain material" (Ray & Seely, 2015, p. 339).

Comprehension Hypothesis: a theory that "language acquisition is the result of understanding messages, or receiving comprehensible input" (Krashen, 2015, p. 168).

Concepts: described events or experiences. Researchers defined and presented them within conceptual frameworks to inform, situate, or explain various studies.

Content-Based Storytelling (CBS): a curricular approach to learn academic content, such as literature, culture, or history, while simultaneously acquiring a target language which is "centered on stories" (Cartford, Kittock, & Lichtman, 2015, p. 3).

Context: "the setting and the participants" (VanPatten, 2015, p. 15) of an event.

Customization: "talking about information or topics that interest your students" (Waltz, 2015, p. 174) which may refer to truth or fictional details.

Directional Gestures: "gestures that express both the Chinese tones of each syllable and the meaning of the word as a whole" (Waltz, 2015, p. 174).

Embedded Reading: "A series of versions of the same reading in which each succeeding version is more detailed than the previous" (Ray & Seely, 2015, p. 339), invented by Laurie Clarcq (2015) and co-developed with Michele Whaley.

Flow: A metaphor used by the phenomenologist Csikszentmihalyi (1997) and by other people to describe "the sense of effortless action they feel in moments that stand out as the best in their lives. Athletes refer to it as being in the zone" (p. 29). Krashen (2015) wrote that "optimal language acquisition puts the language acquirer in a state of flow, a state of mind in which only the activity exists" (p. 169). Some TPRS teachers have said they were 'in the flow' when enjoying a 'home run' lesson when everything went well.

Input: "language that one hears (or sees) that is part of communication, that we attend to for its propositional content and intent" (VanPatten, 2015, p. 391).

Intake: oral or written messages received in the target language that have been processed, comprehended, internalized, and acquired (VanPatten, 2017).

Language: Beyond the common use of the word to refer to languages such as Spanish and English, in second language research, "Language is an abstract, implicit, and complex mental representation" (VanPatten, 2017, p. 19).

Leadership: For this researcher, leadership meant both *influencing by example* and *helping others*, to include students, other teachers, supervisors, administrators, and other stakeholders in world language instruction. Additionally, some of this study's participants used the term 'leadership' to refer to their appointed leaders, department chairs, supervisors, evaluators, and administrators. However, although some people may occupy positions of leadership and subordinates may be required to follow the directives of those individuals who are senior to them, for Maxwell (2013), "Leadership is a process, not a position" (p. 4). For J. Oswald Sanders (2007), "Leadership is influence, the ability of one person to influence others to follow his or her lead" (p. 29).

Legacy Method: "older [traditional] methods of language teaching that do not focus on comprehensible input. Most rely on skill-building" (Waltz, 2015, p. 175).

Learning: For Krashen (2003), 'learning' referred to talking 'about' the language and studying the language's descriptive rules of grammar, contrasting it with acquisition.

Obstacles: resistance, problems, issues, controversies, obstructions, blocks, impediments, snags, hindrances, hurdles, barriers, drawbacks, roadblocks, pushback, disadvantages, difficulties, and challenges encountered when using the TPRS method.

Output: language production, speaking and writing. Swain (2005a) argued that both comprehensible input and 'comprehensible output' have roles in acquisition.

Paradigm: philosophy or belief system about how languages should be taught. A paradigm shift, for this study, referred to changes in thinking that informed practices.

Personalization: making the lessons interesting to students, often by asking students questions about themselves for Personalized Questions and Answers (PQA).

Pop-up Grammar (or pop-up culture): a brief, incidental, less than 15-second comment, drawing student attention to a point of interest while communicating.

Professional Learning Community (PLC): a group of educators who meet in person or online to work together, plan, train, encourage each other, and share materials and experiences. PLCs generally have been formed in individual school districts, but in the TPRS Community the members often came from other schools, states, or countries.

Resistance: Resistance implied that someone intentionally blocked or discouraged another from doing something. In this study, resistance from people who were opposed to the TPRS method also was considered an 'obstacle' to its use (see *Obstacles* above) by some of the participants. In another sense, "self-resistance" referred to this researcher's view that a teacher new to TPRS, before buying in, struggled internally with making a paradigm shift away from theories informing legacy teaching methods toward Krashen's (2015) Comprehension Hypothesis, the paradigm which informs TPRS teaching.

Scaffolding: providing extra support to students to accomplish learning tasks and withdrawing those scaffolds once no longer needed because mastery has been achieved.

Target Language: the language a student is aiming to learn or acquire.

Techniques: activities, approaches, methods, strategies, experiments, computer models, applications, tasks, goals, presentations, and counseling done in the classroom.

Timed Writings: Usually given a time limit of 5 or 10 minutes, students write quickly as many words as they can in connected discourse without regard to form, also called freewrites or speedwrites. They are considered a measure of writing fluency.

TOP: "Tonally Orthographic Pinyin, a system of Romanization based on standard Hanyu Pinyin with enhancements to tone marking" (Waltz, 2015, p. 176) for Chinese.

TPR: or Total Physical Response (Asher, 1966, 1969, 1977, 2009, 2012), a strategy or technique based on student physical responses to teacher commands to indicate the comprehension of vocabulary words and promote long-term retention.

TPRS: Teaching Proficiency through Reading and Storytelling, also called Total Physical Response (TPR) Storytelling (Ray & Seely, 2015). This method included interpersonal interaction, personalization, customization, and story co-construction, among other teaching skills for providing interesting, repetitive, comprehensible input. There have been several variations of the method (Ray & Seely, 1998, 2015). "TPRS® is a method of second-language teaching that uses highly-interactive stories to provide comprehensible input and create near immersion in the classroom" (Ray, 2016, p. 1).

TPRS Theory: Krashen (2015) first referred to the theory informing the TPRS method consistent with his Comprehension Hypothesis as "TPRS theory" (p. 168). Krashen contrasted this theoretical orientation with the Skill-Building Hypothesis.

Zone (in the zone): see *Flow* above.

Assumptions, Limitations, Delimitations

Limitations. The study's findings may not have been generalizable beyond the purposeful sample of participants. The common and differing experiences of teachers may have varied, depending on differences in local school contexts. The data obtained from the experienced TPRS teachers participating in the study may not have been representative of all TPRS teachers. Variability in teacher experiences may have been context-dependent. Experiences were not studied as they were lived, but rather as recollections, providing interview data which qualitative studies have accepted as being trustworthy, dependable, and credible (Brinkman & Kvale, 2015; Hycner, 1985; Richards, 2011; Richards & Morse, 2013; Vogt, Gardner, & Haeffele, 2012).

Delimitations. Even though the triangulation of multiple data sources is not normally a characteristic of phenomenological studies (Creswell, 2013), not having them delimited the study. The researcher's developing skill in interviewing delimited the study. However, this delimitation was addressed by the researcher by studying the strategies and techniques of conducting effective qualitative and phenomenological interviews (Brinkmann & Kvale, 2015; Merriam, 2009; Richards, 2011).

The research design procedures for this study elicited information from teachers with at least three years of experience which delimited the study in terms of experience. Gathering data on experiences and perceptions through interviews, not using other types of data, and performing a quasi-phenomenological data analysis, meant the results only allowed for minimal quantitative measures, such as frequency counts, a further study delimitation. Extensive demographic information on participants was not collected. Quota sampling was not used, but rather purposeful sampling which relied upon the researcher's judgment for sample selection which may have delimited transferability.

The 30 study participants were high school world language teachers who taught five different languages, which included Spanish, French, German, Mandarin Chinese, and English. Twenty-three teachers worked in public and seven in private schools. Study participants taught in 12 states, including Pennsylvania, Delaware, New Jersey, Illinois, Utah, Indiana, Missouri, Idaho, Wyoming, Colorado, California, and Arizona. There were 18 women and 12 men with an average age of 39, ranging from 25-58 years old. Their average years of teaching experience was 14, ranging from three to 36. The TPRS teachers in the study had an average of eight years using the method, ranging from two to 19 TPRS years of experience. These demographics may have delimited the study.

Assumptions. Phenomenological research and this qualitative study using a quasi-phenomenological approach assumed the recalled experiences of selected participants produced credible, dependable, and trustworthy information, that interviewees told the truth, and that common lived experiences revealed useful informational data (Creswell, 2013; Dukes, 1984; Hycner, 1985). It was assumed that the data obtained from face to face, in-person, open-ended, semi-structured interviews was credible and enhanced by member checking (Creswell, 2013; Hycner, 1985; Moustakas, 1994). Through member checking, or "respondent validation" (Merriam, 2009, p. 217), the data were made more trustworthy and dependable, reducing the possibility of researcher bias in identifying, describing, and interpreting each participant's experiences.

Another assumption of this study was that through the primary data collection method of conducting personal interviews, and using a quasi-phenomenological analysis of interview data, that the researcher could answer the research questions accurately, confidently, and findings would be credible (Merriam, 2009; Richards & Morse, 2013).

Summary and Organization of the Study

The introduction described the background for the study in terms of the historical disappointment of student proficiency levels attained, with only 3-4% of students taught in this country successfully learned the target language (Asher, 2011; Robinson, Shore, & Enerson, 2007). With 90% of the students who took foreign language classes nationwide dropping out after three years or less (Asher, 2011), the effectiveness of past methods used to teach languages was called into question (Gross, 2012).

Within that context of disappointing previous results, according to Oliver (2013), Communicative Language Teaching (CLT) approaches and the TPRS method have come increasingly into favor. The TPRS method was theoretically compatible with second language acquisition theory (Krashen, 1982, 1985, 2015) and with brain research for promoting long-term memory (Medina, 2014; Sousa, 2017; Tate, 2016; Zadina, 2014).

While some research has demonstrated that TPRS was found effective in a variety of classrooms (e.g., Beyer, 2008; Braunstein, 2006; Bustamante, 2009, Davidheiser, 2001; Dziedzic, 2012; Garczynski, 2003; Oliver, 2012; Spangler, 2009; Varguez, 2009; Watson, 2009), few phenomenological or quasi-phenomenological studies of this design have been conducted to identify and describe the common classroom experiences lived by TPRS instructors or to identify the obstacles to using the method. Therefore, that knowledge was not available to help educators better understand the phenomenon of using TPRS or to inform their decisions regarding world language instruction.

Chapter I provided the background, purpose, and significance of this study, and defined the key terms. The three research questions that guided the study were listed, the limitations and delimitations were identified, and the assumptions underlying the study's design were clarified. In Chapter II, the professional literature and research studies on TPRS are reviewed to situate the study and to provide the rationale that this study was needed to fill a gap in that literature to inform decisions on language instruction. Chapter III explains the research methodology, design, and procedures for carrying out the study. Chapter IV presents the data analysis and results of the study. Chapter V summarizes the study, discusses implications for practice, makes recommendations for further research, and draws conclusions.

CHAPTER II

LITERATURE REVIEW

Introduction to the Chapter and Background to the Problem

Chapter II of this dissertation was organized by introducing the chapter and providing background to the problem. The theoretical foundations of the study were explained, followed by identifying the early beginnings of TPRS, along with early student achievement data. The literature review included books and book chapters, published journal articles, dissertations and theses, and ended with a chapter summary. The following paragraph addressed the background to the problem.

It has been estimated that only three percent of students who studied a foreign language in American schools reached an Intermediate Low level of proficiency on the American Council on the Teaching of Foreign Languages' (ACTFL, 2012) language proficiency scale (Robinson, Shore, and Enerson, 2007). Another researcher estimated that only 4% of students were successful language learners in school and that 90% dropped out of foreign language courses after three years or less (Asher, 2011). The research consultants from the Center for Applied Linguistics in the nation's capital surveyed 5,000 elementary and secondary schools in the United States and concluded that "overall foreign language instruction has decreased over the past decade and the achievement gap has widened" (Pufahl & Rhodes, 2011). On that survey, teachers self-reported that using the target language over 75% of class time increased from 22% to 36% between 1997 and 2008. However, the ACTFL (2012) guidelines established a 90% target language use goal in class, for both students and teachers (Crouse, 2013). Those numbers called into question the type and quality of instruction that students had been receiving. However, Lichtman (2012a, 2015, 2016) found evidence that at least one method, called TPRS, was effective in several different contexts. However, there were no studies which identified the common lived experiences of TPRS teachers, what the obstacles to using TPRS were, or which effective techniques were missing from the TPRS method. This study was designed to fill that gap by interviewing teachers who could address those concerns.

The literature review included a variety of sources, to include books, journal articles, dissertations, and theses. Search terms for the studies included Teaching Proficiency through Reading and Storytelling, TPRS, TPR Storytelling, and Total Physical Response Storytelling. Among the electronic sources used to search for studies on TPRS were Google, Google Scholar, Linguistics and Language Behavior Abstracts (LLBA), the *International Journal of Foreign Language Teaching* (IJFLT), the references listed by Lichtman (2012a, 2015, 2016), online listings of TPRS research at http://forlangs.niu.edu/~klichtman/tprs.html and at http://tprsplatform.nl/wetenschappelij-onderzoek, ERIC documents, and the ProQuest Dissertations and Theses database. Some studies and books were obtained through interlibrary loan or other sources.

Theoretical Foundations and Conceptual Frameworks

The theoretical foundations and conceptual frameworks for this study were built upon five cornerstones. The TPRS world language teaching method was described in Ray and Seely (1997, 2015) and mentioned its connections to theory. The primary theory of language acquisition informing the method was Krashen's (1981, 1982, 1985, 2015) Comprehension Hypothesis. The Comprehension Hypothesis posited the idea that a language could only be acquired in one way, by understanding messages, or receiving comprehensible input, in the target language. Comprehensible input triggered acquisition, but learning did not. Krashen (1981, 1982, 1985) had previously explained his distinction between learning and acquisition. Acquisition was how languages were 'picked up' naturally and effortlessly by human beings. It occurred at a subconscious level and the language acquirer was generally unaware of the process. Comprehended messages triggered what Chomsky (1965) had called the Language Acquisition Device (LAD) in the brain where the internalization process occurred. On the other hand, learning 'about' a language required conscious effort and explicit instruction.

In addition to the distinction between learning and acquisition, and the need to receive comprehensible input either through hearing or reading, Krashen's (2007, 2011b) Comprehension Hypothesis included the idea that acquisition would be blocked if the person felt displeasure or debilitating stress. An overly stressful environment was thought to raise a person's affective filter which could block the input, so an environment conducive to acquisition was one with a lowered affective filter. Krashen called these three hypotheses the learning/acquisition hypothesis, the affective filter hypothesis, and the comprehensible input hypothesis. He introduced other hypotheses, but those three most informed the principles and practices of the TPRS method.

The TPRS method also integrated multisensory input to include the gestures and movement found to be effective for language learning from Asher's (1965, 1969, 2009) research which also had informed the Total Physical Response (TPR) learning strategy, and the findings from brain research (Jensen, 2009; Medina, 2014; Sousa, 2017) which promoted long-term memory, an important goal of the TPRS method. Acquisition was long-term, whereas learning was viewed as short-term because it was often forgotten.

That explained why TPRS teachers tried to teach for mastery (Hunter, 1982) and guided students through mastery learning (Bloom, 1968, 1971). Taken together, TPRS involved teaching and learning one sentence or phrase at a time, through repetitive, compelling, comprehensible input, with an effort to make the lessons personally interesting and personalized or customized to the students to obtain their engagement. Mastered material and language acquired were not soon forgotten.

In addition to those four theoretical, practical, and research-based foundations that informed the TPRS method, Hycner's (1985) ideas on "phenomenologically analyzing interview data" (p. 279), taken together, formed the conceptual framework which guided and informed this researcher's analysis. The word 'analysis' did involve breaking down the massive amounts of interview data into manageable pieces and reducing the data from general units of meaning down to the units of meaning that were relevant to the research questions and themes of experience. However, Hycner preferred to think of analysis, at least partly, as explicitating the data because he did not want to ever lose sight of the whole phenomenon. Originally used by Giorgi, Fischer, and von Eckartsberg (1971), Hycner (1985) borrowed the term "explicitation, which means an investigation of the constituents of a phenomenon while always keeping the context of the whole" (p. 300). The central phenomenon for this dissertation was using TPRS and the task was to identify the essence or whole of that phenomenon in terms of identifying the common lived experiences of teachers who used TPRS.

From that perspective, the process constantly went back and forth between taking the interviews apart (analysis), locating common experiences and themes, but then going back to view each informant's experience as uniquely situated in his or her own world to get a sense of the whole (explicitation). Hycner's (1985) conceptual framework was visible in the steps he listed for handling interview data. One of those observations was that Hycner did not view phenomenology as a comprehensive theory, but rather a method. Hycner (1985) insisted that the phenomenological researcher's goal was "not to interpret according to some already developed theory" (p. 300), but rather to 'understand' the phenomenon being studied, in this case using TPRS. That meant, at first, the researcher had to "stay quite true to the literal statements and meanings given by the participant" (p. 301). It was also important to bracket out, or set aside, as much as possible, the researcher's experience with using TPRS to capture the teacher informant's experience untainted by premature interpretations (Hycner, 1985). Guarding against researcher bias was necessary to ensure the credibility, trustworthiness (validity), and dependability (reliability) of the data analysis and findings.

The five cornerstones discussed above provided the theoretical foundations and the conceptual frameworks that informed this study. The first cornerstone was Krashen's (2015) Comprehension Hypothesis. The second cornerstone was Asher's (2009) research on the positive effects of providing comprehensible input, kinesthetic learning, tying physical gestures to movement, and multisensory input, which grew into TPR, a strategy which has been used in the TPRS method. The third cornerstone included the findings of brain research (Jensen, 2009; Medina, 2014; Sousa, 2017) which helped to inform the development of the TPRS method and support its legitimacy. The fourth cornerstone was the incorporation of teaching for mastery (Hunter, 1982) and mastery learning (Bloom, 1968, 1971). Taken together, these four cornerstones helped explain the many techniques and strategies that have been incorporated into the changing and evolving TPRS method. The fifth cornerstone informed the way the data were collected, analyzed, and handled.

Review of the Literature

Beginnings of TPRS.

Seely and Romijn (2006) reported that TPR Storytelling was born when "Ray, a high school Spanish teacher… was experimenting with TPR in about 1987" (p. 40). In the first edition of *Fluency through TPR Storytelling*, Ray and Seely (1997) cited some of the early influences on the method's development. Two primary influences were Asher's (1977, 1988, 1996) work and research on TPR, plus Krashen and Terrell's (1983) book which explained the language acquisition theory that informed a natural, comprehension-based, approach to classroom instruction, similar in some ways to how people acquired their native languages. Krashen's (1985) Input Hypothesis also informed Brown and Palmer's (1988) listening approach. Truscott's (1996, 1999, 2007) research finding that correcting students' grammar mistakes had little impact on improving accuracy in their writing and MacGowan-Gilhooly's (1993) use of using freewrites for measuring writing fluency were applied to the method. Krashen (1993) pointed out the key role reading played in language acquisition and reading gradually was increased over time in TPRS. In Carnegie's (1981) book, *How to Win Friends and Influence People,* he discussed how people liked others who encouraged them to talk about themselves, an idea that was incorporated into TPRS. Talking about them (TAT) showed up in many ways, to include personalizing the stories, making students the superstars in them, eliciting story details from the students, co-constructing the stories, and in the genuine desire for teachers to get to know their students' interests through personalized questions and answers (PQA) and then customizing those stories to increase student engagement and active participation. In those ways, TPRS has become increasingly more student-centered over time. In Ray and Seely (1997), Ray explained, "That book had a great impact on my life. Those ideas worked like magic. Students responded to my warmth" (p. 140), but that happened only after learning to put his students first in his teaching.

In the first edition of Ray and Seely's (1997) book on TPRS, the authors stressed the importance of gaining student interest by making them the central focus, making the language input comprehensible, varying the activities, and being careful about the pacing of the lesson by not going too fast. Ray and Seely (1997), with emphasis in the original, wrote, "*The challenge is to keep the class always both interesting and understandable for every student*" (p. 84). There were nine steps for telling a story. Since they recognized that, for most people in addition to reading a book, training in TPRS was necessary to master the new method. Ray and Seely (1997) listed the following presenters. Among the first ten TPRS workshop trainers were Blaine Ray, Contee Seely, Joe Neilson, Valeri Marsh, Susie Gross, Gale Mackey, Melinda Forward, Shirley Ogle, Lynn Rogers, and Carol Gaab (p. 171). Some of the early books and publishers included Ray's (1990), *Look I Can Talk!* that was published by Asher's Sky Oaks Productions and Ray's (1993) book about *Teaching Grammar Communicatively* was published by Gessler. Ray and Neilson's (1994) book *Look, I'm Still Talking* was published by Seely's Command Performance. Neilson and Ray's (1996) *Mini-stories for Look, I Can Talk!* was published by Blaine Ray Workshops. That name was changed recently to TPRS Books® to recognize Ray's collaborators and that the method has grown in popularity and scope to become much larger than the influence of any one person (Coxon, 2017).

Marsh (1998) wrote the first published article on TPRS, peer reviewed by Contee Seely and Carol Gaab. Marsh explained that the method's foundational beginnings were grounded in Asher's (1977, 1988, 2009) Total Physical Response (TPR) learning strategy which paired vocabulary words with physical actions, tapping into multisensory input. Marsh (1998) explained that while TPR helped students retain vocabulary due to the "long-lasting associations between the brain and the muscles," (p. 24) that TPR also had limitations. Marsh stressed that Ray, the developer of TPRS, added "the critical vehicle, storytelling, for utilizing and expanding acquired vocabulary" (p. 24) and developing fluency. TPRS involved using interesting stories, humor, creativity, and delaying grammar, within a low stress environment. Marsh (1998) outlined the five steps that she used in TPRS in 1997-1998. These steps included (1) TPR to pre-teach vocabulary and (2) students practicing vocabulary in pairs. In step 3, the teacher presented a mini-story using props and student actors. Students retold and revised the mini-story. In step 4, they worked with a longer story, adding details, and reading. Step 5 incorporated extension activities to include creative writing, drawing, drama, and other group or pair work. The number of steps in TPRS later expanded to seven (Ray & Seely, 2002) and then condensed to three steps, where it has remained since 2004 (Ray & Seely, 2004). However, despite the number of steps remaining relatively constant, according to TPRS' founder and other practitioners, the TPRS method has continually changed, developed, and evolved over time (Gaab, 2006; Ray, 2013; Ray & Seely, 2015; Sievek, 2009).

Early Student Achievement Data (in the literature).

As early as the 1990s, some TPRS teachers had their students take standardized tests as data to support their using this newer method and document student achievement.

For example, Marsh (1998) reported that her own middle school students, in a pilot program, "scored above the national average" (p. 25) on the National Spanish Exam. Ray and Seely (1997) reported that Joe Neilson's high school students averaged "67 percent… where the national average was 41 percent" (p. 154) on the National Spanish Exam. Ray had "five students pass the Spanish [Advanced Placement] AP test after only two years" (p. 154) of study. Ray had over 50 students performed well on the Advanced Placement (AP) Exam, despite doing "very little homework" (p. 154).

From early on, being supported by student achievement data, both empirical and anecdotal, practitioners began to recognize the potential effective uses of TPRS. For example, following Marsh's (1998) article on TPRS, Cantoni (1999) encouraged the use of TPRS to address the problem of disappearing Native American languages. Cantoni explained that because of the "increasing scarcity of Native-language speakers" (p. 56), fewer children were acquiring their tribal languages at home, so she hoped the schools would fill in that void. A former student of Cantoni, Marsh explained her variation of Ray and Seely's (1997) version of TPRS in its early development. An advocate for bringing school and community members together for positive change, and willing to promote a new teaching method, Cantoni (1999) encouraged school districts to hire TPRS consultants to work with Native speakers of tribal languages to train teachers in the method as well as to develop appropriate programs, materials, and lessons. Cantoni (1999) wrote that the TPRS method was useful because it helped to establish a "positive, collaborative, and supportive classroom climate in which Native American children could develop increasingly complex skills in speaking, reading, and writing their tribal language" (p. 56).

Cantoni (1999) explained that Asher's (1977) teaching technique or strategy called Total Physical Response (TPR) was part of TPRS, especially for pre-teaching vocabulary that would be used in the context of stories. For early beginners, a silent period (Krashen, 1981, 1985) was recognized as not only developmentally appropriate, but also as a practical concern for not embarrassing or ridiculing children who may have mispronounced a word or made a mistake when trying to produce the language. Cantoni (1999) recommended that "all attempts to use the home language be encouraged and rewarded but never criticized" (p. 56), which was consistent with TPRS principles. The method stressed comprehension before production and avoiding the direct correction of student mistakes, preferring recasts in which teachers would model the correct utterances as positive evidence in the input without drawing attention to student errors. Cantoni was unsure that this "polite error correction" (p. 56) would work with all learners. While that technique did avoid embarrassment, Cantoni was in favor of some sort of focused correction. A key aspect of TPRS that Cantoni did appreciate was the "interactive pedagogy principle" (p. 55) which was drawn from Cummins' (1989) work on promoting bilingualism. TPRS provided a "relaxed classroom atmosphere" (Cantoni, 1999, p. 55) where visuals, gestures, and kinesthetic actions were employed to provide input and student responses indicated whether comprehension was occurring. However, Cantoni stressed the importance of moving 'beyond understanding' the language through listening and reading to producing it by writing, and especially in speaking. Cantoni raised this important question about learners, "If they can understand but not speak the tribal language, how are they going to teach it to the next generation?" (p. 55). She expressed that TPRS was a suitable method for achieving those results, especially when scaffolding and cooperative learning strategies were included.

In addition to Cantoni's (1999) advocacy for change in education, Egan (1986, 2005, 2008) also encouraged using stories in the redesign of schools. While not part of the TPRS community, Egan was an educator who believed that stories were useful for learning in nearly all academic disciplines. According to Egan (2008), "Whatever children learn from the stories they are first told becomes quickly fixed and serves as a template for future learning" (p. 13). Egan's work lent support for using storytelling in education. From its early 1990s beginnings through today, TPRS has used stories.

Development of Method and Skills.

Ray and Seely (1997, 1998, 2002, 2004, 2008, 2012, 2015) published seven different editions of their book on TPRS, *Fluency through TPR Storytelling: Achieving Real Language Acquisition in School*. The names of TPR Storytelling® which was abbreviated from Total Physical Response Storytelling® and Teaching Proficiency through Reading and Storytelling® have been copyrighted, registered, and trademarked, with all rights reserved. Official workshop presenters were listed by first and last name.

The second edition of Ray and Seely's (1998, 2000, 2001) book on TPRS came out just one year after the first edition because, in their words, "We keep trying to improve TPR Storytelling" (p. 185). Ray had realized his students did better with TPR and the stories. He recalled having been very unsatisfied with student recall before TPRS (p. 11). Among the changes reported in the second edition were that some people began calling the method 'TPRS' and Krashen had given some presentations with Ray and declared the method was "much better than anything else out there" (p. vii). In addition to Krashen, a few new TPRS workshop presenters were added in the second edition's list, to include Karen Rowan, Michael Miller, and Dale Crum. Another change was that Ray and Seely (1998) placed additional focus on pre-teaching vocabulary, doing "frequent comprehension checks" (p. xii), and watching the "barometer students" (p. 15), while teaching to ensure that all students were understanding the stories. Barometer students were those students who were trying to learn but struggling to comprehend, so the pace and input needed to be slow enough for them to keep up, while the teacher tried to speak "at least 90 percent of the time in the target language" (p. 15). Ray and Seely (1998, 2000, 2001) had become more aware that teacher expectations needed to be high, but they also perceived that "if the stress level is too high, students will drop out and will not learn" (p. 16) at all. Some teachers who wanted to use the TPRS method were "tied to a textbook" (p. viii) and could not, so Rowan and Gross together wrote a new chapter on how to adapt a textbook to the TPRS method to help them make that work.

There were still nine steps in the method, but Ray and Seely (1998, 2000, 2001) noticed that different varieties or variations of TPRS had already begun to appear. Teachers grappled with the question of how much input or output was appropriate, especially for building grammatical accuracy and "confidence in speaking" (p. 106). Educators also had questions about pacing for different level students and how much grammar teaching should be done. Ray and Seely (1998) explained their view, "We have found that the time is better spent on storytelling than on explaining grammar. Studying grammar rules requires a lot of work for trivial gain" (p. 124). They emphasized that grammar was being taught in TPRS classes, but in a different way. When asked about using a textbook, Ray and Seely (1998, 2000, 2001) responded, "There is not enough time to teach your book and use this method too" (p. 178), and that since TPRS was more useful for promoting acquisition, that there was "no excuse for teaching grammar rules to the detriment of your students just to please other teachers" (p. 178). Ray and Seely's (1998, 2000, 2001) primary goal was for students to learn to 'speak' the target language, not just learn 'about' its grammar, and they claimed that TPRS-taught students were more successful than those taught by a textbook approach, although there was a dearth of rigorously-designed empirical research studies at that time to support that contention.

Some changes appeared in the third edition of Ray and Seely's (2002, 2003) book on TPRS. The number of TPRS steps changed from nine to seven. Games, which had been encouraged in the first edition, were eliminated if they failed to provide interesting and comprehensible input in context. Practitioners of TPRS began introducing more reading earlier than before. Teachers increased the use of comprehension checks and looked for points where comprehension broke down to ensure that all students were understanding the story details. A book chapter was added after two teachers, Michael Kundrat and Kristy Placido, started the More TPRS List, an online forum for TPRS teachers to share and support each other at http://groups.yahoo.com/group/moretprs.

Ray and Seely (2002, 2003) introduced the concept of teaching for mastery into the TPRS methodology. With mastery teaching, the goal was long-term memory within a curriculum that preferred going "narrow and deep" (p. 74) rather than wide and shallow. TPRS teachers began teaching one sentence at a time and not moving on until all or nearly all the students had mastered that sentence. To determine whether long-term acquisition was occurring, TPRS tests and quizzes were now unannounced so that students could not study or cram for them, but instead the assessments would reflect what students knew or had acquired. If all students understood everything, then the pacing was appropriate, but if they did not, then perhaps they needed more repetition of targeted vocabulary and high-frequency fluency structures or verb phrases. Also, with the increased emphasis on reading and the lack of materials that were highly interesting to students but written at their levels of understanding, Ray and Seely, among other others, published their own leveled reading materials (graded readers) which limited vocabulary to the high-frequency words, meaning words that were the most used in the language. To help determine which words to teach in school, they consulted books such as Davies' (2006) high-frequency dictionary of core vocabulary.

In addition to those changes, more names were added to the official list of people conducting TPRS workshops in the third edition book, by first and last name, to include Donna Tatum-Johns, Von Ray, Kristy Placido, Carmen Andrews-Sanchez, Julie Baird, Sheila Baumgardner, Kirsten Calkins, Jacqueline King Donnelly, Dennis Doyle, Shaun Duvall, Pablo Muir, Jacqueline Muirhead, María Rosa Sallaberry, Daisy Tingen, Patricia Verano de Varela, Maggie Smith, Jody Klopp, Dr. Shelley Thomas, and Todd McKay.

Between the publishing of the third (2002, 2003) and fourth editions of Ray and Seely's (2004, 2005) book on TPRS, several changes occurred. The number of steps was reduced from seven to three: vocabulary, story, and reading. The name of the method officially changed to Teaching Proficiency through Reading and Storytelling® (TPRS) from Total Physical Response (TPR) Storytelling®. However, some people have continued to use either or both names. Some TPRS teachers have reduced or eliminated TPR in their classrooms, adding to the variations in method application. An increased focus was put on ensuring that the comprehensible input of targeted vocabulary, verb phrase structures, and grammatical features intentionally was provided in the context of stories and through PQA. Additional comprehension checks were being used more often than before to ensure that lower proficiency level students understood the stories as well as the more advanced students, in an increased effort not to leave any students behind. While before some teachers had been mixing the verb tenses, Ray and Seely (2004) reported, "We are now teaching beginning classes with both the past and present tenses from day one or two" (p. 1). That decision was informed by Von Ray's action research project in which he found that the students who learned through a mixed-tense approach used both tenses more accurately than those who limited first-year to present tense only. He found that the mixed-tense group was not fossilized in the present tense as the comparison group was. Other teachers replicated that project in their own classrooms and had similar results, so mixing the tenses, by not sheltering grammar, was added in to the workshops.

New names were added to the list of TPRS workshop presenters, to include Angela Barone, Mary Holmes, Kim Kudym, Nichole Librandi, Sarah Moran, Elizabeth Skelton, Barb Cartford, Jan Kittok, and Jason Fritze. Several new and essential teaching skills were added as chapter 5 in Ray and Seely's (2004) fourth edition of their book on TPRS. In the area of professional development, Jody Klopp organized the first week long national conference (NTPRS) in 2001 and they have continued each July ever since, drawing over 200 teachers not only from the United States but also from other countries, making it really an international conference, but the name has not changed. The use of TPRS has expanded beyond elementary, secondary, and university classrooms, taking the method into adult education as evidenced by Shelley Thomas' summer institute and the Fluency Fast® courses.

In Ray and Seely's (2004) fourth edition, the originator of the TPRS method, Blaine Ray, reflected on his own early teaching experiences. Parts of his story were included here because the theme of this dissertation involved identifying the lived experiences of teachers using TPRS and Ray was the first. Before developing TPRS, Ray had been unsatisfied with previous methods because they did not produce many students who could write and speak proficiently in the target language. After reading Asher's (1977) book on TPR, which applied how babies acquire language to classrooms, Ray tried out TPR and he saw students did much better. One day, a former student visited his room and Ray turned the class over to his students. They gave her fun commands that everyone enjoyed. Tammy commented that Ray's students had learned more Spanish in three months than she did in her first three months living in Costa Rica. However, after a semester his students reached what Asher (1977) called the 'adaptation' point where the previous positive responses to commands disappeared. They were tired of commands, so Ray went back to worksheets but students did not enjoy or learn much from the grammar lessons. Ray read another book that influenced his teaching (Krashen & Terrell, 1983) that discussed the importance of acquiring a language through receiving comprehensible input because the authors believed that people acquired languages by understanding messages in them. Asher had edited a book that contained a story about a man named Mr. Smith who could not find his umbrella. Ray used that story along with TPR and experimented with ways to make it comprehensible that eventually became TPR Storytelling. Ray added other techniques with the stories and three years later wrote his first book called *Look, I Can Talk!* in 1990. He saw that his students enjoyed acquiring Spanish through stories. Ray credited writing that book and combining elements of TPR, the Natural Approach, and storytelling early on with helping him to develop TPRS.

Seely and Romijn (2006) announced that Total Physical Response (TPR) was a more involved process than just teaching commands when they included a description of TPR Storytelling (or TPRS) in chapter 4 of their book on TPR. Moving away from commands to declarative statements, the TPRS stories often contained "some amusing elements, often even zany elements" (p. 43), surprises and fun. Seely and Romijn (2006) detailed ten steps, and sub-steps within those ten, for learning how to tell a story, which showed from their observations that the storytelling process could be considered complex for teachers and students. One goal was for students to hear each new vocabulary word at least 50 to100 times, in context and without boredom, to promote retention so that it was "nearly impossible to forget it" (p. 85) and could correctly emerge in confident fluent student speech without hesitation. Asher (1996) praised Ray for adding the storytelling aspect to TPR because of TPRS' success in moving students from comprehension skills to the production skills, of writing and especially speaking, in the target language.

Seely and Romijn (2006) concluded by mentioning some of the changes or "refinements" (p. 87) that had occurred up to 2006 in the TPRS method. For example, the ten steps were shortened to seven and finally to three, many practitioners were using less TPR than before, there were more questioning strategies added, more details were being elicited from the students making the stories more co-constructed than before, more readings and discussions were added, and "five-second pop-ups" (p. 88) were used to teach grammar in context. In addition to these developments, the weeklong summer national TPRS conferences (NTPRS) began in 2001 and have continued ever since.

Just as Seely and Romijn (2006) noticed how complex the TPRS teaching skills were, so did Slavic (2007) who in his books outlined how to gradually incorporate 49 different TPRS teaching skills of the method into a teacher's first year of using TPRS. Slavic (2008) paid special attention to how to help teachers learn to 'manage' their classrooms and to 'personalize' their lessons for learners in a TPRS class through a strategy called Personalized Questions and Answers (PQA) to make classroom interaction more engaging by having students about themselves and each other in the target language. In discussing his version of PQA, Slavic (2008) wrote that "a story is always best when it has its roots in personalized discussion" (p. 8). To Slavic (2008), a skilled teacher well-trained in establishing a rapport with students was needed to maintain effective classroom discipline and management, adding that "no textbook can deliver personalized comprehensible input to students" (p. 10). Many of the teaching skills that Slavic (2008) mentioned included asking questions to provide students with choices and to elicit responses which focused their attention and encouraged active participation.

While some educators attended a TPRS workshop and immediately could begin teaching with stories, others could not. For those teachers, Slavic (2014) wrote about an alternative way to get started, using stepping-stone strategies to "prepare the teacher in the art of using comprehensible input" (p. 8) in sort of a training-wheel approach with which some of the TPRS teachers on his online Professional Learning Community (PLC) had success. Perhaps somewhat ironically, Slavic (2014) had said, "In my view the need is to simply protect ourselves from too many techniques and strategies" (p. 47), but his books have included several of them. This book was called *Stepping Stones to Stories!* (Slavic, 2014). The first of the stepping stones involved learning six skills which included asking circling questions, teaching slowly, "staying in bounds", demanding choral responses from students, pausing and pointing to words not yet acquired, and establishing the meaning of new vocabulary and structures through multisensory input to make emotional connections with what students were learning. The second stepping stone had ten activities, the third stone six classroom management tools, and the fourth stone consisted of bail-out activities to use in case what they were doing was not working. The final stepping stone contained explanations of the five theoretical hypotheses that informed TPRS teaching with comprehensible input (Krashen, 2013).

To assist educators in their ongoing professional development, in Slavic's (2015) *The Big CI Book: A Step by Step Survival Guide for Foreign Language Teachers*, he described and discussed and 15 teaching skills, 26 learning strategies, eight classroom management techniques, three ways to assess, 37 comprehensible input (CI) activities and four bail-out activities. There were also 14 appendices on areas of concern to teachers. These myriad topics and tools reflected the complex nature of teaching and managing world language classrooms today. Slavic (2015) intended to provide guidance for Teaching with Comprehensible Input (TCI, CI) and perhaps even change the name from TPRS to TCI, but this researcher would argue that the items he covered all appeared to fit in some way within the ever-evolving framework of the TPRS methodology.

Slavic (2015) seemed to agree when he wrote to his readers, "After you read and practice the strategies found in this book, you will be able to do CI instruction, including stories, in your classroom with confidence" (p. 6). If it turned out that he was correct, then he has made a tremendous contribution to TPRS. By isolating, using, and measuring the effects of each facet of the TPRS method, both educators and researchers could better understand the acquisition process and improve world language teaching. An interesting study might be to conduct a content analysis to determine which, if any, of the topics and tools Slavic (2015) presented fell outside of TPRS principles and practices. After all, the TPRS method has since its inception included more than just stories. On the other hand, such a study was not necessary because Slavic (2015) admitted, "There are lots of strategies presented in this book. Each one falls into at least one of the all-encompassing Three Steps of TPRS" (p. 387). Slavic (2015) listed eleven activities for step one, eleven activities for step two, and five activities for step 3, for a total of 37 TPRS activities. Once mastered, there could have been less time needed for extensive lesson planning, preparation, and skill development, with teachers instead being more able to focus on interacting with their students in the target language (TL) in class. As Slavic (2015) reflected and concluded, "The core intent of everything in this book is always the same, to help us get better at communicating in the TL with students" (p. 353). That explained why he discussed so many strategies and skills for providing comprehensible input and personalizing lessons to increase the effectiveness of TPRS teacher-student interactions.

The TPRS method has continued to develop and change over time. In Ray and Seely's (2008, 2009, 2010) fifth edition of their book on TPRS, there was an appendix prepared by Joe Neilson and Karen Rowan listing the grammar items, along with their descriptive metalinguistic terms, included in Ray's (1990) *Look, I Can Talk!* book series for Spanish 1-2-3, which could be a helpful tool for TPRS teachers who were required to prepare a grammar syllabus to support their curriculum. Another book appendix was devoted to classroom management techniques with input from Blaine Ray, Scott Benedict, Tawanna Billingsley, and Ben Slavic. Another appendix topic was written to report the results of an experiment conducted by Meredith Richmond. There were 85 TPRS students who were divided into two groups. The control group was separated by levels Spanish 1, 2, 3, and 4 as usual. The experimental group was taught in mixed-level classes. Both groups were taught using TPRS and at the end of the semester, they all did ten-minute fluency writings and were also scored on a written competency measure using a modified AP-type rubric developed by Joe Neilson. Richmond was surprised to see that the upper-level students were not bored when the instruction was geared toward the lower-level barometer students in level 1 who were their classmates in the mixed-level group. Instead, the biggest gains were made by Spanish 4 students in mixed-level classes. These results indicated that through TPRS, students could learn what they needed to improve (self-differentiate) even in classrooms of mixed proficiency levels. The mixed-level classes outperformed all homogeneous groups at each level, from Spanish 1 to 4, on measures both of writing competency and written fluency. There were also appendix pieces in the fifth edition written by Ray and Noonan (2003, 2008) and by Webster (2003) on how in some schools the student enrollments have increased and the student attrition rates have decreased after changing to a TPRS methodology.

An action research study (V. Ray, 2004, 2008) compared two groups of students taught using TPRS. The control group received instruction using only the present tense for their first year of Spanish and past-tense verbs were introduced in their second year, as normally has been done in regular language classrooms. The experimental group received input in both the past and present tenses in their first year of study. Students were assessed on whether they could correctly translate from Spanish to English correctly using past versus present tenses. The experimental group of true beginners which received mixed-tense input significantly outperformed the control group who had studied Spanish for twice as long, or 200 versus 100 hours. Results indicated that it was more efficient to teach by mixing the tenses. After other teachers replicated the study, TPRS workshops began including training on how to mix the tenses from the beginning and not sheltering grammar or verb tenses. New names appeared on the list of TPRS workshop presenters, by first and last name, to include Debra Allison, Diane Grieman, Melinda Kawahara, Inga Zúñiga, Marjorie LaBella, Deb Read, Andy Trimiño, Robin Young, Elaine Winer, Lynnette Long, Leslie Davison, Laurie Clarcq, and Bryce Hedstrom.

In Ray and Seely's (2012) sixth edition of their book on TPRS, teaching for mastery received a greater emphasis than before, as teachers led students to master one sentence at a time before moving on to the next. The teaching strategies discussed in the book for moving students from slow processing to faster processing helped them acquire the language skill necessary for them to become more confident in speaking and develop their fluency. A new chapter was added on how to elicit or provide background information, get more student repetitions, increase learner interest, and mix the past and present tenses into TPRS teaching. More skills, techniques, and strategies were added to the method. Among those was embedded reading, which was created and developed by Laurie Clarcq and Michele Whaley, and added to the book chapter on reading. Clarcq and Whaley had been conducting TPRS workshops and more names appeared on the list of TPRS presenters, to include Alike Last, Iris Maas, Kirstin Plante, Michele Whaley, and Dr. Karen Lichtman.

In Ray and Seely's (2015) seventh edition of *Fluency through TPR Storytelling*, they included contributions from Rowan on personalization, Hedstrom on personalization, reading, and classroom management, Benedict's views on personalization, and Whaley's discussion on MovieTalk which had been invented by Hastings (1995) for ESL. Ray discussed his new technique for teaching events. Ideas for the elementary school were offered by Davison, Fritze, and Williams. Paskvan discussed how to reach reading in Japanese. Filipescu described her use of embedded readings. Wass shared his experiences with multi-level classes. Peto gave information on leading departments to adopt TPRS and McLean shared adult learner experiences. Slavic, Last, and Krashen contributed their insights to the seventh edition.

Developing TPRS Skills and Knowledge.

In the area of professional development training, some names were added to the list of teachers who have been conducting TPRS workshops and delivering presentations on the method. That list included Grant Boulanger, Mira Canion, Gary DiBianca, Kirsten Eastland, Alina Filipescu, Piedad Gutiérrez, Janet Holzer, Lizette Liebold, Haiyun Lu, Elissa McLean (Express Fluency), Chris Mercer, Betsy Paskvan, Katya Paukova, Michael Peto, Craig Sheehy, Lynnette St. George, Carrie Toth, Jim Tripp, Teri Wiechart, Robin Young, James Wooldridge (aka, Mr. Wooly), and Dr. Terry Thatcher Waltz.

In Waltz's (2015) book on using TPRS to teach Chinese, Krashen (2015) wrote a short chapter about the theory that always has informed the TPRS method which Krashen called the Comprehension Hypothesis. That hypothesis has posited that language was acquired only through understanding messages, or through comprehended input (intake), in the language, by hearing or reading. Output was viewed as the result of, not the cause of, acquisition. Acquisition has only occurred when a person was developmentally ready to acquire any given form because there were developmental sequences and an order of acquisition that limited the learning. Acquisition best occurred in a low-stress environment, that would not raise the affective filter, when the acquirer was relaxed, received compellingly interesting comprehensible input, and was focused on the message, not the form, of the language. Acquisition was considered a subconscious process. Those views contrasted with what Krashen called the Skill-Building Hypothesis which purported that grammar rules must first be consciously learned through production practice, by writing and speaking, until the linguistic forms became automatic in use.

Krashen (2015) mentioned that three methods consistent with the Comprehension Hypothesis were TPR, the Natural Approach, and TPRS because they focused on providing students with comprehensible input and did not encourage forced speech. While grammar study was not prohibited, its value was considered limited to monitoring or editing output. Krashen explained that the stories in TPRS were "co-created by the teacher and the students" (p. 170) and they were personalized or customized to student interests to make them more compelling. Krashen (2015) discussed the challenges of teaching Chinese today, recognized the contributions of Terry Waltz in making Mandarin comprehensible to students using TPRS, and coined the phrase "TPRS Theory" (p. 168).

In her book, *TPRS with Chinese Characteristics: Making Students Fluent and Literate Through Comprehensible* Input, Waltz (2015) both described the TPRS method and explained her strategies for dealing with the special challenges of teaching Chinese. In Mandarin, there were very few cognates, tones affected the meaning of utterances, the non-Western writing system did not have a Roman alphabet but rather sight words, and lower-level reading materials were not widely available that were appropriate for true beginners. To address those challenges, Waltz (2015) created the Cold Character Reading (CCR) method, the Tonally Orthographic Pinyin (TOP) system, "which means tones through spelling" (p. 148), and using capitalization and colors to visually signal the tones for non-native speakers and students of Chinese. Waltz (2015) also introduced using directional (hand) gestures for "linking the tone to the specific word being acquired" (p. 151) or even at the syllable level. Directional gestures were used to help students notice, understand, and remember the tones, tapping into kinesthetic learning. Waltz has incorporated those and her other contributions into TPRS, used the method in her own teaching, trained and coached teachers in workshops, and written, illustrated, and published her own reading materials in Chinese (e.g., Waltz, 2011, 2013, 2014). In those materials, she followed the TPRS principles she wrote about in Waltz (2015).

Similarly, VanPatten (in preparation, 2017) drew from the principles derived from second language acquisition research. VanPatten synthesized some second language acquisition (SLA) research, writing primarily for a target audience to include language teachers and teachers-in-training. He wrote to help language professionals understand or to review accumulated knowledge from the field of SLA. His focus was on six principles that he interpreted as informing communicative and proficiency-based teaching today, directly derived from research. In describing those six principles, the role of *input* in instructed SLA repeatedly emerged. In discussing the role of input in the classroom, VanPatten mentioned TPRS as an example of where "input is central to the curriculum" (p. 71).

VanPatten (in preparation, 2017) examined TPRS through making comparisons with the six principles below that he argued were among the basic findings which inform "contemporary communicative and proficiency-oriented language teaching" (p. iii) from an SLA research perspective. Those six basic principles, obtained from empirical research studies on SLA, as discussed and interpreted by VanPatten (2017) follow:

> *1. If you teach communicatively, you'd better have a working definition of communication. 2. Language is too abstract and complex to teach and learn explicitly. 3. Acquisition is severely constrained by internal (and external) factors. 4. Instructors and materials should provide student learners with level-appropriate input and interaction. 5. Tasks (and not Exercises or Activities) should form the backbone of the curriculum. 6. A focus on form should be input oriented and meaning based.* (VanPatten, 2017, p. iii, emphasis in original).

VanPatten (2017) did not write on every component of TPRS, but his analysis went beyond the three basic steps of establishing meaning, asking a story, and reading. He reported, "In a typical TPRS lesson, there is constant expression, interpretation, and negotiation of meaning appropriate for the context of the classroom" (p. 72). VanPatten also wrote, "What is clear from an examination of TPRS is that the input and its use in the classroom clearly reflect the ideas about making input comprehensible" (p. 72). He acknowledged that TPRS teachers communicated by "talking with students, not at them" (p. 72). Regarding the nature of that communication, he questioned whether there was always a communicative purpose or intended outcome beyond learning the language or telling a story. Nevertheless, VanPatten (2017) concluded that "TPRS classrooms are 'more communicative' than most 'traditional' language classrooms and involve a good deal more input and interaction with that input" (p, 72). Case studies of TPRS teachers' knowledge of SLA research, guided by these six principles, have not yet been conducted.

The previous section discussed several of the developments that have occurred in the TPRS method over time and the many TPRS teacher skills and knowledge there are to acquire. The following sections reviewed some of the studies that have been conducted on the method, discussed teacher experiences using TPRS, the obstacles and resistance some teachers have faced which appeared in the literature, areas of potential growth for TPRS, and some evidence of its effectiveness from empirical research.

Empirical Research.

Documented Effectiveness of the TPRS Method.

Lichtman's (2012a) first review of the literature on TPRS was published as a research appendix (in Ray & Seely, 2012). Her review included a total of 17 works, 12 of which were empirical studies where TPRS students outperformed students taught by another method in seven studies (Bustamante, 2009; Dziedzic, 2012; Garczynski, 2003; Oliver, 2012; Spangler, 2009; Varguez, 2009; and Watson, 2009) and mixed results were found in three studies (Beal, 2011; Foster, 2011; and Perna, 2007). TPRS students did as well as or better than others in all 12 empirical studies. From her analysis of the studies in her review, Lichtman (2012a) concluded that "TPRS® students often outperform and rarely underperform traditional students" (p. 311). Her review provided research-based evidence which provided collective empirical evidence that the method was effective.

Lichtman (2012a) noted that TPRS was "implemented in different ways by different teachers, in part because it keeps evolving and in part because every individual is different and every teaching situation is different" (p. 310). Despite some variation in method delivery, she found favorable evidence from several different educational contexts. She synthesized the studies and noticed that students taught with TPRS, or some variation of it, generally performed as well or better than non-TPRS students.

Ray and Seely (2015) expressed their pleasure and gratefulness "to see the results of the considerable amount of research that Karen Lichtman has found, summarized and analyzed" (p. xi) on TPRS. Lichtman's (2015) second review of the literature on TPRS was published as an updated research appendix (in Ray & Seely, 2015). Since her first review (in Lichtman, 2012a), she noted that "there has been an explosion of research" (Lichtman, 2015) into TPRS, at least in part due to teachers who have been publishing their master's degree theses and doctoral dissertations. Lichtman (2015) summarized her review by writing that "TPRS students keep pace with (or outscore) traditionally taught students on a variety of assessments" (p. 376). She concluded that TPRS was effective.

With an interest in studying implicit and explicit learning (see Lichtman, 2012b) in children and adults, she has been collecting a growing list of TPRS research studies online where researchers and others can contribute related studies that they have encountered (at http://forlangs.niu.edu/klichtman/tprs.html). The evidence of the TPRS research explosion came through comparing the number of studies in her first review with the second. The first one "contained seven published articles and ten theses" and the second review included "fourteen published articles and twenty-one theses" (Lichtman, 2015, p. 365). The second review included descriptive articles and studies on TPRS, studies on TPRS with no comparison group, and sixteen empirical studies comparing TPRS with other language teaching methodologies.

Lichtman (2015) found that TPRS students did better than students taught through other methods in 15 out of 16 empirical studies in at least one area. In four of those studies, TPRS students clearly outperformed others (De Vlaming, 2013; Nijhuis & Vermaning, 2010; Oliver, 2012; and Watson, 2009). In six studies, TPRS students outperformed others in one language skill and performed equally in another skill (Castro, 2010; Dziedzic, 2012; Garczynski, 2003; Roberts & Thomas, 2015; Spangler, 2009; and Varguez, 2009). In five studies, there were mixed results where TPRS outperformed another method in at least one language domain, but also another method outperformed TPRS in a different domain (Beal, 2011; Foster, 2011; Jennings, 2009; Murray, 2014; and Perna, 2007). In one peer-reviewed study, TPRS students performed equally with students taught by another method (Holleny, 2012). Taken together, in no study was there found to be a clear advantage of another method over TPRS. In other words, TPRS students equaled or outperformed students taught through other methodologies.

Lichtman (2015) also discussed three published journal articles (Armstrong, 2008; Brownstein, 2006; and Miller, 2011), five master's theses (Beyer, 2008; Bustamante, 2009; Jakubowski, 2013; Webster, 2003; and Wenck, 2010), and one bachelor's thesis (Brune, 2004), all with no control group. Lichtman (2012a) reviewed a book chapter (Cantoni, 1999) and five descriptive articles on TPRS (Alley & Overfield, 2008; Bernal Numpaque & Garcia Rojas, 2010; Davidheiser, 2001, 2002; and Lichtman, 2014). In addition, Lichtman (2015) discussed three descriptive master's degree theses (Rapstine, 2003; Sievek, 2009; and Taulbee, 2008) and one descriptive dissertation (Oliver, 2013).

Taken together, Lichtman (2015) reported on the past, current, and developing state of research on TPRS and she did point out the need for additional research to fill some gaps. However, the results of her first and second reviews of the professional literature and research on the method clearly showed, in her own concluding words, that "TPRS is at least as effective as, and often more effective than, other second language teaching methods," (p. 376) especially in speaking, reading, and grammar.

Comparing TPRS with Other Methods.

In the following section below, 22 empirical studies were reviewed comparing TPRS with other methods in studies that were conducted between 2003 and 2016. Some of the topics included were the effects of methods, socioeconomic status, explicit and implicit instruction, age, gender, the presence or absence of grammar instruction, dialogs, motivation, proficiency testing, adapted TPRS, special needs strategies, and accelerated learning gains. Among the target languages included in those research studies were Spanish, French, Mandarin Chinese, Italian, and English. While there were some mixed results, much of the empirical research studies found positive effects for teaching using TPRS in public and private schools at the preschool, secondary, university, and adult levels of learning.

Middle School International Baccalaureate Spanish Program.

In the title of Garczynski's (2003) empirical study she included the words "Audio Lingual" but she explained what she meant was "traditional textbook teaching" (p. 6) which included workbook activities and "memorization of vocabulary and grammar drills" (p. 7). Given that clarification, Garczynski compared TPRS with a grammar-textbook approach. There were 152 beginning-level middle school Spanish students enrolled in an International Baccalaureate (IB) program who participated in the study. It was a convenience sample consisting of her own students of 83 TPRS students and 69 textbook-taught students. They were all given a pre-test which most students failed. A potentially contaminating factor or confounding variable was that all students were taught Chapter 1 through the textbook approach which included subject pronouns and how to conjugate verbs which the researcher thought all students should know. In the TPRS-principled approach, there was generally a primary focus on meaning, not form, in the experimental group. The textbook (control) group's instruction continued with Chapter 2 of Prentice Hall's *Paso a Paso*, level one, as the textbook-grammar taught students worked through the textbook drills and workbook activities. The TPRS group used the book's TPRS supplement as a resource, but that instruction included TPRS strategies such as PQA (personalized questions and answers), story and comprehension activities, readings, whole group and pair work, and they told stories to parents for homework.

Garczynski (2003) had learned about TPRS by attending a four-hour workshop taught by Susie Gross before conducting her study. She noticed there were "quite a few skeptical teachers" (p. 5) there. She was surprised at the number of teachers who "openly challenged the ideals of TPRS… One teacher was so passionate about her opinion that she got up and left the workshop" (p. 6). Garczynski (2003) wrote that TPRS was controversial because it challenged the "many years of traditional textbook teaching which have been firmly implemented by the majority of second language teachers in our country" (p. 6). That experience and personal observation motivated Garczynski to study the effects of a traditional textbook approach with a focus on learning grammar explicitly with TPRS's emphasis on acquiring language through implicit instruction using stories. She aimed to empirically determine which method achieved better results with students.

Garczynski's (2003) study had a pre/posttest design and she compared the TPRS and non-TPRS student post-test scores. The groups' mean scores were 2.45 and 2.50, with no significant differences found on the teacher-made test of listening and reading comprehension. Garczynski (2003) wrote that the "TPRS students performed slightly higher" (p. 2) than those taught with a textbook but the treatment only lasted six weeks, covering the material in chapter two of the Spanish textbook. Garczynski (2003) also was interested in which group improved the most from pre-test to post-test by two or more grades. The TPRS group outperformed the textbook-taught students 63% to 49% by that measure of learning gain. Garczynski (2003) interpreted those results of improvement as a "good indication that the TPRS group was more successful overall in reading and listening comprehension" (p. 33). She had the students in her study complete an opinion survey and Garczynski (2003) reported, "Overwhelmingly, both groups chose TPRS as their preferred learning method" (p. 34) on the survey.

Garczynski (2003) also surveyed teachers (n = 24) on the internet who had experience teaching with both methods. She found that "most if not all agreed that until they started teaching with TPRS strategies they did not witness a lot of student success" (p. 34). After synthesizing the teacher survey responses, she reported that TPRS "created a more comfortable and enjoyable atmosphere in their classrooms. Some of these teachers also indicated that by using TPRS methods their students have performed better on AP tests" (p. 36). Her experiences in conducting her study helped Garczynski (2003) appreciate the way "TPRS lessens anxiety" (p. 38) which led her to participate in more TPRS professional development opportunities to improve her teaching skills.

An obstacle to using TPRS which Garczynski (2003) uncovered included the school district's requirement to use a textbook, but the textbook-taught students in her study failed to outperform the TPRS-taught students and no advantage was found for explicit grammar instruction. While there were no significant differences on test scores, the TPRS students showed a higher learning gain. The teacher survey showed that teachers had been unsatisfied with student success before using TPRS and that one effect of TPRS was an improved classroom climate more conducive to learning, with less student anxiety. In listening and reading comprehension, TPRS students performed as well or better than students taught through a method using textbook grammar drills.

High School Italian / Method Fidelity Issue.

In Perna's (2007) dissertation, she compared the effects of three methods in an empirical study of a convenience sample of her own 118 high-school students in their third year of studying Italian. She taught three grammar lessons and three vocabulary lessons using each method in classes on a four-day rotation for a treatment lasting five weeks, with teacher-made pretests and posttests. All students were taught through all three methods to control for any possible effects of method novelty. There were no significant differences found on grammar tests. However, the method which took considered the learning styles (and perceptual strengths) of learners produced significantly higher results on an analysis of variance (ANOVA, $p < .001$) than the other two methods. The TPRS method came in second, above the traditional method, meaning there were mixed results for TPRS in this study. On the other hand, as Lichtman (2015) observed, "Since TPRS does not typically break lessons into grammar lessons vs. thematic vocabulary lessons, Perna's instruction may not have been typical of TPRS classrooms" (p. 368). That observation called into question any conclusions which could be drawn from the data in terms of validity and fidelity of method delivery. The observation also highlighted the need for a rigorous study design and the importance of describing just how the construct of TPRS was operationalized as a treatment in any given empirical research study.

Another observation this researcher made of Perna's (2007) study design involved how she attempted to ensure that all students were actively engaged in the stories, an action that was not present in any other study reviewed. Perna explained, "Due to the nature of TPRS, students must be actively engaged" (p. 36). To increase engagement, she evaluated students daily on their class participation when taught through TPRS, which she did not do during the other methods. This extra evaluation could have unintentionally introduced a confounding variable if students were worried about their participation grades rather than focusing their attention on message comprehension and enjoying the Italian class. That worrying over grades and academic performance may have raised the students' affective filters (see Krashen, 1994, 2013) which could have limited the possible positive effects of TPRS teaching as operationalized in her study.

Rural High School Spanish / Low to Middle Income.

Kariuki and Bush (2008) compared the effects of TPRS and a traditional teaching approach in a rural Tennessee public high school of 450 mostly low-to-middle income families that were 98% Caucasian. From a total of sixty Spanish I, beginning-level, students in the school's college preparation program, 30 were randomly selected as subjects for the study after receiving permission, consent, and assent from the school's administration, parents, and students involved. Students were informed that they could drop out of the study at any time without any negative consequences. From the 30 students selected, two groups of 15 students each were randomly selected for the experimental and control groups. The control group received traditional language instruction for the one-unit treatment of only one week, which focused on learning vocabulary and grammar rules through textbook drills and worksheets.

Kariuki and Bush (2008) described the traditional approach in four steps. First, students heard the instructor and other students speaking the target language. Second, students were encouraged to speak in class and in small groups to practice pronunciation. Third, students read and interpreted sentences and paragraphs with teacher questions to guide their reading comprehension. Fourth, students practiced applying the rules of grammar to writing tasks. Students in the traditional (control) group were responsible for memorizing vocabulary and learning the rules of Spanish grammar to prepare for tests.

In the Kariuki and Bush (2008) study, both the control and experimental groups took the same teacher-made unit test after one week of instruction, which provided the primary quantitative source of data for analysis, plus qualitative teacher observations. The test had two parts, translating sentences from Spanish to English and vocabulary matching. The experimental group received instruction from an instructor using TPRS. The article did not mention whether the same instructor taught both groups.

Kariuki and Bush (2008) described the TPRS method as including Asher's (1966, 1969, 1977, 1988) Total Physical Response (TPR) plus stories. This TPR technique used commands aimed at connecting the learning of vocabulary to physical gestures and motions to help students learn, practice, and retain the new words. The researchers further described TPRS as a "stress free teaching style" (p. 5) and cited Ray's (2006) book for the mini-stories, of 2-3 paragraphs each, which student volunteers acted out and the dramatized with the teacher. Personalized questions and answers (PQA) were used in class, as described by Slavic (2007, 2008), to elicit more student interest, participation, engagement, and attentive involvement in the communicative nature of the lessons.

Kariuki and Bush (2008) wrote that when using TPRS, "Spanish class becomes a time where anything can happen" (p. 7) and that for the teacher the method could be "physically and emotionally exhausting" (p. 6). The goals of TPRS were for students to be engaged, pay attention, participate, and have fun. The teacher used a combination of both classical and hand TPR, Spanish cognates, which are words that look or sound similar to their English equivalents, and props or real items as visuals. Homework was not required "because it is hard when students are at home completing homework when they do not understand, [so] the students' job is strictly in the classroom" (p. 8). Students were expected to be present in class because absences were difficult to make up, to be creative and to actively participate meaningfully in order to "keep the class interesting" (p. 9). Students added details to the stories co-created with the TPRS teacher in class.

In their study, Kariuki and Bush (2008) found that students taught with TPRS scored significantly higher (at the $p = .05$ level) on both the Spanish-to-English sentence translation part of the test (mean scores of 93.87 vs. 77.87%) and on the vocabulary matching section (96% vs. 76.33%). In addition, researcher observation comments included that TPRS students, per Kariuki and Bush (2008):

> appeared positive and engaged… remained motivated throughout the lesson and were excited to enter the classroom and volunteered new gestures for the new vocabulary words and volunteered to be a part of the mini-stories that were acted

out. They were not afraid to fail. The [TPRS] students perceived learning to be fun (p. 19).

On the other hand, traditional students "appeared bored and unmotivated. The students knew the routine … and tended not to be fully engaged" (p. 19). Kariuki and Bush (2008) concluded that the "results indicated a significant difference between TPRS and the traditional style of teaching on the overall performance of students" (p. 20) in favor of TPRS. The Kariuki and Bush (2008) study did not support the conventional wisdom that by focusing on learning grammar and vocabulary through textbook drills and worksheets, practicing speech and pronunciation in class, applying grammar rules to writing tasks, and doing homework would provide students with success.

Instead, TPRS teachers used a method that observers noted was both physically and emotionally exhausting, leading their students to significantly higher achievement on vocabulary and translation tests. Despite doing no homework or small group work in class, TPRS students were perceived to be more actively engaged and motivated than others, answered teacher questions in Spanish, contributed details to add fun and interest to the stories, acted them out dramatically, and they outperformed the non-TPRS group.

High School Spanish / High Income Community.

Watson (2008) conducted an empirical research study for her master's degree that was published in a peer-reviewed journal a year later. In that study, Watson (2009) compared the effects of TPRS and traditional teaching, for one academic year, for high school Spanish 1 students from high income, affluent, families. Two class periods were taught by the same teacher using TPRS and one period was taught by a different teacher who used a traditional teaching approach. The TPRS (experimental) group had only 4%

of its 50 students who "spoke Spanish at home or used Spanish frequently outside of school," (p. 22) while the traditional (control) group of 23 students had 15% heritage speakers, indicating no language advantage for the TPRS group. There were no attitude or motivation surveys given, so those factors were not considered. However, students were asked to estimate how much time they spent studying or reading Spanish outside of class and no significant differences were found, so time spent on homework was not considered a confounding variable. The sample size for the study was modest ($n = 73$), but there were significant differences found between the two groups on two post-tests, with effect sizes equal to one standard deviation for each measure.

In Watson's (2009) study, at the end of the school year, the TPRS group scored significantly higher, at the $p = .05$ level, on both the speaking test and on the final exam which tested listening, reading, vocabulary, and grammar. The final exam was a common and an objective measure, so the scores were comparable. No inter-rater reliability was computed since each student had only one rater, but both raters were trained to use a scoring rubric with agreed-upon criteria for the speaking test and no teacher scored his or her own students. Another way to ensure that the groups could be compared and draw valid and reliable conclusions was to establish fidelity in method delivery to ensure that both groups received different instruction during the treatment.

Watson (2009) audio recorded four class meetings each for both the experimental and control groups and she analyzed the discourse and interaction between teacher and students. That analysis included the use of questions, vocabulary repetition, the amount of group work, and teacher talk during class. One session per teacher considered to be the "most representative of that teacher's typical teaching style was analyzed in detail"

(p. 21). Watson (2009) found that the experimental group teacher delivered instruction that was comprehension-based in a manner "characteristic of a TPRS class," as described in Ray and Seeley (2008, p. 23). The storytelling teacher asked 141 questions in class compared with 18 asked by the traditional teacher. The traditional class had more group work and was teacher-fronted only 29% of the class period, compared to the TPRS class which was teacher-fronted 68% of the time. The TPRS teacher spoke "nearly entirely" (p. 22) in the target language, more often than the traditional teacher, who mixed Spanish language practice and instruction with grammar explanations in English. In the traditional classroom, there was more corrective feedback from the teacher, more language production, drills, direct grammar instruction, student output, games, projects, technology, and interview interaction between students. Both groups read the beginner-level reader *Pobre Ana* (Ray, 1999, 2007), but the TPRS group also read the novella *Patricia va a California* (Ray, 2001). The TPRS group read more in Spanish.

Watson (2009) took the time to establish fidelity of the different methodological treatments received by the experimental and control groups. She described how each method construct was operationalized in her empirical study and how comparisons were made possible through a careful study design. Her findings, based on student results on two post-tests, supported previous research of studies reviewed by Krashen (2003, 2013). Those studies had found that students taught with repetitive, comprehensible input had outperformed students taught through a traditional, output-based, method. She explained that the practices of the TPRS method were informed by language acquisition theory that supported comprehension-based methods. In Watson's (2009) study of high school students, she found empirical evidence that TPRS was more effective than a traditional approach for developing listening, speaking, reading, vocabulary, and grammar. The Kariuki and Bush (2008) study had shown that TPRS worked well in lower SES neighborhoods and Watson's (2009) study showed that TPRS achieved significantly better results than grammar-textbook teaching with more affluent students as well.

High School Spanish / Proficiency Testing / Effects of SES.

Varguez (2009) compared the effects of TPRS with traditional teaching in high school, testing 83 beginners using the University of the State of New York's standardized Second Language Proficiency Examination in Spanish, on listening and reading, after one academic year of instruction. Of the ten schools invited to participate, only four sent in test results. Schools A and B had been taught through a traditional approach and schools C and D used TPRS. School A had 32 students and B had 16, so the comparison (or control) group had 48 students. School C had 13 students and D had 22 (experimental group of 35 students). There were incidental differences in socio-economic status (SES) within the experimental (TPRS) group. As determined by free or reduced lunch criteria, the TPRS students in school C had a lower SES than students in schools A, B, and D.

Varguez (2009) found no significant differences found in test results for the traditionally-taught group and school C, the TPRS school with students from a lower SES. However, significant differences were found between the traditionally-taught students and school D, the TPRS school with a higher SES. High school TPRS students in school D significantly outperformed the traditionally-taught students on the standardized proficiency exam in both listening and reading. Varguez (2009) concluded that when "demographic factors were similar, [her study] provided clear support for the efficacy of TPRS and the validity of the underlying theory" (p. 5).

Varguez (2009) had situated her empirical study by contrasting two theoretically opposing views, or paradigms, of language and pedagogy. The traditional classroom environment treated language as an object to be analyzed and taught through a "concept explanation-concept practice model" (p. 2). In the TPRS classroom second language classroom acquisition was viewed as a process similar to the natural way people have picked up their mother tongue, by being immersed in contextualized and "understandable language" (p. 2). In order to identify appropriate teacher participants for her study who represented these two opposing ways of thinking, Varguez sent out surveys designed to elicit their beliefs about language learning and their teaching practices to teachers in several states. Teacher participant selection criteria for her study included "reputable recommendation, survey score, and a personal description of typical classroom activities" (p. 3). Varguez selected two traditional teachers (survey mean score = 47.5) and two TPRS teachers (mean score 23.5) that she determined as representative of the two different theoretical paradigms to ensure the fidelity of method delivery treatment.

In describing the two methods, Varguez (2009) explained that traditional teachers "tended to elicit practice of reading, writing, listening, and speaking skills" (p. 3). Those traditional students learned through a focus on classroom production-based activities and drills, memorizing vocabulary, consciously learning the rules of how the language works through explicit grammar teaching, and error correction. In contrast, the TPRS teachers spent the "bulk of class time on language comprehension activities including storytelling, teacher-led class conversations, and reading, citing target language comprehension as an essential precursor to target language production" (p. 3). Grammar descriptions were brief and usually emerged from readings. In TPRS class, the focus was on limiting vocabulary to high-frequency phrases, meaning those often used in the language, that were embedded into and repeated within the lesson conversations on meaningful topics and stories. The TPRS teachers spoke mainly in Spanish (90% goal), but English was used sparingly to establish and clarify meaning or for comprehension checks so that students understood nearly everything that was said in the target language in a low-stress environment. Rather than directly correct student errors, the TPRS teachers would use grammatically correct recasts when repeating or verifying story details to provide an incidental focus on form during classroom communication.

Varguez's (2009) study was relevant to this dissertation in several ways. Varguez used a standardized proficiency test to measure student performance in listening and reading, adding increased validity and reliability in instrumentation to her study. Varguez (2009) carefully selected her study participants, systematically identifying teachers who were representative of the opposing theoretical paradigms which informed traditional versus TPRS teaching. Krashen (2015) later articulated those differences in thinking as the Skill-Building Hypothesis and the Comprehension Hypothesis. Varguez (2009) described key differences in the teaching methods which resulted directly from those two opposing theoretical foundations. Those descriptions offered insight from the professional literature on what teachers experienced when using TPRS to provide comprehensible input to students in high school Spanish classes.

High School Spanish / Communicative Language Teaching.

Spangler (2009) called Communicative Language Teaching (CLT) and Teaching Proficiency through Reading and Storytelling (TPRS) "the two dominant methodological frameworks that many foreign language classroom practitioners use to teach second language (L2) in the United States" (p. 60). Spangler (2009) studied two convenience samples of beginning-level Spanish students of 162 total students from two public schools, one in California and the other in Rhode Island. Of the 129 high-school student participants in California, 51 learned through CLT and 78 through TPRS in different classes. Of the 33 middle school students in Rhode Island, 14 of them received instruction in CLT and 33 through TPRS in different classes. Spangler's (2009) work filled a gap at the time because no empirical study yet had compared the effectiveness of the two methods.

Spangler (2009) designed a quantitative, quasi-experimental study to examine student results in three areas which included reading achievement, speaking and writing proficiency, and the students' anxiety levels. The language skill domains were measured using the Standards-based Measurement of Proficiency (STAMP) Test (Avant, 2002) and the students' anxiety levels were measured using the Foreign Language Classroom Anxiety Scale (Horwitz, Horwitz, & Cope, 1986). After the 14-week treatment, there were no differences found for reading, writing, or in anxiety levels, but TPRS students significantly outperformed CLT-taught students in speaking fluency.

While Spangler's (2009) student participants came from convenience samples, the teachers were chosen purposefully. One teacher in each school taught using each method and the effects of each method were compared using a proficiency test and an anxiety scale. Using the same teacher in each school reduced the possibility of teacher quality impacting the student results. Spangler's study design required the teacher participants to know and be skilled in using both methods, without favoring one over the other, which was not always an easy combination to find. As Spangler (2009) related, most university

(like mine)

methods courses mainly encouraged the use of CLT, but some teachers turned to TPRS because they were "dissatisfied with the amount of progress their students make using CLT strategies and textbooks" (p. 3). Teachers of both approaches valued providing comprehensible input, but they differed in their views of what was an appropriate role for output. In the CLT approach, there was a "fundamental belief that *both* input and output facilitate language acquisition" (p. 4) and that both types of activities were necessary in class. However, in the comprehension and content-based TPRS method, "production of the language, or output, is delayed for the students… [because] *only* comprehensible input results in language acquisition" (p. 3). For TPRS teachers, output was considered an indicator, the result, or evidence that second language acquisition had occurred, but not the cause of acquisition. Thus, the teaching practices and philosophical foundations, or the theoretical paradigms informing CLT and the TPRS method, differed.

As Spangler (2009) explained, teachers "staunchly support the use of one methodology to the exclusion of the other" (p. 6). Magnan (2005) called these polar opposite views the "paradigm wars" (p. 315). Therefore, the pedagogic decisions were very different about what was considered the best use of class time. From the beginning, teachers using CLT approaches required students to produce output through speaking and writing, often working with partners or in small groups doing active cooperative learning activities. In contrast, TPRS teachers focused on providing students with repetitive, comprehensible input, related to their interests, without requiring forced output, allowing them to speak and write extensively only when they felt ready and confident. TPRS incorporated brief, frequent, oral, visual, and kinesthetic responses from students to teacher statements, commands, and questions as comprehension checks during TPR and stories. However, extensive language production early on was not demanded of students in TPRS classes in order to avoid raising a student's anxiety level or affective filter (see Krashen, 1982, 1985, 1994, 2013). Previous research had found a negative correlation between a learner's foreign language anxiety level and student achievement. As anxiety levels rose, students learned less (Horwitz, 2008; Horwitz, Horwitz, & Cope, 1986).

Since Spangler's (2009) study design required the two teacher participants to use both the CLT and TPRS methods skillfully, she used purposeful and criterion sampling (Hatch, 2002) and asked for teacher participant recommendations (Miles & Huberman, 1994) from a second language acquisition (SLA) researcher who was knowledgeable about CLT (Bill VanPatten) and TPRS workshop presenters (Blaine Ray and Susie Gross). Spangler (2009) articulated the differences in their pedagogical approaches and listed the classroom activities by the selected teachers for each method (in her Appendix G, and see below). That list showed how the constructs of CLT and of TPRS were operationalized in her study. To ensure the fidelity of each method's delivery, Spangler (2009) not only collaborated on the lists with the two teachers before the study, but she also collected from them the techniques, strategies, activities, and tasks they were using throughout the 14-week treatment. It had been observed that TPRS has been changing and evolving over the years and there have been variations in how the TPRS method has been applied in different teaching contexts by different teachers (Lichtman, 2012a), so Spangler's (2009) readers benefitted by knowing how TPRS was applied in her study.

Some of the TPRS teaching strategies and pedagogic practices that Spangler (2009) included on her list included using TPR, gestures, personalized stories, PQA, circling questions, asking students for story details to include 'bizarre, exaggerated or personalized' (BEP) information to co-construct stories, pop-up grammar, changing the point of view in stories, songs, reading to students, students reading, students acting out stories told by the teacher, and students responding to all teacher statements and questions verbally and nonverbally to demonstrate comprehension (pp. 177-178).

Spanish-speaking Adult English Learners.

Castro (2010) studied one group of learners, comparing the percentage-increase gains from pretest to posttest scores of 13 Spanish-speaking, adult English language learners who attended an evening class once per week for four weeks. The researcher also served as the study's teacher participant for both methodologies. Castro taught three 60-minute classes using the Grammar-Translation (GT) method and three classes of the same 13 (out of 25) students who met the study's selection criteria using TPRS. Their percentage gains obtained through using TPRS were compared with the gains made through the GT method. Students achieved a 49% gain, from 13 to 62 percent, through GT. They made a 45% gain, from 25 to 70 percent, through TPRS instruction. Both methods produced large gains in student learning for the 24 vocabulary words targeted. While Castro (2010) perceived that TPRS was "more engaging" (p. 43), no statistically significant difference was found comparing the learning gains of the two methods, so he concluded, "Neither TPRS nor the Grammar-Translation approach proved more efficacious in vocabulary and retention, but there was far more enthusiasm in learning under TPRS" (p. 42). However, the treatment was short, lasting only four weeks.

Castro's (2010) increased interest in storytelling led him to interview Kieran Egan. While not a TPRS teacher, Egan (1986, 2005, 2008) has authored books advocating the use of stories to transform the way school subjects were taught. Portions of that interview were included in an appendix of Castro's (2010, pp. 46-51) study. Egan emphasized, "My work has been about using the structure of stories to shape regular curriculum content to make this more emotionally and imaginatively engaging to students" (p. 49). Egan (2008) commented that "a good story has the power to reach across time and place. Consider the universal appeal of such fairy tales as the Grimm tales" (p. 50). In discussing the various responses of people to stories, Egan further explained that "the story is simply the main tool we have for organizing content in a way that brings out its emotional force, and delivers information to engage the emotions of the hearer" (p. 51). Castro's (2010) inclusion of the Egan interview with his TPRS study showed how stories could benefit more than one context or educational framework.

High School Spanish / Processing Instruction.

Most of the empirical studies in this review compared TPRS with output-based methods, but Foster (2011) compared TPRS with traditional teaching and another input-based approach. There were mixed results, as discussed below. VanPatten's (1996, 2004) Processing Instruction (PI) framework, which he later called an intervention (in VanPatten, 2017) was both similar to and different from TPRS because PI included some explicit instruction, especially on a limited number of grammar features in Foster's (2011) study. Both TPRS and PI put a primary focus on providing comprehensible input through interpersonal classroom communication that was focused on the meanings of communicated utterances, but there were differences. For example, TPRS used brief (pop-up) grammar comments that were intentionally held to under 15 seconds in order to minimize interference with communicative activity and yet aid student comprehension and lower the affective filter. However, VanPatten's (1996, 2004) PI framework sometimes included more direct, explicit, grammar explanations given which sometimes preceded the performance of communicative tasks in class which students processed to understand the targeted grammatical structures when they subsequently appeared in classroom activities. Those short explanations were given by the PI teacher especially when a contrastive analysis would have determined that those particular grammar structures were formed differently in the learner's first language and target languages. At other times, the explanations were given as an instructional intervention to address prior incorrect student usage to guide their processing of meaningful messages in class.

Even given this difference in approaches, in Foster's (2011) study, there were only 10 minutes total of PI explicit-grammar explanations given compared with two minutes of brief pop-ups total for TPRS. Foster's (2011) study, focused on the acquisition of three target structures which included the preposition /a/, the indirect object pronouns /le, les/, and the verb is pleasing to (*gusta*) or likes. With no prior grammar explanations, the TPRS students read, heard, and responded to sentences containing those structures which were provided to them in readings and oral stories within grammatically-correct sentences such as: *No le gustó bailar a Miguel* which meant Mike did not like to dance. Those targeted structures also were incorporated into the personalized question and answer (PQA) sessions of the teacher with TPRS students.

In Foster's (2011) study, the researcher was also the teacher participant. It was a convenience sample of her own beginning-level high school Spanish classes. A pretest was administered to ensure that the 61 students, ages 14-18, started at the same level and no one scored above 50% on knowledge of the targeted grammar. One group of 20 was taught through PI, 24 using TPRS, and a control group of 17 students was not taught the target forms during that time frame. Students were tested immediately following the limited 130-minute, 3-day, treatment and took a delayed posttest eight weeks later to see if any gains attained were durable. The results were mixed. The students taught using TPRS significantly outperformed the PI group in written fluency ($p < .05$) as measured by total word counts on a ten-minute timed writing test, at the discourse level beyond individual sentences. There were no statistically significant differences found for reading comprehension or on the aural grammaticality judgment test. The PI group had greater gains in speaking and writing accuracy, at the .05 level, which proved durable over time.

While not advocating for any lengthy explicit grammar lessons in the first language, Foster (2011) did conclude, "Practitioners of TPRS could improve their methods by not shying away from some explicit grammar instruction and by considering learners' processing strategies in planning instruction" (p. 46). Foster mentioned that those processing strategies were grounded in principles obtained from SLA research as synthesized by VanPatten (1996, 2004, 2014, 2016, 2017; VanPatten & Williams, 2015). That conclusion implied that teachers should consider incorporating the principles and findings directly derived from SLA research studies into the TPRS method.

Among those PI principles that Foster (2011) mentioned that reflected differences in grammar usage between the first and target languages included the "first noun principle" (p. 10), the "availability of resources principle" (p. 21), the "sentence location principle" (p. 22), and the "lexical preference principle" (p. 24). The first noun principle pointed out that the first noun to appear in a sentence was generally assumed to be the subject, or agent, in the sentence by English speakers, but that was not always the case for other languages. The availability of resources principle reminded teachers to avoid overwhelming learners with too many new unfamiliar terms when teaching new material. The sentence location principle stressed that that word order often differed between languages. The lexical preference principle indicated that certain statements simply sounded better, or were preferred to the ear of a native speaker, even though other utterances technically could be considered as good grammar usage. In other words, VanPatten's (2004) decisions of which structures to explain explicitly to learners were highly selective and principled. The PI framework did not advocate for any widespread or lengthy explicit instruction of all forms. On the contrary, VanPatten's (2004) primary stated goal was to provide comprehensible input within meaningful contexts to promote the acquisition of implicit knowledge. VanPatten (2002) had pointed out that explicit knowledge cannot become implicit knowledge or directly cause acquisition. However, since Foster (2011) found that accuracy, in the production skills, was improved after receiving some explicit grammar explanation through PI, her study did support the inclusion of some brief grammar discussions at least slightly beyond the limited 15-second pop-up comments used in TPRS. Foster's (2011) study drew additional attention to studying the effects of instructional techniques and classroom learning strategies, which were supported or refuted by SLA research, on student achievement.

Secondary School Student Survey / TPRS / BEP.

Beal (2011) was interested in investigating some of the positive claims made by TPRS practitioners with the goal of supporting or refuting them with empirical data. Beal found no evidence that TPRS reduced student anxiety levels or that TPRS promoted improved student retention in the Spanish program from lower to upper levels of study.

Beal found mixed results on the district's final exam, with the middle school TPRS students outperforming traditional students, but not at the high school.

Beal (2011) had separated his convenience teacher sample obtained from one school district into three groups, by how often the teachers used a 'bizarre, exaggerated, and personalized' (BEP) storytelling technique and only "to introduce and reinforce vocabulary and grammar" (p. 68). Beal (2011) wrote that "traditional exercises in speaking, reading, and writing" (p. 8) could follow the BEP, a notion which helped to clarify why no teacher used TPRS exclusively in his study because traditional exercises have not been accepted as part of the TPRS method. Twenty-eight teachers participated, two men and 26 women, who taught Spanish, French, or German. There were 18 high school teachers, nine middle school, and one who taught in both the high and middle schools. The three groups included six teachers who did not use the TPRS BEP storytelling technique at all, 16 were partial users, and there were six regular users. In Beal's (2011) teacher sample, there were no exclusive users of TPRS in any district school and no middle-school teachers reported themselves as complete non-users.

Curiously, Beal (2011) cited Ray and Seely's (2003) book, *Fluency through TPR Storytelling*, as his main source for claiming that BEP was an essential element of TPRS, rather than a more current edition. The 2003 book was the third edition and the fourth came out in 2004. In the fifth edition (2008), three years before Beal's (2011) study, Ray and Seely (2008) mentioned that some teachers preferred the term "*unexpected* instead of bizarre" (p. 251), making bizarre stories an option rather than a central component of TPRS, as Beal claimed. That change created space within the TPRS method for more content-based instruction, nonfiction and authentic texts, folktales, and lessons on culture.

Given the context of the above-mentioned comments, Beal (2011) reported the following findings. The independent variable in Beal's (2011) dissertation was the BEP storytelling technique that was described for the groups above. No significant differences were found in student anxiety levels, as measured on the Foreign Language Classroom Anxiety Scale (FLCAS), constructed by Horwitz, Horwitz, and Cope (1986). There were no significant differences found in the middle school for continued enrollment plans on an independent samples chi-square test, but the non-use high school group had the highest levels of students who intended to take the next level foreign language class. Relying on self-reports, the non-use group rated their own skills higher than did other groups in reading and listening. Academic success was measured by scores on a multiple-choice semester exam that included discrete point grammar questions and scores on the reading sections. These were common assessments for the school district, with the high school non-use group scoring the largest adjusted mean. When the middle school students were considered separately, the regular use group had significantly higher scores.

Beal's (2011) intended purpose for his dissertation was to "research some of the claims of TPRS supporters" (p. 2), but he admitted, "Since the teachers in the present study use[d] the various aspects of the method inconsistently, it was decided to only examine one part of the method" (p. 68). Beal did not adopt Spangler's (2009) approach to operationalize the entire construct of TPRS as a whole, nor did he cite her study. Neither did he purposefully search for TPRS teachers to ensure the fidelity of method delivery, as Spangler (2009) had done. Instead, Beal opted for a convenience teacher sampling from a school district that agreed to cooperate; he admitted, "None of the teachers surveyed for this research rated themselves as exclusive TPRS teachers" (p. 77).

A teacher participant sample which included one group that used TPRS exclusively could have made his purpose statement attainable, but his decision to reduce the TPRS method to only one technique (BEP) made it difficult to draw any valid findings from his data for the method as a whole that could refute or support the positive claims of TPRS supporters. Beal's (2011) study had mixed results and it reflected higher levels of engagement from using BEP storytelling for the younger children only, not yet in secondary schools. In addition to Beal (2011), other researchers have been interested in comparing the effects of using different language teaching methodologies, or types of instruction, and the potential impact of learner age on second language acquisition.

Effects of Implicit and Explicit Instruction / Age of Learner.

Lichtman (2012b) investigated the questions of what gains have been attained through explicit and implicit instruction, for learners of different ages, and whether there were limits in acquisition through explicit teaching. Lichtman (2016) discussed and summarized her own dissertation findings first published in Lichtman (2012b). Two commonly-held beliefs were that children learned languages more easily than adults and that they did not benefit from explicit instruction. Lichtman (2012b) found that children were generally not provided with explicit instruction but when they received it, they could learn grammar rules as adults did. She also discovered that adults usually were taught through explicit methods, but that they could also acquire languages slowly and robustly through implicit instruction too. For her study, she obtained her groups taught without explicit grammar instruction from TPRS classes. TPRS students were taught through an implicit grammar approach. She concluded that adults could learn and acquire language implicitly when provided with appropriate acquisition-rich classroom environments.

In a second part of her study, Lichtman (2012b) used an artificial language, called *Sillyspeak*, and found additional evidence that both adults and children could learn language with accuracy through explicit instruction. However, the explicit knowledge did not result in better language production, so she concluded that teaching explicit grammar rules did not improve performance. Implicit instruction enabled students to acquire an additional language in the classroom. Lichtman (2012b) concluded that adults' supposed reliance on explicit learning was caused more by what instruction they were given rather than any innate change related to age, a myth many people had believed before her study. In other words, both children and adults can learn about languages through explicit teaching and acquire their use through implicit instruction.

Explicit and Implicit Instruction in High School Special Education.

In Holleny's (2012) study, her special needs students received both implicit and explicit instruction. Holleny, a special education teacher, taught Spanish to four classes of high school students (n = 44), with mild to moderate learning disabilities, in a resource room. In her empirical study, two classes scored higher on unit tests "when taught through TPRS techniques" (p. iii) and two classes did better learning through traditional methods. There were no significant differences found. Both groups received instruction, on four units of thematic vocabulary (on action verbs, rooms, food, and activities) and took unit tests for each which included sections on listening, picture identification, and translations. Average (mean) test scores were compared. Overall, the results "slightly favor[ed] the TPRS techniques" (p. 43) as 24 out of 44 students performed better with

TPRS (81.1% to 78.9%). She concluded that "both methods could be effective" (p. 45). Despite no significant differences in test scores, Holleny (2012) wrote that her study "found the TPRS storytelling technique to be slightly more effective, engaging, and efficient than the traditional methods… in students with mild disabilities" (p. 50) or special needs students.

In her study design procedure, Holleny (2012) decided to switch the control and experimental groups so that all students received two units of instruction using TPRS and two using traditional methods. "Each class was the experimental group [TPRS] twice and the control group [traditional] twice" (p. 36). While that procedure may have provided equity of exposure to both methods, it was confusing to many students who asked why the researcher "stopped showing pictures, teaching with gestures, and playing review games. The students stated that they enjoyed these activities and felt that they learned the vocabulary better this way" (p. 49). The researcher also "noticed an increase in attention and participation when [she] used the TPRS techniques" (p. 49). Holleny did not explain her decision to mix the methods, but from the theory informing TPRS, it could have been counterintuitive to do so and perhaps introduced a confounding variable.

As Krashen (2015) pointed out, TPRS is not just a technique, but a complete language teaching "method consistent with the Comprehension Hypothesis" (p. 168). His hypothesis assumed that acquisition is a subconscious or unconscious process activated by receiving comprehensible input in the target language. Krashen (2015) further explained that its rival is the "Skill-Building Hypothesis [which] says that in order to develop competence in a second language we must first consciously learn the grammar rules and then practice them in output until they become automatic" (p. 168). These two sets of competing assumptions have resulted in radically different teaching and learning approaches. When mixed in a study design with the same students, neither approach or separate theoretical paradigm could be tested separately on its own merits, calling into question researcher conclusions drawn from method comparisons. Holleny (2012) mixed the approaches, a design flaw discussed earlier that some other researchers also made.

University Spanish / Adapted TPRS with Grammar.

In Oliver's (2012) study, the adapted TPRS group (experimental, 44 students) scored significantly higher (at the $p = .05$ level) than the control group (83 students), that received traditional instruction, on the college course final (semester) exam which was written by the department coordinator and tested only reading, writing, and fill-in-the blanks. There were no sections on listening or speaking and no pre-test to ensure all students began at the same beginner level of Spanish proficiency. There was a convenience sample comprised of six intact classes ($n = 127$). Four sections were taught by three self-described 'traditional' teachers and two sections by a teacher who wanted to try out TPRS for the first time. However, despite these delimitations, Oliver (2012) could correctly conclude that college students exposed to an adapted version of TPRS teaching had significantly outperformed traditional students on a final exam ($p < .05$) in Spanish at the university level. "Additionally, the students' attitudes were generally very positive in the Storytelling classroom, according to their class evaluation forms" (p. 56).

Oliver (2012) had wanted to compare traditional and pure TPRS teaching in six beginning-level college Spanish classes, but settled for an adapted version of TPRS. The department coordinator placed certain 'restrictions' on Oliver (the teacher-researcher) who taught the TPRS sections, so rather than those classes being run entirely following the method's principles (from Ray & Seeley, 2009), students in her study received an 'adapted' or modified form of TPRS. She was not given complete academic freedom. The restrictions imposed included being required to teach the textbook vocabulary and grammar, that students take common assessments, and that all students be prepared for the subsequent courses in the curricular sequence. Learning activities outside the TPRS paradigm included having students work in small groups to practice questions and answers with embedded target grammatical forms, but their 'small group work' was more of a traditional strategy, rather than TPRS, because the quality of input was lowered in the forced student-to-student interaction and contained errors and mispronunciation.

Oliver (2012) explained that in TPRS classes normally the teacher provided most of the quality, correctly-formed, engaging, input and the students' role was to listen for understanding rather than force output before beginning learners were developmentally ready to produce structures they had not yet acquired. Oliver's department coordinator required her to cover thematic textbook vocabulary, but in TPRS vocabulary came from high frequency usage lists (i.e., Davies, 2006), not from themes or a grammar syllabus. Oliver's (2012) Spanish coordinator also required students to take common assessments, which tested grammatical forms out of context, but these exams did not include language proficiency. Traditional courses have 'covered' grammar items from simple to complex forms, often explained in English, rather than the TPRS approach of 'mastering' high frequency fluency structures needed for communication, one sentence at a time in the target language. Oliver (2012) had to cover every textbook chapter and required her students to complete textbook exercises and electronic workbook activities to practice grammatical forms out of context for homework, which was not normally part of TPRS.

At the time of that study, Oliver (in 2012) was just beginning to try out TPRS and had not yet acquired all the essential teaching skills of the method. When she had difficulty sustaining the high energy demands of storytelling, she sometimes "shifted to [teaching] traditional grammar" (p. 56), in English, which was not in line with TPRS principles. In those moments, she watched the student "energy level of the class drop and eyes droop as they lost interest in textbook activities and grammar explanations" (p. 56). However, despite these occasional departures from using pure TPRS, guided by its principles, Oliver (2012) perceived that students did succeed from her efforts to learn and use the method, even when TPRS was new to her and her skills not yet fully developed.

Oliver (2012) described her own experiences using TPRS and her observations of students being taught by a teacher beginning to use the method. Before TPRS, she was a veteran teacher who had become dissatisfied and "frustrated with the lack of proficiency and retention" (p. 54) in her students and their lack of vocabulary and grammar mastery despite her use of a grammar-oriented approach. Since her students were "reluctant to speak the language" (p. 54), she sought a more communicative method and discovered TPRS. She did not mention attending any workshops, but she studied the 5th edition of Ray and Seeley's (2009) book, *Fluency through TPR Storytelling*, and wanted to try out the method. As mentioned above, her department coordinator allowed her to use TPRS, but only within certain parameters, somewhat limiting her academic freedom, but she did work within those restrictions in both her teaching and for her research study. Oliver (2012) wrote stories using the textbook vocabulary about college life and added some "unusual and unexpected elements in the stories to keep the students' interest [because] their active participation was essential" (p. 54) for TPRS to succeed.

Oliver (2012) discovered that storytelling required concentration and practice, but her TPRS teaching skills did improve. She used TPR gestures, asked students questions, demanded their choral responses in Spanish, and observed that they were "all speaking Spanish more" (p. 54) than her previous students who were taught using other methods. Oliver found that her new TPRS classroom "atmosphere was fun and supportive" (p. 54). Her TPRS-taught students incorporated the fluency structures acquired through listening and reading into their writing tasks, which became more creative over time. Oliver (2012) reported that she saw a "marked improvement in composition writing" (p. 55) because her students could compose with fewer grammatical errors than before TPRS.

For Oliver (2012), the "most surprising and encouraging grammar acquisition came from the three novels the students read [that contained] indirect and direct object pronouns in context with repetition. Grammar seemed to come naturally to them in context" (p. 55). Before encountering these pronouns in the textbook, her students already had acquired them and wrote them correctly in their final exam compositions. Although direct error correction was not normally considered part of TPRS principles, Oliver (2012) explained that after TPRS her confident students were "more willing to correct errors in their compositions because they could see the relevancy of the correction in context" (p. 55) as her students experienced success through TPRS.

High School Spanish / Proficiency Assessment.

For a one-year treatment, Dziedzic (2012) compared the effects of Teaching with Comprehensible Input (TCI) to traditional language teaching, in high school Spanish 1 classes. The TCI group outperformed traditional students in speaking and writing proficiency, but no significant differences were found on listening or reading tests.

While no pre-test was given, only students who were true beginners and had not taken a Spanish class before or had exposure to the language were included as participants in the study. The researcher was the teacher for both groups (n = 65) so that differences among teachers would not be an issue in this empirical study. The fidelity of method delivery was ensured by having experienced and knowledgeable instructors observe his teaching. Patricia Shikes, who had 30 years of Spanish teaching experience, verified his 'traditional' approach. For this study, traditional was defined as "grammar-based instruction that focuses on student output [and] on teaching grammar rules" (p. 4), language was studied as an object, and students learned 'about' the language using the textbook, *¡Buen viaje!* (Schmitt & Woodford, 2008). Traditional learning activities included "warm-ups, rehearsed conversation, grammar explanation, and vocabulary repetition" (p. 5).For the instruction received by the TCI-taught group in this study, Karen Rowan, Diana Noonan, and Donna Tatum-Jones observed his instruction to verify the fidelity of how the teacher (researcher) provided students with comprehensible input (CI), used TPR techniques with the TPRS method, and included Sustained Silent Reading (SSR or Free Voluntary Reading, FVR).The experimental (TCI group) treatment was provided through a combination of CI strategies, TPR, and TPRS for one academic year.

According to Dziedzic (2012), in the typical TPRS/TCI class, the "focus is on storytelling, reading, and the personalization of class topics" (p. 4). The teacher's stated goal was to provide comprehensible input (CI) to students 85-90% of class time in the target language. Dziedzic taught the TPRS stories from Ray's (1990, 1992) *Look, I can talk!* books and the TCI students read Ray's (2007) *Pobre Ana* novella and Canion and Gaab's (2008) reader *Piratas*. In this study, however, the reading of short novels was not limited to the CI-taught group alone because both the experimental and control groups had ten minutes of daily recreational reading (SSR/FVR), of ten minutes per class for three months in the second semester, when they could select what they wanted to read from a classroom library of 150 children's books.

Dziedzic (2012) decided not to limit SSR (FVR) class time to the TPRS/TCI group alone as existing research already had established its effectiveness. In all 23 comparison studies of English-as-a-foreign (EFL) contexts, that he reviewed on SSR, Krashen (2011a) found that no matter how the groups were compared, the students using SSR outperformed all others. Therefore, to deny SSR to any group could have been considered unethical since it was known to be effective. However, since both groups received SSR (and not just the TCI group), that fact may be considered a confounding variable and could partially explain why no significant differences were found in the 'input' skills (listening and reading) for Dziedzic's study.

Dziedzic (2012) found significant differences in 'output' production skills on the Denver Public Schools Proficiency Assessments. The TPRS group scored significantly higher than the traditionally-taught control group in both writing (large effect size = 0.70) and in speaking (effect size = 0.99). This finding, that focusing on input resulted in more proficient output, which may have surprised some people, was consistent with previous research on comprehensible-input approaches leading to higher results on measures of output and production (Krashen, 2003, 2011b, 2013; Varguez, 2009; and Watson, 2009).

Secondary School EFL / Proficiency and Motivation.

Safdarian (2013), in an EFL (English as a foreign language) secondary school context in Iran, compared the effects of storytelling on proficiency and on motivation.

An experimental group of 60 students taught using stories significantly (at the .05 level) outperformed control group of 42 students, taught without stories, on a post treatment (semester) language proficiency test. The post-test included vocabulary, grammar, and reading comprehension. All students (n = 102) were boys, aged 11 to 14, who were all identified by pre-test to be at the same elementary English proficiency level before the treatment period. Based on the post-test scores, Safdarian (2013) concluded that "storytelling can be used as an effective pedagogical tool in EFL settings" (p. 202).

In Safdarian's (2013) study, the two groups, both experimental and control, were demographically similar and received the same traditional teaching approach, other than the presence or absence of stories. Their teachers followed the same course syllabus, textbook exercises, homework assignments, assessments, and grammar coverage for both groups. Safdarian (2013) defended his design of not having the story group 'exclusively' use the TPRS method by writing that would be a "departure from the way languages are generally taught currently" (p. 220). However, that decision resulted in all students receiving a combination of methods (TPRS and traditional), with a possible confounding variable in that all students received the first TPRS step (of three) of establishing meaning by pre-teaching unit vocabulary.

Safdarian (2013) noticed that since all teachers in the program were required to cover the same curriculum, the storytelling teachers lacked sufficient time to fully implement the TPRS method in class because they had to "hasten to catch up to the schedule" (p. 240) in order to ensure coverage of the explicit grammar syllabus. That potentially confounding variable was a concept contrary to the TPRS strategy of mastery learning and may have served to raise the affective filters the students and faculty. TPRS teachers were not free to choose and personalize their own stories or to fully co-construct them with their students because the stories were "specified by the school English department" (p. 229). Further, Safdarian (2013) perceived that the "type of stories chosen" (p. 239) and the "way the storytelling was carried out in the classroom triggered the motivation problem" (p. 240). The results of the Attribute/Motivation Test Battery (AMBT) questionnaire indicated that there were no significant differences found in student motivational levels between the experimental group taught using stories and the control group taught without stories. However, as pointed out by Safdarian (2013) and throughout this literature review, the TPRS method involves more than the presence or absence of pre-prepared stories.

Secondary EFL in Turkey / Vocabulary.

Cubukcu (2014) studied two groups of secondary school students learning English vocabulary in an EFL (English as a foreign language) context in Turkey. Of the 44 study participants, 22 students received instruction from a textbook approach and 22 were taught through TPRS. The control group students did substitution drills in the textbook and used memory aids to learn the vocabulary. The textbook-taught control group was not exposed to storytelling and the TPRS-taught treatment group did not use the textbook. The same twenty vocabulary words were taught to each group during the short three-week treatment using a pretest/posttest study design to measure improvement, but specific information about those tests was not provided. Cubukcu (2014) found that the TPRS-taught group significantly outperformed the textbook-taught group. Cubukcu (2014) concluded that "vocabulary instruction through TPRS has a significant impact on the lexical knowledge level" (p. 89) and that her study's results "corroborate the success of TPRS on vocabulary teaching competence" (p. 84).

In designing her study, Cubukcu (2014) went beyond Safdarian's (2013) approach in that she operationalized the construct of TPRS to include more than the mere presence or absence of stories. Cubukcu (2014) described how TPRS was delivered in her study as including storytelling, questions and answers, interpersonal interaction, personalization, establishing meaning of target vocabulary, TPR, gestures, eliciting unusual responses, making students look good, using barometer students to check for story comprehension, asking parking and circling questions, and story dramatization.

Preschool EFL in Turkey / No Differences Attributed to Gender.

Demir and Cubukcu (2014) studied EFL students learning vocabulary in Turkey, at the preschool level to determine whether TPRS should be used at that level. They found empirical evidence to support a positive response to that question. Twenty high-frequency vocabulary words (commonly used words in the language) were selected from a book about an island from their school's regular curriculum. In their study, those 20 words were incorporated into a pre/posttest design for the four-week treatment period, with 16 total hours of instruction. The multiple-choice test was locally prepared and the same test was administered both before and after the treatment. Two intact preschool classes were randomly assigned to two groups (39 students total). The control group students were taught through a Communicative Approach (CA) and the intervention (experimental) group through TPRS. The CA sessions included role plays, games, and some information gap activities. For this study, TPRS was described as including stories, personalization, rhymes, songs, reading, and acting out. TPRS lessons included establishing meaning, asking a story, reading, gestures, short explanations, a focus on meaning, contextualized language use, students sharing ideas, teacher questions, fun answers, and some translating of the story into the mother tongue to ensure comprehension. Pretest results had shown no significant differences between the two groups, so posttest scores were used to measure student vocabulary learning. Preschool TPRS-taught EFL students significantly outscored the CA control group on the posttest ($p = .013$) and no gender differences were found. Demir and Cubukcu (2014) concluded that the "TPRS method has a notable impact on lexical development" (p. 194) for both boys and girls and was an appropriate methodology even for young children in preschool.

French / Motivation to Continue Study / Increased Confidence.

Murray (2014) compared a typical French 1 class with TPR and TPRS added. The treatment was limited to six weeks and 27 students. The experimental group received an instructional treatment which included TPR, TPRS, and a "traditional teaching approach" (p. 22), along with using a textbook, workbook, doing homework, and partner work. The control group treatment was limited to the "traditional teaching approach" (p. 22). Pretests and posttests were used to measure gains and the students in the experimental group made significant improvement in language skills. In addition, the results of a Likert-scale attitudinal survey indicated that their confidence grew in speaking and comprehending French and they were motivated to move on to French 2. Murray (2014) concluded that TPR and TPRS were "effective methods that should be incorporated into the world language classroom" (p. 41) for high school students.

Murray (2014) admitted that she believed "that students of world languages need to be taught in a variety of ways" (p. 5). She also expressed her opinion that TPR and

TPRS "were never intended to be the 'sole' teaching strategies applied when using these teaching approaches" (p. 20). Murray (2014) did not explain where she got the idea that TPRS was 'not' a complete method, but she did admit her only training in TPR or TPRS was limited to a "basic one-day seminar given three years ago," (p. 6) before conducting her own study. Because of this, Murray (2014) did not compare a pure TPRS approach with a traditional approach, as the title of her study suggested, limiting the conclusions that can or could be drawn from her study. Qualified global conclusions could be drawn comparing a traditional approach with a somewhat unique mixed-methods eclectic approach, as defined above, but it would be unclear which elements of the experimental group's treatment impacted the results.

TPRS + COLA / Effect of Dialog within TPRS.

Murray (2014) added TPRS to a traditional approach, but Cox (2015) added Context-based Optimized Language Acquisition (COLA) to the evolving TPRS method. In Cox's (2015) study, there were 52 Spanish 2 students, ages 15-19, mostly high school sophomores, 35 in the experimental TPRS + COLA group, and 17 in the regular TPRS control group. No information was provided on what type of instruction they had during Spanish 1 classes the previous year, so no long-term effects were possible to determine. In a treatment limited to 90 minutes of instruction, both groups were taught 20 new vocabulary words and given a pretest and posttest, with no delayed posttest used to test for retention. Students were given picture prompts and asked to speak about those as the number of words they uttered was counted as the only measure of speaking fluency used in the study. No time limit was set, so students could speak for as long as they wished. No differences were found in learning gain when the TPRS group was compared to a combined (experimental) TPRS + COLA group. In Cox's (2015) study, the presence or absence of COLA dialogs in the instructional treatment had no significant effect.

Cox (2015) introduced her TPRS study by declaring that, especially in her home state of Colorado, "gone are the days of verb charts and explicit grammar instruction and its place is a focus on communication" (p. 1). Cox explained that both her state school system and school district now "require the use of TPRS" (p. 1). She included a copy of her state's Department of Education's 2014 "Position Statement on World Languages Standards-Based Teaching, Learning and Assessment" (p. 53) as Appendix K of her study which clearly defined the expectations of teachers and learners. Paraphrasing that paper, teachers were expected to speak the target language at least 90% of class, to provide learners with opportunities to acquire language through meaningful contexts, and to use authentic resources to promote cultural awareness. Teachers were to have their effectiveness measured through student growth measures. Learners were expected to perform tasks using the target language, to show their growth in formative and summative assessments, and to acquire the levels of proficiency needed for college and career readiness in programs from elementary through high school. Learner assessments were to include presentational, interpretive, and interpersonal modes of communication to assess the language domains of listening, speaking, reading, and writing. The Colorado position statement concluded, "Therefore, discrete measurements of isolated skills, such as grammar points, vocabulary knowledge and cultural facts are NOT ACCEPTABLE [emphasis in original] measures of student proficiency" (p. 53). The position statement was endorsed by the state's Commissioner and Deputy Commissioner of Education.

Within the above-mentioned political climate, Cox (2015) argued that previous "researchers have found that TPRS at least matches other methods of instruction or outperforms it" (p. 30). However, Cox noted there were several evolving variations of TPRS and many researchers failed to describe exactly how TPRS was operationalized in their studies. From Cox's view, with the effectiveness of TPRS already sufficiently established, it was now time for research to isolate particular aspects of the method and to determine which ones had greater impact or effects on acquisition. Cox (2015) advocated "examining specific facets and newer variations to create the most effective version of TPRS" (p. 33). Without a written source, but rather citing a personal telephone interview in 2015, Cox credited Gaye Jenkins with being the founder of "Context-based Optimized Language Acquisition" (p. 10) or COLA. The COLA method has been called the "newer upgrade" (p. 1) of TPRS, as well as the "next step in TPRS or TPRS 2.0" (p. 10). As such, in Cox's (2015) study, COLA also incorporated TPRS, so the mix has been more accurately called "COLA + TPRS" by (Lichtman, 2016) but herein and moving forward it has been simply called COLA for purposes of brevity. For her contribution to this new path in research that she envisioned and has begun to carve out, Cox (2015) decided to conduct the first empirical COLA research study and to "tackle the most obvious and the largest difference between TPRS and COLA: the use of dialogues" (p. 15).

Cox (2015) described COLA as (1) having more repetitions than regular TPRS because the students acted out the story twice rather than once, (2) the students saying or repeating the new vocabulary words as they gestured them, (3) using dialogs that in Cox's (2015) view, were similar to those that had been used in the audiolingual method, and (4) that COLA always used a pre-prepared story rather than the regular TPRS technique of the teacher and students working together to co-construct a story through interactional communication during class. In other words, COLA was "more of a formula where the method required that the teacher do each step in a certain sequence [and] COLA dialogues encouraged the practice of output" (p. 11). More partner work was used in COLA and fewer questions were asked of students than in regular TPRS.

The changes incorporated into Cox's (2015) study involved TPRS taking on COLA characteristics where differences existed, rather than COLA conforming to regular TPRS principles, strategies, and techniques. One might jokingly, but accurately, have said that the TPRS group was invited to drink the 'cola' in order to control the other variables in order to isolate the impact of dialogs. This conflating of the methods could have called into question any conclusions that might have been drawn had there been significant differences found between groups. However, as the study turned out, "both groups improved the same over time" (p. 25), even though the students reported on a survey that they enjoyed the dialogs more than the stories which indicated that they had experienced both, perhaps in itself a confounding variable.

The researcher attempted to hold all variables constant except for the dialogs in order to measure their effects. However, in so doing the fidelity of method delivery of the TPRS method may have been compromised in part because the circling questions, personalized questions and answers (PQA), and the co-construction of stories were all eliminated from the typical TPRS instruction in Cox's (2015) design. In addition, before the study, students in the TPRS (control) group "had done dialogues before" (p. 31) of the type used in COLA instruction, which was a possible confounding variable.

Cox (2015) had attempted to compare the possible differential effects of TPRS and COLA dialogs on "speech production in a Spanish 2 high school classroom" (p. iii) for a short, two-day, treatment. However, in order to isolate the impact of dialog, the TPRS group had only two days of atypical TPRS instruction. The COLA group had TPRS on their first day, but on their second day they had COLA dialogs while the TPRS group did another story. Despite the short treatment time, from pretest to posttest, both groups demonstrated statistically significant improvement in speech production. The COLA dialog group gained 1.6 more words than the regular TPRS group, which did not reflect a significantly significant difference, so the COLA group did not do better after having practiced dialogs, as the researcher had expected. Cox's (2015) study revealed the difficulty of designing a quasi-experimental study that properly isolated a single variable, holding all other variables constant, and eliminating potential confounding variables, from which valid and reliable findings could be drawn. One of her main contributions was to challenge other researchers to isolate and study the effects of different aspects of TPRS to determine which were more effective, moving the research agenda forward. Cox (2015) declared with optimism, "With future research, storytelling can be streamlined to potentially create the most effective language instruction ever used, revolutionizing the field and second language instruction" (p. 35).

University French / Presence or Absence of Stories.

Merinnage De Costa (2015) compared TPRS with traditional instruction in a beginning-level university French class and used teacher-made tests for vocabulary, culture, listening, writing, and grammar. Twenty students participated in the study, with ten randomly assigned to two groups, an experimental TPRS (story) group and a control group that did not use stories. Before the study, they all had studied French for two months using a traditional approach with the same teacher-researcher. There was a pretest/posttest design to compare learning gain. The results were mixed. In vocabulary learning, the TPRS group had a larger learning gain than the traditional group (58.83 to 45.80), but the difference was not statistically significant ($p = 0.517$). Similarly, for cultural knowledge, the TPRS group had a higher learning gain (70.84 to 62.50), but the difference was not statistically significant ($p = 0.780$). However, in the listening domain, the TPRS group outperformed the control group (24.07 to 22.60), with a significant difference ($p < .05$). On the other hand, the traditional group significantly outperformed the TPRS group in both grammar and writing ($p < .05$), with mixed results for stories.

Merinnage De Costa (2015) had intended to compare TPRS with traditional instruction. However, in the study's abstract, the researcher reduced the study to comparing TPRS with a method that did "not incorporate a story" (p. iv) because the researcher had thought that TPRS was "fully reliant on the common and familiar communicative device of the story" (p. 9). Therefore, Merinnage De Costa (2015) did not operationalize the construct of TPRS more broadly in her study which could have included other essential elements such as circling, personalized questions and answers (PQA), and co-constructing the story during class through referential questioning with the students. A close reading of the lessons plans revealed that the main difference between the methods in this study was limited to the presence or absence of using a story, but stories have been used in contexts not involving TPRS. That oversimplification of the TPRS method was reflected in the instructional treatment as several classroom activities were the same for both methods, many of which may have violated TPRS principles, as discussed below. Among those were the following activities not generally considered to be part of the TPRS method (see Ray & Seely, 2015).

Merinnage De Costa's (2015) provided the lesson plans for perusal which showed how TPRS was operationalized in the study. On the first day of the instruction, the TPRS story group used flash cards, conjugated verbs, were limited to the present tense, did textbook exercises, and produced a similar story to the one they were told. In other words, even on the first day, the story group received traditional instruction not typical of TPRS. In most variations of TPRS, textbooks and flashcards generally have not been used because they promoted short term, not long-term retention. Output was not forced in the TPRS applications outside of this study because that could have raised the affective filter and would have ignored the limitations of the natural order of acquisition (Krashen, 1981) and learner developmental sequences.

Unlike Merinnage De Costa's (2015) study, in most TPRS applications, it has been vocabulary and not grammar that was sheltered from learners, and students were not expected early on to produce extended discourse until they were ready and volunteered to do so. The researcher in Merinnage De Costa's (2015) study taught vocabulary from the textbook and did not limit it for the story group. The researcher told, and did not ask, the students a story. The researcher explicitly taught and reviewed grammar for its own sake, outside of meaningful classroom communicative contexts. There was not a myriad of questions and brief answers to check for understanding and comprehension as normally were considered essential parts of the TPRS method by its practitioners (see Ray & Seely, 2015). Throughout most of the Merinnage De Costa's (2015) study's lesson plans, the student learning objectives were the same for both the story or experimental group and for the control (traditional) group as well. The only real difference was that stories were not used in the traditional approach. Therefore, any conclusions that could be drawn from the study's data would have to be limited then to measuring the effects of traditional, but not TPRS instruction, or isolating the presence or absence of stories, because this study conflated the two treatments. TPRS has always been much more than the mere presence of stories.

In Merinnage De Costa's (2015) lesson plans, on the second day, the experimental group conjugated new verbs, reviewed verb conjugations from the previous class, and completed additional textbook exercises in the book for the purpose of practicing those verb forms which focused on form, and not on communicating meaning in context. The students played a game to practice the verbs and did worksheet exercises. Generally, TPRS practitioners have rejected worksheets in favor of using instructional strategies more compatible with brain research, as contained in Tate's (2016) book, *Worksheets Don't Grow Dendrites* and informed by Medina's (2014) book on *Brain Rules* which generally was included in TPRS workshops. Merinnage De Costa (2015) did not mention having attended a TPRS workshop. The researcher cited the 2012 version, rather than the most-recent seventh edition of Ray and Seely's (2015) book on TPRS, *Fluency Through TPR Storytelling*, which in part could have explained why the TPRS variation used in the study did not reflect the most-recent changes to the method.

The third and fourth day of Merinnage De Costa's (2015) experimental (story) group instructional treatment continued with more activity worksheets and the objective was to review the "target elements of the chapter" (p. 30). In other words, this was more of a textbook, and not a TPRS, approach. Textbooks were often not necessarily used at all in typical TPRS teaching. The teacher's plan indicated that a story was told, but since no details were given as to how that was done, it could not be determined whether that storytelling was consistent with TPRS principles. Students shared sentences that they wrote in front of the class, perhaps another opportunity to raise the affective filter unless volunteers were used. On day 5, the students took the posttest.

In Merinnage De Costa's (2015) study, a possible confounding variable was identified. The researcher included The Natural Approach as part of the traditional instruction group treatment and asked lots of yes/no questions and comprehension questions, strategies perhaps more consistent with TPRS principles than traditional instruction. On the other hand, precisely how the teacher researcher applied The Natural Approach (by Krashen & Terrell, 1983) with the traditional group was not discussed, so it could not be determined whether it was applied in ways consistent with Krashen's (1978, 1981, 1985, 1989, 1992, 1993, 2006, 2009, 2011b, 2013, 2015) theories and research.

The researcher, Merinnage de Costa (2015) who had hypothesized that the TPRS group would outperform the traditional group on all measures offered some possible explanations for the surprise results. Among those was the small sample size of only 20 total study participants. That small sample size did not warrant wide generalizability of the results. The treatment time was limited to less than a week, when "the researcher would have preferred a study of a four-month time frame in order to fully implement all aspects of the TPRS method and the traditional method" (p. 48). Despite some of the results not being statistically significant, the researcher did note that in her study TPRS "demonstrated improvement" (p. 47) for in listening, learning culture, and vocabulary and recommended that "all educational fields could benefit from the TPRS approach when vocabulary is being taught" (p. 49). The researcher also recommended that since the TPRS method "makes a comfortable environment for students to practice the language" (p. 49) that college language teachers should be trained in TPRS. The researcher, Merinnage De Costa (2015), wrote that the study's "results demonstrated that combining these two methods could be useful for teaching new language to college level students" (p. 47). Given the above-mentioned accidental conflation of the two methods that was present in Merinnage De Costa (2015) and the learning gains achieved if viewed as one method rather than two, that may have been the actual, unintended, finding of the study, since the treatment was mostly the same for both methods. However, given the limitations admitted by the researcher, a more rigorously-designed study which included a concern for the fidelity of method delivery would be required to test that hypothesis.

Describing the Method / The Fidelity of Method Delivery.

Blanton (2015)'s dissertation compared the effects of two mostly implicit language teaching approaches, Communicative Language Teaching (CLT) versus TPRS on motivation and proficiency in high school level 3 Spanish classes. There were 117 students total in the study, 72 girls and 45 boys, mostly 10th and 11th graders, with an average age of 16 and an age range of between 13-18. There were 64 CLT students and 53 TPRS students. Student participants were tested after the one-year treatment.

To test for motivation, Blanton (2015) administered the Language Learning Orientations Scale--Intrinsic Motivation, Extrinsic Motivation, and Amotivation Subscales (LLOS-IEA) Motivation Scale (Noels, Pelletier, Clement, & Vallerand, 2003) Motivation Scale. Blanton (2015) found that, compared to CLT-taught students, the TPRS students had "statistically significant higher levels of L2 motivation for IM

Accomplishment, IM knowledge, and IM stimulation" (p. 1). While TPRS students scored higher in motivation, the study results were mixed because there were significant differences found for CLT students in three of the four basic language skill domains.

Blanton (2015) administered the STAMP 4S Test and she found no significant difference between students taught using CLT or TPRS in Speaking. Her analysis did show that CLT students significantly outperformed TPRS in Reading, Writing, and Listening. Blanton (2015) concluded that the "students' level of motivation was higher in the TPRS classroom" (p. 96), and she speculated as to why they did not do as well as the CLT students on the standardized proficiency test.

In addition to drawing conclusions from statistical interpretations, Blanton (2015) also reported test score results in terms of how the students' results on the STAMP Test aligned with ACTFL benchmarks. When compared through the benchmark lens, TPRS students only underperformed CLT in one area, Reading, with CLT barely reaching the 'Intermediate Mid' level of 4.0, with a 4.032 mean. The TPRS Reading mean fell within the 'Novice Mid' range, at 2.667. Since TPRS stands for Teaching Proficiency through *Reading* and Storytelling, it raised the question as to whether the amount of reading done in Blanton's study was typical of other TPRS contexts. Both the TPRS and CLT mean scores fell within 'Novice Mid' for Listening (TPRS= 2.211, CLT= 2.754) and both groups fell within the Novice High benchmark for Writing (TPRS= 3.050, CLT= 3.466) and in Speaking (TPRS= 3.069, CLT= 3.229). The ACTFL goal for oral proficiency after two years of high school study was Novice Mid and after four years the students were expected to reach Intermediate Low (Swender, 2003) which showed that both groups met the ACTFL goals for Speaking on or ahead of the benchmark schedule.

Another area that Blanton (2015) provided information about, but chose not to consider in her speculations as to why TPRS students did not score as well on the standardized tests as did the CLT students was that the two participating school districts had very different demographics coming into the study. That demographic data showed the two groups were unequal in the following areas. In Blanton's (2015) study, the TPRS students came from a school district with 93% African American students and 83% received free or reduced lunch. The CLT group was comprised of 60% White students, 5% African Americans, and 12% received free or reduced lunch. Blanton did not refer to previous research on student achievement gaps to explain the differences in standardized test scores. According to Chan (2015), "Black students generally score lower than white students" (p. 3). Additionally, students of lower socio-economic status (SES) "often need additional supports to be successful" (p. 5). In short, factors other than the method of instruction may have affected the TPRS student results on the standardized tests.

Blanton (2015) failed to provide any information on how the Spanish 3 students were taught in their first two years or the proficiency levels they had reached up to that point in her convenience sample. With no clearly-defined starting point, or pre-test, Blanton's comparisons of student proficiency could not reflect any learning gains made during the students' third year of Spanish or show longitudinal progress within one approach. With no pre-test given and since learning gains for the study's treatment phase were unknown, any conclusions drawn from the post-test data comparisons were suspect. In other words, due to the design choices made by the researcher, Blanton's (2015) study's purpose could not be attained. Students only took the STAMP Test, version 4S, at the end of the study's one-year treatment. The post-tests merely indicated the mean (numerical average) proficiency levels of students who were taught through CLT and TPRS at the end of their third year of Spanish study. Since no information was provided on their previous instruction, there was no way to know whether the students taught with CLT in their third year had received TPRS classes during their first two years, or vice versa, so that may have been a confounding variable making any longitudinal or short-term learning gain claims of either method impossible.

Blanton's (2015) intention to measure the effects of their third year of instruction and draw conclusions about the effects of the CLT approach versus the TPRS method were also confounded by her decisions not to provide much information about how the methodological constructs of CLT and TPRS were operationalized in her study. Blanton had compared her study to Spangler's (2009) study of first-year students who were taught through either CLT or TPRS, but Spangler took steps to ensure the fidelity of method delivery. Not only did Spangler work with the teachers before her study to produce a list of typical classroom learning activities typically used for CLT or TPRS, but the teacher participants in Spangler's (2009) study also provided information on what and how they were taught during the treatment phase. Blanton (2015) chose not to contact the teachers in her study, but rather interviewed their department chairs about their instruction.

Blanton (2015) mentioned that each of her two participating school districts provided in-service training on both CLT and TPRS, but what that training included or who conducted it was not described. There was no mention of whether the TPRS teachers had ever attended a TPRS workshop taught by an approved presenter or attended a national TPRS conference (NTPRS). Just why Blanton (2015) selected the teachers she did for her study was unclear, but she did admit that her sample only represented a convenience and "experimentally accessible population" (p. 166). About the teachers in her study, she admitted that she was unaware of the "unique principles that their teaching approach holds as well as knowledge and practical ways to implement the teaching approach within their classrooms" (p. 118). The treatments, CLT versus TPRS, were not fully described in Blanton's study, so it would be difficult to replicate.

Blanton (2015) explained that in the case of TPRS "its application varies from teacher to teacher" (p. 117), but she failed to fully describe the application or variation that was used in her own study. She admitted that her "study did not seek to examine the entire TPRS approach" (p. 117), yet she attempted to draw generalizable conclusions. Despite Blanton's study being published in 2015, in her dissertation she cited an older fourth edition of Ray and Seely's (2004) book on TPRS to explain her view that TPRS "pre-teaches vocabulary out of context" (p. 105), rather than cite the 2008 fifth edition, the 2012 sixth edition, or the 2015 seventh edition. Failure to cite the most current edition could have reflected that Blanton may have been unaware of the changes that had been made to the TPRS method or perhaps she chose not to consider them in designing her comparative study.

In Blanton's (2015) brief description of CLT and without citing a source, she wrote, "Practitioners of the CLT approach teach grammar systematically and stop the learning process to examine how the language works" (p. 107), an apparent conflation with a traditional grammar approach. Blanton wrote that CLT focused on "form and error correction, whereas TPRS focuses on communication" (p. 144), which would not be consistent with Long's (1991) description in his seminal book chapter on that topic that a brief 'focus on form' typically arose unobtrusively and incidentally during classroom

(CLT) communication. That would have made Long's (1991) focus on form notion in CLT similar to the "pop-up grammar" (Ray & Seely, 2015, p. 229) used in TPRS. Blanton's (2015) discussion of CLT was inconsistent as she cited Richards and Rodgers (1987, 2011) to emphasize that the CLT approach allowed "much greater room for individual interpretation and variation than most methods permit" (p. 83), yet she also wrote that "CLT is more rigid and systematic" (p. 111) than TPRS. In any case, she did not list those rigid and systematic steps or fully describe how CLT applied to her study. From the information, both provided and not provided in Blanton's (2015) study, it could not be determined precisely what instruction her student participants actually did receive for their CLT versus TPRS treatment or what accounted for the differences in test scores.

Accelerated Acquisition Without any Explicit Grammar Instruction.

The Roberts and Thomas (2015) empirical study originally had been published in 2014, but was republished with minor corrections in the same peer-reviewed journal. The researchers were interested in studying the rate of learning, in terms of gains per hour of instruction, within their Center for Accelerated Language Acquisition (CALA) where students were taught through implicit language instruction rather than an explicit approach. The implicit instruction of high-frequency vocabulary and grammar was focused on providing students with comprehensible input (CI) in the target language in communicative classroom contexts. The implicit instruction included TPRS, TPR, songs, games, hands-on interactive activities, reading, teacher-led conversations with students, and both personal and comprehension questions. The implicit language instruction was accomplished with no homework and "without the use of explicit grammar explanations, memorization, or drills" (p. 25). Positive results were reported from two CALA studies.

In one study, Roberts and Thomas (2015) tested 325 adults who received implicit instruction for 5 days, for only 22.5 total hours. In terms of hours per instruction, the average CALA student scored significantly higher (1.25 points/hour) than high school students (0.20 points/hour) who had studied 180 hours, for one full academic year, on the National Spanish Exam. Those numbers indicated an accelerated rate of learning for CALA students who were taught through implicit, not explicit, language instruction.

In a second study, Roberts and Thomas (2015) tested 16 adult learners after they received 35 hours of implicit language instruction in a ten-day summer CALA program. All sixteen CALA students tested out of 1-4 semesters of college Spanish based on their scores on the WebCAPE Computer-Adaptive Placement Exam. When compared to secondary students with 1-3 years of world language study, CALA students scored at or above non-CALA students and the implicitly-taught students "were far superior in gains per hour" (p. 24). Taken together, these two studies supported the notion that the rate of acquisition could be increased through an implicit approach, without receiving any explicit instruction at all during the entire program.

High School AP / Scored at National Norms Without Grammar Instruction.

Pippins and Krashen (2016) were interested in the longitudinal effects of TPRS. Whereas most TPRS studies had treatment periods of one year or less, in this case study, thirteen students took Spanish classes together from grades 8 to 12. Those students had a traditional beginner class and in their senior year took an Advanced Placement (AP) exam preparation course. However, levels 2 through 4 were all taken with the same TPRS teacher (Pippins) who also taught their final course. Levels 2, 3, and 4 were all taught using TPRS "with no error correction, no teaching of explicit grammar (but pop-up grammar was included), no grading of writing for accuracy, no grammar worksheets, and no textbooks or verb charts were used" (p. 27). Their TPRS classes focused on providing students with comprehensible input and included reading, discussing and acting out the novels they read in Spanish, personalized questions and answers (PQA), songs, and DVDs. The DVD materials were made for providing comprehensible input through "funny, creative, and absurd stories with unexpected twists" (Wooldridge, 2016).

Pippins and Krashen (2016) compared the TPRS students' scores with 41,627 non-native Spanish speakers who took the AP exam in 2014. The exam measured language proficiency in listening, speaking, reading, writing, and assigned an overall score ranging from 1 to 5. The researchers mentioned that some colleges have granted credit, or advanced placement, to students who scored 3, 4, or 5, and so they regarded a score of 3 or above as passing. In their study, 84.6% of the TPRS students scored 3 or above, the same as the nationwide mean. From these results, Pippins and Krashen (2016) concluded that "an extensive grammar foundation is not necessary for success in developing academic language" (p. 29). TPRS students taught through "comprehensible input made compelling through taking students' interests very seriously and through personalization" (p. 29) did as well as others on a standardized proficiency exam without receiving three years of direct, explicit, grammar instruction. The study results further supported the notion, previously expressed in the professional literature, that input made compelling and comprehensible through 'personalization' could benefit students in class in acquiring the target language (Hedstrom, 2014, 2015; Krashen, 2011a, 2011b; Pippins, 2015; Rowan, 2013; Slavic, 2007, 2008, 2014, 2015; and Waltz, 2015).

In the section above, there were 22 empirical studies reviewed comparing TPRS with other methods in studies that were conducted between 2003 and 2016. While there were some mixed results, the majority of the research demonstrated positive effects for TPRS instruction at the preschool, secondary, university, and adult levels. Some of the topics included were the effects of methods and SES, how TPRS was described, the fidelity of TPRS method delivery, explicit and implicit instruction, age, gender, the presence or absence of grammar teaching, dialogs, motivation, proficiency testing, adapted TPRS, special needs strategies, and accelerated learning gains. Among the target languages included in those studies were Spanish, French, Chinese, Italian, and English.

On TPRS Alone Without Comparison Groups.

The empirical studies reviewed above were experimental, or quasi-experimental, but the following studies were not experimental because they each lacked a control group. Despite that delimitation, the following studies contributed to the growing body of research on TPRS by providing information from studies focusing on TPRS alone. The levels and settings studied varied, to include adult English as a Second Language (ESL) in the United States, English as a Foreign Language (EFL) in Indonesia, Chinese as a Foreign Language (CFL) in Tennessee, university and secondary school classes in Spanish and German, classroom management in the middle school, and Content-Based Storytelling (CBS) in the elementary school. Among others, topics varied from an instructor studying her own teaching practices, to secondary student performance on the National German Exam, to the impact of using illustrations in TPRS classes for vocabulary retention. The studies on TPRS itself provided insight into the method.

Braunstein (2006) had experienced previous success teaching young children, but she wondered whether the TPR and TPRS methods would work with adults. She was surprised to find that those methods were preferred by older students over a more traditional approach. During a practicum, she taught 15 Latino adults in two beginning English as a second language (ESL) sessions, for a total of five contact hours, using TPR and TPRS. She employed six sources for data collection in her study of adult students' responses to those methods.

First, Braunstein (2006) administered a survey to determine the adults' learning preferences. Before the treatment, they had preferred "explicit grammatical instruction, lecture, and written work" (p. 11). Second, adult ESL students completed a reaction questionnaire after learning the vocabulary of body parts through TPR. They reacted to TPR instruction with interest, enthusiasm, and happiness. No one reported feeling bored, embarrassed, or stupid when using TPR. Third, questionnaires revealed that ESL adult learners reacted to TPRS storytelling instruction with interest, happiness, and enthusiasm, with no one feeding stupid or bored from TPRS teaching. Fourth, over 90% of the students agreed that the combined TPR/TPRS instruction helped them learn nouns, verbs, listening comprehension, and understand better when watching classmates act the story out and doing a picture sequence activity. Fifth, the researcher's cooperating teacher, peer observer, and practicum professor all completed observation reports. These reports revealed that students volunteered, laughed, smiled, were on task, and made eye contact with the teacher during class sessions. Viewing a videotape of one session supported those observations. Sixth, the researcher reflected daily in her journal upon the data collected and added her own perceptions and interpretations.

Braunstein's (2006) results indicated that, before the treatment, students had preferred learning through a traditional approach. However, after receiving TPRS and TPR instruction, adult students' attitudes toward those kinesthetic and implicit methods were "overwhelmingly positive" (p. 7). A strength of the study was that triangulation was provided by using multiple data collection sources, which both increased the content validity of the data and the reliability of the findings. However, the researcher admitted to a few weaknesses of the study. For example, the external validity and generalizability were limited due to the small sample size of only one class of 15 adult ESL students. Other possible threats to validity included the short treatment phase of only five total hours over a two-day period, with only one experimental group of a convenience sample, and no control group or random assignment. Despite these possible shortcomings in the study's design, the multiple data sources increased the reliability of the findings and supported the researcher's interpretations.

Braunstein (2006) concluded that students' incoming preferences or expectations may not match their actual reactions to non-traditional methods, such as TPR and TPRS. "Therefore, it may be necessary to inform the students on the usefulness of methods that are distinct from what the students prefer" (p. 16). This would be especially true in cases where previous research has supported the effectiveness of the non-traditional methods that were not preferred by those students. Braunstein's (2006) conclusion regarding the need to inform students supported VanPatten's (2017) observation, "In trying to develop contemporary communicative and proficiency-oriented language curricula, a good number of teachers run into trouble… students, colleagues and others think they know as much about language, communication, and acquisition as the teacher!" (p. 54).

Funded Action Research and TPRS.

Armstrong (2008) reported on elementary and middle school student enjoyment when learning Spanish through TPRS. Armstrong's (2008) TPRS study, despite having no control group, resulted in a descriptive article of her two-semester funded action research project being published in an undergraduate research journal. In her project, she worked to improve her students' learning at the elementary and middle school levels, along with developing her own TPRS teaching skills through an ongoing process of "planning, acting, observing, and reflecting" (p. 1) on her goals and student performance. In cycle 1, Armstrong (2008) was able to use the target language, Spanish, for 90% of class time at the elementary school. In cycle 2, she added using Spanish to give instructions supported by providing pictures and visuals of the classroom learning activity steps, thereby reducing English use. Students were observed to be on task and less confused as they referred to the visuals when moving to the next step. In cycle 3, the teacher used chants ("*¡Olé, olé!*") to gain and maintain the students' attention and she gave them jobs to help facilitate movement to new activities. Cycles 1-3 were conducted during the first semester at the elementary and the second semester at the middle school.

In cycle 4, Armstrong (2008) had to address the new problem of the older children being more reluctant in student participation. She focused on getting all the students engaged and involved through differentiated question asking, by varying the classroom organizational structures to allow for different student groupings to include some pair work, and by allowing the use of signals, gestures, or manipulatives rather than always demanding verbal responses from students to check for understanding. Middle school students' participation did increase through those strategies and the classroom climate for learning improved. In the final cycle 5, the teacher's challenge was to implement strategies to encourage and enable target language use even during pair work. Her strategies included the pre-teaching of vocabulary and grammar structures, a list of words students needed with written translations to refer to if they forgot them, and a classroom management point system called TALK. In the acronym, the /T/ stood for talking in the target language, the /A/ meant accurately, the /L/ reminded students to listen, and the /K/ meant to be kind to one another (talk, accurately, listen, kind). Pair work improved and through those strategies student target language use increased, and the teacher was able to use Spanish, the target language, almost exclusively in class.

Armstrong (2008) found, through surveys and tests, that her students increased their knowledge of Spanish and they liked Spanish, gestures, acting out plays, reading, books, speaking, and writing in Spanish more than before the project. The test scores revealed that her students, on average, could identify vocabulary words correctly through pictures (10.39 out of 20) more than translations (8.64 out of 20), but they could remember the most words they learned through TPRS with gesture cues (15 out of 20 words targeted). She found that elementary and middle school students of Spanish enjoyed learning through TPRS. In describing the methodology, Armstrong (2008) explained that "within TPRS, students learn Spanish through stories, dramatic play, and body movements. Using TPRS, teachers provide instruction [almost] exclusively in the target language, foster a brain-body connection, and engage students in developmentally appropriate activities" (p. 1). Even action research contributed to the literature on TPRS.

Beyer's (2008) study measured how well TPRS "helped students conjugate verbs in the preterit tense" (p. 3). Suburban high school level 2 students retold "The Three

Little Pigs" (p. 4) story in Spanish. The students heard the past-tense verbs in the context of a story and they watched classmates reenact it. They revised and rewrote the story. The teacher's role was to provide meaningful, interesting, repetitive, and comprehensible input interactively to the students in the past tense. The teacher-researcher asked several questions about story details to check for understanding and the students responded briefly to yes/no, either/or, and other comprehension questions. Gestures were used to help students understand the vocabulary, messages, and story events in Spanish and to signal back to the teacher that they were, or were not, understanding them.

Beyer's (2008) study design provided for triangulation through multiple data sources that included a teacher-made test, an oral interview, and a four-point Likert-scale questionnaire. The researcher used a convenience sample, one of his Spanish 2 classes, so one limitation was the small sample size and there was no control group. There were only "18 students, consisting of 3 sophomores and 15 freshmen, 8 females, and 7 males" (p. 10) whose individual data were kept confidential. The treatment was limited to four weeks, with five class periods per week of 42 minutes each. The class also used a textbook, which was potentially a confounding variable since TPRS did not require textbook use. Students practiced story vocabulary on a website (www.storyplace.com) and did homework, also not required but not prohibited in most variations of TPRS. The teacher used four steps. First, the students watched and listened only as he told the story using picture visuals and props. Second, the teacher began sentences, paused, and students briefly finished them orally filling in the blanks one at a time to check for story comprehension. Third, Beyer asked students several questions about the story details. Fourth, the students acted out the story using props as the teacher narrated the story.

Beyer (2008) reported the results from three data sources. The four-point Likert-scale questionnaire revealed the students' perceptions. They reported that acting out the story helped them better understand the past tense verbs (M=3.8, SD=0.39). Writing their own extra scenes helped them better understand the past tense (M=3.6, SD=0.47). They thought the oral interviews were beneficial (M=3.5, SD=0.5) and they preferred TPRS to the textbook activities (M=3.50, SD=0.5) because it was more fun, easier to learn, and "because books are boring" (p. 15). "All students also answered 'yes' to preferring reenactment over book-centered activities" (p. 16). The high mean scores (out of 4.0 possible per item) indicated how much the students perceived that those TPRS activities helped them learn to conjugate verbs in the past tense and the low standard deviations meant that their agreement levels on those points were high. The results of the teacher-made post-test included a mean score of 90% level of mastery, which reflected that the students knew the story content and the verb conjugations. They learned grammar incidentally while focusing on story content. Beyer (2008) concluded that students preferred TPRS to a textbook approach and that the TPRS method did help students learn to conjugate verbs in the past tense through stories at the high school level.

College Spanish and TPRS.

Bustamante (2009) tried out the method in college. Bustamante (2009) measured the effectiveness of TPRS using multiple data sources in a semester-long pilot course for beginning-level college Spanish students. She found that the TPRS college students improved significantly in several areas to include reading, writing, grammar and vocabulary. Both before and after the semester-long treatment, the Brigham Young University's Spanish WebCAPE Computer-Adaptive Placement Exam, commonly called the CAPE Test (Larson, Smith, & Bach, 1998, 2004) was administered to determine student proficiency levels. Student mean scores improved from 61.06 to 121.82 after the 16-week instructional treatment and paired two-tailed *t*-tests determined that student improvement for the Spanish 100 pilot course was statistically significant (p = .005). Compared to college benchmarks, overall the students moved from Novice High (100) up to Intermediate Low level (101) through TPRS instruction. In terms of writing fluency, TPRS students improved from an average of 19.17 words written up to an 87.06-word count for five-minute timed writings. A paired t-test analysis determined those differences to be statistically significant. TPRS students moved from the Novice High (100) to the Intermediate Low level (201) in writing fluency. In the number of words read aloud, students significantly improved from 56.68 to 72.11 words per minute. In terms of how many words were read aloud correctly, TPRS students also significantly improved from 50.87 to 63.33 which indicated a rise from the Novice High (100) up to an Intermediate Low level (200) college benchmark for reading. Each measure used in the study documented that the improvements that were made by TPRS students during the 16-week pilot course were all statistically significant.

Bustamante (2009) surveyed the nineteen student study participants and discovered that twelve had taken a Spanish course before, either in high school or college. Bustamante reported, "All 12 students felt like they were learning Spanish better with the TPRS method" (p. 57). The researcher made some observations from the TPRS lesson plan compared with a non-TPRS plan. She noticed that for six steps of "setting the stage, providing input, guided participation, extension, informal assessment, and formal assessment" (p. 50) that TPRS had 21 activities to accomplish those while the non-TPRS approach had only six. In terms of differentiation and meeting the needs of students, Bustamante (2009) wrote, "The activities in the traditional lesson did not address all the learning styles like the TPRS" (p. 59) lesson had. She observed that the TPRS students were "more able to remember the vocabulary" (p. 62) and the TPRS teacher spoke in Spanish more, at least 85% of class time, because she was not having to give lengthy grammar explanations in English as was often done in more traditional classrooms. Bustamante (2009) perceived that the improved class attendance indicated that the "students were more motivated to attend a TPRS class" (p. 65). While not a research question, Bustamante (2009) perceived that "female students obtained better results than male students" (p. 67).

Studying One's Own Teaching Practices with TPRS.

To obtain permission to do a master's study where she worked, Wenck (2010) explained to her building principal that the university required, in her words, "that I conduct a systematic study of my own teaching practices" (p. 139). Wenck (2010) collected the perceptions of the 16 students, eight girls and eight boys, in her German 2 class about which instructional strategies they felt helped them learn best. Among the multiple data sources included were student surveys, questionnaires, interviews, and student work, plus a field log of student observations and a reflective researcher journal. She did not set out to focus on studying the TPRS method because admitted her bias before conducting the study was that a "variety of approaches" (p. 6) would likely work best. Wenck's (2010) planned research timeline (p. 39) limited her combined use of TPR and TPRS to six of the 12-week treatment for the purpose of introducing new vocabulary and textbook unit vocabulary through commands and stories. Wenck (2010) analyzed and coded her data from the aforementioned data sources in answer to her primary research question: "What will be the observed behaviors and reported experiences when I use various language acquisition approaches in my German class?" (p. 6). She used "peer debriefing" (p. 38) to verify her analysis and obtain additional insights.

From that analysis, she identified five themes, to include: comprehensible input, student perception, classroom climate, readiness of students, and teacher reflections. Presented in theme statements and as findings from her study, Wenck (2010) wrote:

> Strategies that ensure student understanding of a second language are imperative in order for these students to start believing that they are capable of communicating in that language. Students need to perceive themselves as capable of learning another language in order to view it as a worthwhile endeavor. Student centered approaches are necessary to set the stage for an atmosphere where the students are the most important component for beginning to progress in the language. Students who demonstrate a lack of confidence and who are pre-occupied with personal issues struggle to learn another language. Over time, the use of natural language acquisition strategies results in less dependence upon isolated grammar drills and textbook activities (Wenck, 2010, p. 108).

Wenck (2010) valued the perceptions of students, as evidenced by the number of data collection sources she used in her study. She also trusted in her own data analysis skills, but increased the reliability of the study by verifying her analyses and findings using a peer review process called "peer debriefing" (p. 38). As a result, Wenck (2010) confidently concluded that "when students focused on the meaning of a conversation, they used vocabulary more correctly than they had in the past" (p. 126). However, that solid and boldly-stated conclusion, which emerged directly from her data, did not lead Wenck to totally abandon grammar drills and teaching from a textbook altogether or to adopt the exclusive use of the TPRS method, as some of her colleagues did. Despite Wenck's (2010) own conclusion from her own study and despite having cited Wong and VanPatten's (2003) conclusion that "the evidence is IN: Drills are OUT," Wenck continued to teach explicit grammar through mechanical drills.

In addition to the connections to TPRS, Wenck (2010) included a discussion of her own unsatisfying teaching and language-learning experiences. She described her father's touching story of how he saved Kurt Vonnegut's life in 1944 during the war in Germany and how that story motivated her to learn German in high school and college. After working hard doing drills from the textbook, she "could still not speak the language" (p. 4). After six years of drills and mastering the grammar, in her own words, she "could not speak a full sentence" (p. 6) in German when she went to Germany to study there. Yet later, when she became a German teacher, she taught the way she had been taught in high school and in college, fully aware that it did not work, even for her, a student who was motivated to learn the language.

When she became a teacher, Wenck (2010) wrote that her own students "began to complain about the 'stupid' grammar rules" (p. 1). It was having those experiences that led her to TPR and TPRS, for her students, in her own words, "to acquire German instead of learning grammar and vocabulary in isolation" (p. 6). Unsatisfied with the student results obtained from traditional teaching, plus her own negative experiences with learning through a grammar-focused approach, Wenck (2010) searched for more effective acquisition strategies which led her to TPRS. However, she still had difficulty buying into the idea of managing a world language classroom without including direct, explicit, grammar instruction. Wenck (2010) never completely made that paradigm shift.

TPRS and Classroom Management / Dissatisfied Before TPRS.

Roof and Kreutter (2010) had their article published in a teacher research journal. Roof, the primary researcher, had been dissatisfied with student learning before finding TPRS and she wanted to teach with the method. However, she did encounter discipline difficulties when teaching with TPRS in a middle school Spanish class. She explained, "Classroom structure dissolved during the interactive storytelling sessions when students' disruptive responses overshadowed the benefits of the teaching method" (p. 1). For this reason, teaching with TPRS was "overwhelming" for her. Ironically, the students were disruptive "because they became absorbed in the story" (p. 2), so Roof set out to solve the puzzle of how to modify her TPRS teaching to improve classroom management rather than abandon the method, hoping to make student participation less disruptive.

Roof and Kreutter (2010) designed an action research project and studied an intact TPRS class, without modifications in the first lesson and with them in the second. There were five modifications made. These included adding visuals and asking more questions, encouraging choral responses, communicating clear expectations, and stating rules for student conduct, especially during storytelling time and when acting out the stories. One rule was that students had to respond to questions without using English, either in Spanish or visually by using whiteboards. The teacher awarded extra points when they responded to questions in Spanish. She also increased Spanish use and student engagement by having someone hold up a sign, when she or he felt it was appropriate in the story, with three funny phrases. Those phrases included the Spanish equivalents for 'that's funny, too bad, and you're kidding' which cued the whole group to repeat the phrase in Spanish rather than "yelling out comments in English" (p. 8). The teacher also used pictures projected on overhead to guide the story and help students understand it. The researchers videotaped three class periods and analyzed student participation.

By reflecting upon those observations and analyses, Roof and Kreutter (2010) were able to monitor students and modify the classroom interaction practices in one middle school class. Roof and Kreutter (2010) found through "directly stating the rules, monitoring expectations, and reinforcing the rules" (p. 4) that students remained engaged, were more often on-task, they spoke less in English and more in Spanish, and the teacher "felt more comfortable" (p. 9) with TPRS and improved her classroom management.

Junior High TPRS Students and the National German Exam.

Miller (2011) compared 13 years of TPRS-taught seventh and eighth graders' scores on the National German Exam (NGE) from one school with national norms. Normally, the NGE has been taken by high school students. The NGE tests listening and reading comprehension, and fill-in-the-blank grammar. The junior high students in this study had about 203 hours of instruction compared to 225 hours for high schoolers. All the students from the school studied had begun as true beginners and received all their German instruction through TPRS. Over the thirteen-year data collection period, about 75% of the students in this study took the exam yearly, but those volunteers were not limited to the top students and the sampling was considered as representative by their teacher. On average, "TPRS students scored at the 41st percentile, doing better than 40% of the high school students who took the exam [and] percentile scores increased between 1998 and 2011 ($r = .76$)" (p. 11). While not a true experiment and there was no control group, Miller's (2011) data demonstrated that "TPRS students can perform reasonably well on standardized tests... with little or no grammar study" (p. 11), through TPRS only.

Using Visual Illustrations with TPRS.

Jakubowski (2013) studied whether "using illustrations during TPRS instruction would help learners to process vocabulary into long-term memory" (p. 61). Sixty-seven middle school Spanish 1 student participants were taught two stories by the researcher during the one-month TPRS instructional treatment. Having only one teacher provided consistency in lesson delivery, but the research may have been "less biased if multiple teachers provided TPRS instruction instead of one teacher-researcher" (p. 64). The independent variables were the use or non-use of illustrations and the dependent variables were the test scores. Students were given vocabulary tests four days after instruction to assess short-term learning and again after four weeks to test for long-term retention.

Jakubowski's (2013) study findings that were derived from the test scores indicated that the illustrations helped with short-term learning, but not with long-term retention because "students relied on the direct translations more than the illustrations when communicating" (p. 63). Qualitative data was obtained from videos of students retelling the stories who used the targeted vocabulary words in that activity in the short term, but less so in the long term. The researcher noticed that during the study, "the direct translations were no less effective than the illustrations to prompt student responses" (p. 57), implying that the illustrations were not needed since the translations were all that was necessary for "long-term vocabulary acquisition" (p. 63).

However, when designing the Jakubowski (2013) study, it was a challenge to hold all other potentially confounding or possibly contaminating variables constant in order to isolate one independent variable, such as the use of illustrations. For example, if the targeted vocabulary words were retained in long-term memory, that could have been more due to the repetitions of the words in context or to muscle memory from acting out the stories or from using gestures, rather than the presence or absence of illustrations, which the study intended to measure. On the other hand, if the words were not retained, it could have been because the teacher's TPRS skills were underdeveloped and the input provided may not have been engaging, interesting, repetitive, or comprehensible to the learner or learners. Roof and Kreutter (2010), Miller (2011), Jakubowski (2013), and Susan (2013) all found positive effects of TPRS with junior high school students.

татьTPRS and English as a Second Language in Junior High.

Susan (2013) was interested in determining whether TPRS would improve students' listening comprehension. She also wanted to know the advantages and the disadvantages of the TPRS method, from both the teacher and student points of view. She designed a mixed methods study to find out the answers. The 20 students were tested on listening comprehension both before and after receiving the TPRS treatment. The difference between the pretest and posttest scores of 13.70 (SD = 6.85) and 31.35 (SD = 4.76) was found to be statistically significant at the 95% level of confidence. Therefore, the null hypothesis that there were no differences between scores was rejected. Therefore, Susan (2013) concluded that there were "differences in students' listening comprehension before and after the TPRS was done, and TPRS can improve students' listening comprehension" (p. 107).

Susan (2013) conducted interviews after the treatment to identify the advantages and disadvantages of using TPRS. Of the 20 junior-high EFL student participants in the study, ten were randomly selected to be interviewed, including five boys and five girls, plus the instructor, who were all asked, "What do you think about TPRS?" (p. 108). Among the advantages, students perceived that the method was interesting and a "good, fun, stress free technique" (p. 104) through which students could build their vocabularies and understand stories. Students perceived some disadvantages as well, saying that for some students TPRS could be complicated and the pre-teaching of key vocabulary "created confusion" (p. 111) if done out of context or if the stories were too long. One student said TPRS was childish and "more suitable" (p. 110) for children than teenagers. The teacher perceived the advantages of TPRS included learning vocabulary, improving listening comprehension, and getting students to become more involved in class, helping them to "feel invited in the teaching-learning process" (p. 110). As a disadvantage, the teacher said that TPRS was limited because it "could only be applied in story based materials" (p. 110). The researcher added that TPRS required teachers to "have good competence in telling stories [and to] base their teaching materials on stories" (p. 112).

Chinese as a Second Language through TPRS with Adult Learners.

Nguyen, Yonghui, Stanley, and Stanley (2014) investigated the perceptions of Chinese-as-a-second language (CSL) teachers and students of storytelling. There were 30 students (ages 18-35) who came to China from different countries to learn Mandarin and 15 university professors (ages 24-36) who taught them were surveyed. The intact class of 30 CSL students taking a 14-week course at a university, for 280 total hours of instruction, was a convenience sample. In the study, TPRS was not the primary method of instruction, but rather TPRS was sometimes used as a supplemental method in class. The teachers were allowed to use stories, but were constrained by a prescribed curriculum that they were expected to cover, as well as its scope and sequencing. As one explained, "I would use storytelling more, but our school's plan is a tough offering. We need to follow the schedule of lessons in class" (p. 463). Due to these curricular and time constraints, the TPRS lessons tended to use short stories. The regular curriculum was "considered traditional and typical of what students encounter in most foreign universities. The emphasis was on developing reading, writing, speaking, and listening skills with focused instruction on phonetics, vocabulary, phrases, grammar, and calligraphy" (p. 460). The teachers used lectures, grammar exercises, and provided students with corrective feedback on their errors. Given that context, the storytelling lessons deviated somewhat from typical TPRS classes because the above-mentioned elements were integrated into the stories or taught directly. For example, the professors corrected pronunciation mistakes and there was forced output demanded of individual students and in pair work, which was not normally considered to be part of TPRS. However, realizing that the "traditional Chinese teacher centered, traditional curriculum can hinder opportunities for student engagement through storytelling" (p. 464), professors in this study did follow the regular 3-step process of TPRS. They used TPR gestures to teach four new phrases and vocabulary for each unit lesson, asked and answered personalized questions, created and dramatized stories, and the students applied what they learned in extension activities.

Nguyen (et al., 2014) found that storytelling was widely accepted by both professors and CSL students alike, but how often stories were told was unclear. All 15 professors reported using stories "very often" (p. 461), but 11 (out of 30) students said that stories were used frequently, 15 said occasionally, while 4 indicated at least once.

Interestingly, since teachers integrated stories into their regular academic lessons within an otherwise traditional CSL approach, students did not always recognize that a story was being told because they were focused on understanding the academic message content. Teachers' and students' memories varied on how often they were used in class, but everyone agreed that they liked stories. There was wide acceptance in CSL classes.

In the Ngyuen (et al., 2014) study, students reported that they enjoyed and accepted storytelling because it helped them learn language, enjoy class, and learn about each other's cultures. They perceived several benefits from storytelling. The benefits included "language learning, comprehension, community building, and multicultural understanding" (p. 458). Teacher goals also included teaching vocabulary, grammar, critical thinking, and reducing learner stress. Among others, the students' perceived benefits included humor, building confidence, fluency, and social skills. "The instructors and learners in the interviews all reported that doing storytelling helped the learners' language skills develop... while interacting and communicating" (p. 462) in Chinese.

Ngyuen (et al., 2014) found that storytelling materials often were lacking in Chinese, so most CSL teachers obtained their resources from books and the internet. Some used folktales or literary stories, but many 10 (out of 15) teachers and 13 (of 30) students told personal stories. A typical CSL class story involved a "family member overcoming challenge" (p. 462). For example, perhaps an uncle immigrated to China, learned the language and culture well, made friends, and he succeeded in his business. The researchers perceived that some CSL classrooms "have changed from a grammar translation approach" (p. 464) and lecture format to more storytelling. They suggested also using stories for learning outside of class through social media, digital storytelling, and other technological applications. In short, CSL teachers, adult students, and researchers appreciated the benefits, but concluded that "storytelling is not used as it could be and its full potential has not been realized" (p. 466) yet in CSL classrooms.

Chinese as a Foreign Language in Tennessee.

Chang and Chen (2015) described a one-week summer program where students in Tennessee learned Chinese-as-a foreign language (CFL). In a CFL context, students were not normally exposed to the target language outside of class as they were in CSL (Chinese-as-a-second language) programs. In the CFL summer study, there were two groups of students in grades 3-5 and two groups in grades 6-8. While total numbers were not provided in the journal article, class sizes varied from 8-12 students per class. The summer program goals included having fun and learning language. The TPR and TPRS methods were chosen as the combined instructional approach because previous research had shown their popularity and effectiveness and for "engaging students in fun activities in a stress-free and supportive learning environment" (p. 2). The separate effects of TPR and TPRS were not teased out for comparisons of effectiveness in their study.

Summer school students in the Chang and Chen (2015) study were in class for five days and received a total of 3 hours and 15 minutes of CFL instruction for beginners. In addition to TPR and TPRS, their instruction included drills, pronunciation practice, and forced output in the form of creative writing tasks. Students learned to introduce themselves in the target language, listened and responded to TPR commands followed up vocabulary drills and picture cues. Sentence-level learning put the word learning into context with pictures posted during expanded TPR practice. TPRS was used to move students into the discourse level as the teacher told stories in Chinese and students acted them out. Students demonstrated comprehension physically and through brief spoken responses in the target language (Chinese), giving comments equivalent to good, not good, or terrible during storytelling when appropriate. Student reading was done through Pinyin, rather than in traditional Chinese characters, due to the summer time constraints and included both silent reading and reading aloud following the teacher's model. After reading, students wrote 8 stories and drew 8 story pictures to refer to when retelling them.

Chang and Chen (2015) observed that students could follow teacher commands, give appropriate comments, demonstrate story comprehension, and signal when they did not understand. The researchers found some variation in early student outcomes, but the "speaking outcome was still striking considering the limited learning time" (p. 3). Ten minute timed writings ranged from 27-40 words. While a limitation of the study might be that student feedback was not systematically elicited, the parent survey results were positive overall. One mother said that "her son was totally engaged and wanted more training" (p. 3). Due to parental requests, the director decided to double class length.

With positive feedback from the children's study, Chang and Chen (2015) followed up to see whether TPR and TPRS would be effective with CFL adult learners. Eight adults, ages 19-36, had six hours of instruction. The adults "outperformed the children in understanding [Chinese] and their writing was longer and more complicated" (p. 3), but the younger learners did better in pronunciation. From their two studies taken together, Chang and Chen (2015 found that students could listen, speak, read, and write with some confidence following summer instruction in Chinese. Learning gains were obtained in each of those four language domains. They also found that using TPR and TPRS could be challenging for the teacher if underprepared or if materials supporting that instruction were lacking, and that there was some variation in student proficiency development. From their CFL studies, Chang and Chen (2015) concluded that TPR and TPRS were effective methods with children, teenagers, and adult learners.

Writing Fluency through Content-Based Storytelling in Elementary School.

Cartford, Holter Kittok, and Lichtman (2015) investigated Content-Based Storytelling (CBS) classrooms in elementary school. CBS is a method that teaches language through content. TPRS and the study on CBS were both theoretically informed by Krashen's (1981, 2015) Comprehension Hypothesis. The CBS students focused on understanding the stories and the academic course content while simultaneously acquiring Spanish incidentally by understanding the messages communicated in the target language, both orally and in writing. The researchers followed the progress of 137 fourth-grade students through fifth grade who received foreign language instruction 60 minutes per week for two years, totaling 70 hours. The researchers found significant gains over time in 'writing fluency' which were "attributed to the instructional approach" (p. 8). Writing fluency was measured by comparing the word counts for ten-minute timed writings in the longitudinal study of Spanish language classroom learners. The CBS course curriculum included fiction and nonfiction stories, plus cultural information all taught in Spanish, the target language. The instructional approach included TPR, TPRS, and other strategies for providing students with comprehensible input (CI, as defined in the definition of terms of this dissertation). The student role was to learn the message content of seven units. The units consisted of stories about the Mexican flag, a llama in Peru, a beverage (mate) in Argentina, a ghost story on the Day of the Dead, a mouse that barked in Cuba, the Wizard of Oz from the U.S., and the Elian Gonzalez custody battle. There was no direct, explicit grammar instruction.

The language gains documented in the Cartford (et al., 2015) study were all incidental while students focused on learning the content information of each story. Study results indicated that students developed writing fluency through CBS. To measure writing fluency, seven freewrites were elicited, one after each unit. The students were asked to write complete sentences about each story, giving as many details as they could. They were permitted to use pictures of the stories as memory prompts, if needed. Researchers noted that no two writing samples were identical and student writings did not reflect mere memorization, but rather contained recombinations. Word counts were collected for all students, averaged for the whole group, and compared. The averages were 74, 98, 91, 87, 129, 130, and 99. Learning gains were significant ($p<.01$), with a large effect size ($\eta p^2 = .555$) for the group studied, but there was no control group. However, the 7 to 13 words per minute that students in the Cartford (et al., 2015) study wrote in their timed writings "were close to grade-level expectations" (p. 7) for native speakers of English. The results showed that "elementary students can develop a measure of written fluency in the target language and that their fluency can improve, even in a program with minimal instruction time" (p. 6), by focusing on learning content information only and "without direct grammar instruction" (p. 7).

In addition to the improvements in word counts, a document analysis of the freewrites revealed that CBS students in the Cartford (et al., 2015) study could also communicate story elements and details, create original sentences, correctly use Spanish syntax, and proper word order, with improving grammatical accuracy. In their portfolio reflections, "students reported that they felt they had not only learned a lot of Spanish, [but] they also learned a lot about Spanish-speaking cultures" (p. 7). Cartford (et al., 2015) concluded that for "educators looking to develop students' fluency and content knowledge at the same time, Content-Based Storytelling is a promising approach" (p. 8).

Elementary School EFL in Indonesia.

Nurlaili, Nurani, and Yohana (2015 were interested in studying vocabulary learning and acquisition in young children who could read and write in the first grade. The Indonesian EFL student participants in their study took an English vocabulary test, both before and after receiving an instructional treatment of the TPRS method which included TPR. Using a pre/posttest design, they found significant learning gains for TPRS-taught first graders in vocabulary. Not much information on that vocabulary test was provided, other than it covered "Math-shape" (p. 63) vocabularies, so the type of test used was unclear. In one place in the journal article, vocabulary "comprehension toward the vocabularies' meaning" (p. 63) was mentioned, but in another place comprehension was reflected from a student's "capability in defining vocabulary" (p. 68). What students actually did on the test to demonstrate mastery of English Math-shape vocabulary was unclear. The type of test questions was not mentioned. A list of the tested vocabulary words was not given. Posttest scores were significantly higher than pretest scores, at the .05 level, so the researchers concluded that TPRS "worked well in teaching English Math-shape vocabularies for the first-grade elementary students" (p. 66). The Nurlaili (et al., 2015) study could prove difficult to replicate due to the limited information provided.

Nurlaili (et al., 2015) described their study as experimental, but there was no control group or random sampling taken. Rather, a purposive sampling was taken using the construct of literacy, the ability to read and write, as the sole criterion for subject selection. Thirty-one elementary school students from the first grade were identified as literate, although the test name used to determine their literacy levels was not given. Preliterate students were excluded from participation in the study. The 31 literate students were taken from a school site population of 41 total first-grade students who were studying English-as-a-foreign language (EFL) in Indonesia.

In operationalizing the construct of the TPRS treatment for their study, Nurlaili (et al., 2015) described the TPRS method as including TPR and storytelling "where the teacher narrates a story by using visual aids, checks and repeats the story several times" (p. 65). They listed the three main steps of TPRS of establishing meaning, the story, and literacy, adding that "there are many different ways to accomplish these steps and every teacher can do it in their own way by adding a little personal flair" (p. 65). In their study, the TPRS teacher used flashcards (not normally part of TPRS) and asked the students questions about the shapes being taught. While their study included only students who could read and write, the Nurlaili (et al., 2015) EFL study was important because the researchers also discussed strategies for working with preliterate students using TPRS, noting the method's adaptability to various educational contexts to include first graders.

In addition to the research studies discussed above which compared the effectiveness of TPRS with other language teaching methods and empirical studies with no comparison or control groups, this literature review included descriptive articles on the method and experiences using TPRS. In the following section, teacher experiences with TPRS that appeared in the professional literature were discussed, along with studies and written works which described the changing elements of TPRS in a variety of contexts and variations of the method as they have continued to develop over time.

Teacher Experiences and Method Descriptions.

The seven editions of Ray and Seely's (1997, 1998, 2002, 2004, 2008, 2012, 2015) book on TPRS, *Fluency Through TPR Storytelling: Achieving Real Language Acquisition in School*, taken together always have been and remain the definitive source for describing the evolving TPRS method over time. Evidence for that assumption was heard when TPRS teachers often have referred to it as the Green Book or the Green Bible, a name which reflected the color of its cover and the authority of its authors. Even with that being the case, Ray and Seely (1998) observed that there have always been variations and different versions of the method as individual teachers put their mark on how the method was delivered in their educational contexts. For example, even in Marsh's (1998) descriptive article on TPRS, as discussed earlier in the beginnings of TPRS section of this chapter, there were already subtle differences from the first Green Book when she reduced the number of steps.

That trend of differences in method delivery has continued among teachers as well as with researchers. As seen in this review, the construct of TPRS has been operationalized differently in different studies, so the reader must beware to carefully read how TPRS was described and operationalized when interpreting each research study. How TPRS was understood and implemented could have affected the experiences teachers had when using the method. Since studies on TPRS usually have been conducted by teachers, it could be argued that nearly every study reported at least some teacher experience using TPRS. In this section, researchers described experiences that educators had using TPRS to teach several languages, such as Spanish, Russian, English, Latin, and German at the elementary, secondary, adult, and university levels of instruction. Davidheiser reported on his own experiences.

University German Classes with TPRS.

Davidheiser (2001) tried teaching with TPRS and he perceived that the method was effective with his class of beginning students at the university level. He believed that TPRS was a more natural way to learn than his previous approach; his students were more comfortable and less anxious than before in class; and that they were more actively engaged in their own learning. Despite not practicing pronunciation, his students did improve their pronunciation primarily from hearing the target language spoken often by the teacher. Due to the repetitive comprehensible input received by students in class, they could remember more vocabulary than through methods he had used previously. However, even though the teacher had seen those benefits, he (see Davidheiser, 1996) still believed that teaching grammar was important, so he looked for ways to blend grammar teaching with the TPRS method of world language instruction.

In a second descriptive article on TPRS, Davidheiser's (2002) was purpose was to "contribute both to a better understanding of the method and to foster its wider use in German classes" (p. 25). He noted that several high school and university teachers had posted favorable comments about their experiences using TPRS on the American Association of Teachers of German (AATG) Listserv and that the method was growing in popularity. He reported that many German programs had increased their student enrollments and retention rates by using TPRS. Davidheiser discussed the origins of TPRS, to include TPR (Asher, 1965, 1966, 1969, 1988, 2000; Garcia, 1988, 2000), storytelling (Forward & Ogle, 1997; McKay, 2000; Ray, 1998; Ray & Gross, 1998; Ray & Seely, 1997), and the language acquisition theory which informed The Natural Approach (Krashen & Terrell, 1983; Terrell, 1977) and the TPRS method (Krashen, 1978, 1981, 1982, 1985, 1989, 1994, 2002, 2009). Ray and Seely (1998) had noted that, even from early there have been several variations of TPRS which have deviated from their original method description (in Ray & Seely, 1997) and the TPRS method has continued to develop and evolve over time (Cox, 2015; Gaab, 2006; Ray, 2013; Sievek, 2009; Taulbee, 2008). Therefore, it helps readers when researchers describe how the TPRS method is operationalized in each of their studies.

Grammar Groups and TPRS.

Davidheiser (2002) described his own teaching approach which included variations of TPR and TPRS. He began by showing a demonstration of TPR on video (Asher, 2000) during their first class session. His classes stayed in the target language, German, the for most of class time through connecting words with physical movements which he found helped students remember the words and verb structures. Davidheiser departed from classical TPR by giving his students handouts on vocabulary and by including some explicit grammar teaching, and he would "allow students to speak when they felt the need" (p. 27). He added grammar in context through TPRS after attending a workshop taught by Carol Gaab, Shirley Ogle, and Valeri Marsh. Davidheiser (2002) used Ray's (1998) early TPRS textbook, *Look I Can Talk*. He perceived that his adaptations of both TPR and TPRS, when used together, not only fit within the early research and theories of both Asher (et al., 1974) and Krashen (1978) which have endured, but also resulted in instruction that his college German students enjoyed.

Davidheiser's (2002) variation of TPRS included practicing in student pairs, storytelling, and drawing eight-picture "frames" (p. 28) to guide the acting out and writing of stories, plus homework. During class, he asked different types of questions about each story to help students focus on message content, story details, co-constructing different versions of a story, and because he perceived that "[a]rtful repetition is the key to retention" (p. 29). Among the comprehension checks that Davidheiser used was to encourage students to correct him when he gave incorrect story details on purpose. He found that humor and props added to student interest, involvement, and engagement.

Davidheiser (2002) justified his "brief allusions to grammar" (p. 31) by reminding his readers that even Krashen (1978, 1981, 2002) had conceded there was some limited value in learning grammar, particularly for editing and output-monitoring purposes (Krashen, 1992, 1993). Davidheiser (2002) further argued that "[n]either TPR nor TPRS proscribes grammar teaching" (p. 30) and he had attempted to develop a "communicative approach to grammar" (p. 30), which he had described previously in Davidheiser (1996).

Davidheiser (2002) listed five reasons why he perceived that TPRS was both successful and useful. First, TPRS encouraged active learning, movement, and social interaction in class. Second, he observed that "students take ownership of their learning" (p. 32) through listening to, acting out, telling, and writing stories. Third, through TPRS students received more comprehensible input than through other methods or textbooks. Fourth, TPRS helped students to "feel included and validated" (p. 32) in class. Fifth, he said simply that "TPRS is fun" (p. 32). Davidheiser (2002) did recommend more reading and writing, but he concluded that "it behooves us at all levels to consider strengthening our German curricula via TPRS" (p. 33). Davidheiser believed so strongly in his version of the TPRS method that he not only wrote journal articles to promote its use for increasing student enrollment and retention, but he also became a leader by presenting TPRS workshops to encourage others to use TPRS at the university and other levels.

Curriculum Development / Student Retention in High School.

Webster (2003) was interested in developing an entire TPRS curriculum that could support program growth at the high school level. Webster's (2003) study provided anecdotal evidence from his own survey and observations that TPRS significantly raised student retention and enrollment rates, both in terms of total numbers and from the lower levels up to the higher-level language courses, with substantial percentage increases. Webster (2003) perceived that high school TPRS-taught students were well-prepared for college language courses. An excerpt from Webster's (2003) master's thesis on TPRS was later published in Ray and Seely's (2012) sixth edition of *Fluency through TPR Storytelling* because it provided some evidence that student retention and enrollments increased through TPRS.

Since many of the early research studies on TPRS have been accomplished by teachers working on master's and doctoral degrees, Lichtman (2016) and Lichtman and Krashen (2013) recommended that teachers work with university professors to get those studies published and to increase the rigor of their research designs. Webster's (2003) thesis was not rigorously designed enough to withstand the close critical scrutiny expected of second language acquisition (SLA) researchers and was not published in a respected, peer-reviewed professional journal. While teachers may not have been interested in conducting research before, in this day of data-driven decisions and the requirement that instructional programs and lesson plans must be research-based, teachers doing research could give them a greater voice in curricular decisions.

Cognitive versus Communicative Paradigms.

Kaufmann (2005) discussed the polar differences between a traditional and a comprehension-based approach such as TPRS. Traditional language teaching and legacy methods generally involved the practice and manipulation of grammatical forms in isolation. However, comprehension-based approaches reflected the theory that speech emerges naturally, even without production practice or output, when people receive enough comprehensible input. Traditional approaches typically have involved forced output learning activities, production-based exercises, grammar-based drills, an emphasis on grammatical accuracy through corrective feedback, and they have been theoretically informed by a cognitive or communicative paradigm. On the other hand, comprehension-based methods, including TPRS, have relied on acquisition-based strategies for providing plentiful amounts of repetitive, interesting (or even compelling), comprehensible input in a meaningful context, such as a story, to promote long-term retention, second language acquisition (SLA), and proficiency through a primary focus on meaning, not on grammatical form.

Similar to Kaufmann's (2005) perspective, Krashen (2015) has described the traditional approaches as being informed by the Skill-Building Hypothesis and the TPRS method as informed by Krashen's (1981, 1982, 1985, 1989, 1992, 1993, 2013, 2015) Comprehension Hypothesis. These two approaches represented two very different ways of thinking about how languages are best acquired in classrooms. Therefore, mixing the two teaching approaches within the same treatment group in a research study which aimed to make method effectiveness comparisons, as in the Holleny (2012) study, could be considered counter-intuitive to Kaufmann (2005), Krashen (2015), and some TPRS teachers. Since the construct of using TPRS has been operationalized differently, perhaps even incorrectly in some studies, those variations in method delivery may have made analyzing TPRS difficult, as both Rapstine (2003) and Taulbee (2008) discovered. However, descriptive studies on TPRS variations have contributed new knowledge from a variety of perspectives and from contributors with different levels of experience.

Beginning with TPRS / Getting Started.

Decker's (2008) beginning expertise in teaching through TPRS grew through conducting her action research study and by reporting her experiences using the method. Before that, she had no previous experience using TPRS when she first taught a lesson using her version of TPRS. She compared that TPRS lesson with an explicit grammar lesson in a Spanish III class taught by their regular teacher. Decker taught the TPRS group a 14-sentence story which contained 5 reflexive verbs and asked 16 questions. However, Decker did not ask any questions for *se llamaba, se sentía*, or *podía peinarse*. She only asked 3 with *se sentó* and four with *se peinó*. Decker (2008) wrote up her study claiming that she was "ensuring that they orally hear and then verbally repeat the conjugated reflexive verbs multiple times" (p. 3), but the numbers indicated that this input was more limited than repetitive. The TPRS lesson included choral responses to questions and student actors. Decker assessed the students with a teacher-made verb conjugation grammar quiz and a freewrite. Despite this limited exposure of teaching only one lesson, Decker (2008) concluded that the "TPRS lesson did not have an immediate effect on the students' ability to correctly conjugate reflexive verbs in writing, [and that] "during the grammar lesson continuous participation was not an expectation" (p. 6). Decker (2008) observed that students were "more engaged with the TPRS lesson than with the explicit grammar lesson" (p. 7) and she valued her early learning experience.

Retirement Delayed.

Whaley (2009) described her own teaching experiences using TPRS. She had taught secondary school Russian for 23 years and intended to retire. However, after a two-day TPRS workshop, she decided to continue teaching, but in a very different way. Not only did Whaley think and teach differently, but she also brought in a new grading system that was standards-based. She received student support from beginning students who competed to have their own ideas, which were fun or interesting to them, accepted into the stories that the teacher and students co-constructed in class. Her lessons limited target vocabulary to three new structures per story, but she did not shelter grammar. Rather than limit first-year students to the present tense as before, students now heard and responded with both past and present tense verbs as needed to express the natural and logical meaning of story events in context. The repetition required for long-term memory and retention of high frequency vocabulary was achieved through personalization, by asking multiple questions, and by adding parallel characters or other details to stories. Daily comprehension quizzes held students accountable for these story details and the teacher used comprehension checks to ensure the students understood the messages.

Whaley's (2009) new goal, in teaching with TPRS principles, was to do "whatever it [took] to make sure that every student [understood] every word" (p. 2). She trained her students to stop her whenever they did not understand a detail, or if she was going too fast, so that she could clarify the meaning for them and so they would not "shut down" (p. 2) or get discouraged when others were laughing and understanding the story. She began teaching for mastery, one sentence at a time, and only moving ahead when "80% of the students" (p. 3) earned 80% or higher on quizzes or other assessments. Rather than receiving grades for completed work, as before TPRS, the teacher provided feedback for students and their parents for the language proficiency domains of reading, writing, speaking, and listening which reflected standards-based goals, with statements such as "meets standards" on every assessment or "almost meets standards" (p. 1).

Whaley (2009) met with some resistance to the new method from upper level students who had been taught with an explicit grammar textbook approach. The new system had "turned up a lot of weaknesses" (p. 1) for some of these students who had become accustomed to getting good grades, despite previously not being able to "display proficiency in any number of grammatical or lexical areas they had covered" (p. 1). Under the new system, mere coverage of material was no longer sufficient, the new goals were now proficiency, retention, long-term memory, mastery, and language acquisition. Despite some initial upper level student resistance, they "grudgingly admitted that they were learning a lot" (p. 1) with TPRS. Both the teacher and the students noticed that "everyone was doing well, not just the super stars" (p. 1) and those labeled as special education students were "almost indistinguishable" (p. 1) from other students. The TPRS teacher's confidence rose and her "insecurity in the classroom [took] a nosedive [as] the old teacher became the new teacher" (p. 2) because her students were having success.

Whaley (2009) did encounter some obstacles and challenges when beginning to use TPRS. There were few graded reading materials available in Russian that were of high interest to her students or written for their low levels. She did not know many other

Russian TPRS teacher colleagues, but she did discover that the TPRS "community seems to attract people who want to share," (p. 2) and she found support and encouragement online from <*benslavic.com*> and at the <*moretprs.net*> forum. Despite these difficulties, Whaley (2009) who had planned to retire in 2008 before finding TPRS has since won awards for excellence in teaching, is a regular presenter at NTPRS, and continues to teach Russian eight years later. In Whaley's (2009) experience, using TPRS, in her own words, was "like dancing. Sometimes everything flows so well that it feels as if you are floating, and the class is pure enjoyment. Sometimes the music is unfamiliar and you get out of step and knock your partner's knees. But it's still dancing, still music, and it's still way more fun than teaching the way I used to" (p. 4).

Teaching English as a Foreign Language (EFL) in Colombia Using TPRS.

While Whaley (2009) danced (her analogy) away from retirement by teaching Russian in Alaska, Bernal Numpaque and Garcia Rojas (2010) discussed teaching EFL in Colombia. Bernal Numpaque and Garcia Rojas first read about TPR (Asher, 2000, 2009), TPRS (Ray & Seely, 2008), and the five theoretical hypotheses of second language acquisition that informed the Natural Approach (Krashen & Terrell, 1983). They then synthesized those three principled influences to develop what they called a "methodological procedure" (p. 159) or "new proposal adaptation" (p. 160) that they decided was appropriate for their particular EFL program in Colombia, for both children and adults. Their adaptation of TPRS included pre-teaching vocabulary, story modeling, story mimicry, retelling in pairs and individually, rewards and compliments, writing, creating and acting out new stories, followed by reading and translations.

Bernal Numpaque and Garcia Rojas (2010) wrote about their perceptions of the advantages of using their adaptation of TPRS. Among those was that vocabulary and stories were retained by the students who could then speak with fluency and grammatical accuracy after experiencing TPRS. For them, the fun and humor contributed to long-term memory and positive student attitudes, especially when interesting, relevant to their lives, entertaining, or about real-life experiences. The researchers added that TPRS encouraged students to "use their imagination and creativity; it also encourages them to take on a large part of their responsibility for learning and building their confidence when speaking" (p. 161) in a low-stress, acquisition-rich, classroom environment.

Sustaining TPRS through an Online Professional Learning Community.

Black (2012) situated his descriptive dissertation study on TPRS in socio-cultural theory, or SCT, especially as influenced by Bakhtin's (Bakhtin & Holoquist, 1981; Bakhtin, Holoquist, & Emerson, 1986) perspectives because the ways "people create meaning through interaction have been increasingly used by educational researchers as the sociocultural turn in the field has increased" (Black, 2012, p. 2). He studied the interactions of an online Professional Learning Community (PLC). Using Bamberg's (Bamberg & Georgakopoulou, 2008) positioning analysis, Black (2012) interpreted the interactions of how six secondary-school TPRS teachers, who participated in the online PLC, a video study group, as its participants reconstructed their professional identities through sharing their TPRS teaching experiences and responding to each other's narratives and videotaped classes. They encouraged one another to sustain TPRS use.

Black (2012) recruited his study participants through online listservs and blogs. There were six teacher participants in the study whose experience using TPRS ranged from one to eight years. Five were women Spanish teachers, four in high school and one in middle school. One man, the researcher participant, taught middle and high school German. Three worked in urban and three in rural schools. Two teachers were from the Midwest, two from the South, one from the Southwest, and one from the Pacific coast. Those who worked in urban schools were required to use a textbook, so they sought ways to incorporate TPRS within a textbook approach. They met seven times from March to June 2011 "online using the Adobe Connect forum which enabled participants to interact using webcams, microphone and text typed in a chat box" (p. 98). They shared teaching challenges, tensions, resources, advice, and they discussed 5-10 minute videos of their classroom teaching. Black's (2012) systematic data analysis included transcriptions, using NVIVO version 8 for the coding of speaker turn-taking and responses to identify positioning moves during interactions, to notice instances of identity construction, and to develop individual profiles, identify themes, and interpret the conversational data.

Black (2012) closely examined how all six teachers interacted with three focal participants in the group, noting how they developed professional personas or identities, through their own personal narratives and positioned themselves or renegotiated their roles within the video study group dynamics. Individuals were not seen as having fixed identities because they changed often in response to others and were highly dependent upon new social contexts. Black explained that "strong environmental changes, as in times of reforms or crisis, can correspondingly create identity crisis for participants as they struggle to organize their identities to adapt to the changing conditions" (p. 4). The locus of learning about oneself occurred between participants through social interaction as one person gave a narrative (or told one's story), others responded to it, and then after receiving those responses, the personas had changed. In that three-step way, Black (2012) wrote that "storytelling was a core component of how they made sense of their experiences" (p. 5). These instances sometimes occurred in online focus group sessions. Since the learning was accomplished through this trio of dramatic social interaction, then "speakers can never claim full ownership of ideas" (p. 14). Therefore, learning and cognition, as well as personal identity construction and the repositioning of someone's role within a group, were not limited to the internalization of any one person's new thoughts, but rather happened between communicators through "the social nature of dialogic activity" (p. 15).

Black (2012) discussed how one teacher developed a new identity, through social interaction with other enthusiastic workshop attendees, as a new TPRS teacher, only to discover that the skills were difficult to master upon returning to her classroom. At that point, she met with self-resistance because of her previously-formed internal narrative and identity from the past contrasted with her new socially-constructed persona. In deciding whether to accept or reject the TPRS method, she realized that the new philosophical paradigm and values which informed TPRS teaching collided with and were in "conflict with values embedded in common past practices of the teacher, such as structuring communicative speaking applications of grammar points" (p. 18). Another one of the study group's members, Kendra, through her online narratives, "consistently portrayed herself as well-informed through regular references to various workshops that she attended" (p. 216) and she cited influential TPRS presenters to support her ideas. In Black's (2012) study, Kendra provided an example of how "learners must negotiate their place into social circles" (p. 10) through their own narratives to gain group acceptance.

Another member of Black's (2012) online study group, Elaine, also positioned herself as well-informed, with a special interest in reading books on literacy development and TPRS blogs, but she also "undertook the role of adapting the resulting ideas for world language instruction herself" (p. 216). Elaine provided an example of finding one's voice through speech acts and growing beyond the constraints of the group to arrive at an "ideological consciousness" (p. 17). In finding one's own voice, what may have begun as an "internally persuasive discourse may later develop into an authoritative discourse to be resisted and questioned" (p. 21) by others. Celina's narratives mostly described what she did in her classroom, simply telling what worked for her students' learning, as she did not feel the need to invoke the authoritative voices of experts. Celina's narratives showed that her focus was on "classroom interactions or on developing tools or techniques to support her teaching" (p. 176). Celina emerged as a natural group leader early on because she was skilled at interactively engaging others.

Black (2012) observed that group interaction both "enabled and constrained the discourse of individual group members" (p. 223). In the first video session, Kendra had directly criticized Hannah's classroom management and offered suggestions on how to better engage students, while others offered supportive comments. Black surmised that Kendra's remarks negatively impacted Hannah and "constrained her further participation to a degree that it may have contributed to her spotty attendance" (p. 223). When Nathan (Black) asked Elaine for details on how she coached her students when they expertly acted out stories, he had intended to learn more about how to do that, but when Nathan mentioned his difficulties, the group wanted to offer him support and so they "veered sharply away from Elaine's prepared talking points" (p. 224) and she lost the opportunity to shine. This provided an example of how the participant researcher's role proved complicated, at times contributing to and sometimes hindering the group discourse.

Black (2012) contributed to the field by situating his study within a socio-cultural paradigm, which future researchers might consider. His video study group model could prove useful for supporting university and certification programs, student teachers, providing skill building programs for those new to TPRS or as follow-up to their first workshop, for practicing teachers interested in continued professional development, and for teachers looking for ways to learn about and learn through new technologies.

Several studies in this review contributed information on the experiences students and teachers had using TPRS. For example, Oliver (2013) wrote an autobiographical dissertation discussing her first-hand experiences using several methods to teach world languages over several decades in the profession. As a teacher who had seen popular methods come and go over the years, she could communicate the lessons she learned and share the perspectives attained through her many teaching experiences. Oliver (2013) described the benefits of using different methods and concluded from her own experience that TPRS was the best method for developing oral proficiency.

Describing TPRS for ACTFL Readers.

Lichtman (2014) described TPRS and her early experiences using the method in an ACTFL publication. Lichtman reported on how much her teaching had changed after attending at a TPRS workshop where she learned the teaching strategies for providing plentiful amounts of interesting, repetitive, and comprehensible input through stories. Lichtman (2014) perceived that her students could retain more structures and vocabulary when learned in context. One of her students remarked, "I've taken Spanish for three years, but this is the first year I can *remember* the words!" (p. 1). Lichtman reviewed the empirical research studies on TPRS (see Lichtman, 2012a, 2015, 2016) which, in her own words, "have shown that it offers significant advantages for students' speaking, reading, and grammar skills" (2014, p. 1). Lichtman also noticed that in the studies she reviewed that there were variations of TPRS and adaptations made to local educational contexts.

Lichtman (2014) described the three basic steps of teaching through a story which included clearly establishing the meaning of new vocabulary, telling or asking a story, and reading and discussing the story. She discussed the importance of the teacher and students both sharing in the interpersonal creation of the story together. While the teacher guided the story's basic direction, students also contributed their own ideas and detail suggestions during class, so neither the teacher nor students knew beforehand exactly where the story might go or what details would be included in the final version of their co-constructed story. This meant there was some real interpretative, interpersonal, and communicative interaction inherent in the process. The final step was to read and discuss the original story, plus perhaps a longer version of the story, graded novellas, free reading, or even authentic readings could be used. At times, students acted out stories or changed the endings. Through retelling and rewriting stories, students practiced their presentational skills. By changing some story details, alternate versions became possible, allowing for creativity and differentiation for students at different levels of proficiency.

Lichtman (2014) discussed "three major worries that dissuade some teachers from using TPRS strategies: translation, grammar, and culture" (p. 2). She explained that translation should only be used sparingly so that the target language is used most of the time in class. Justifiable uses of the first language could have included establishing meaning to avoid student frustration, to save class time, and choral story translations. Some teachers may have rejected TPRS because they believed that grammar should be taught directly and explicitly. However, Lichtman (2014) cited the National Standards (1999; see ACTFL 1999, 2012) which "stress communicative language use" (p. 3) and she explained the TPRS use of 'pop-up' grammar which has involved briefly drawing the students' attention to formal features in the context of classroom interaction. Lichtman (2014) did agree that it was important to teach or to "infuse culture into the stories" (p. 3) and for teachers to provide students with comprehensible input.

Elements of TPRS / Connections to Marzano.

Welch's (2014) study was descriptive of the TPRS method and her master's thesis appeared in Spanish. A paraphrased translation of a portion of that description included:

> TPRS is a teaching method that has influenced the pedagogic world in a positive way and it strives to be an innovative method of telling and reading stories as a principal fountain of teaching. The structure of the stories offers various repetitions of certain grammatical structures. That repetition helps in the acquisition of a second language. There is now a lack of authentic literature, so I have taken stories, poems, and a dramatic work and have converted them into TPRS stories and readings. The stories and readings included will help students in the acquisition of Spanish as a second language. That will happen by way of grammatical structures that are repeated several times in each story and in each prepared reading, in this way, for the student to read and comprehend the original work (Welch, 2014, p. 1).

Above, Welch (2014) stressed the need for not only including authentic materials in Spanish lessons in school, but she also contributed by modifying those works so that those modified readings aligned with TPRS principles, beginning with providing a myriad of repetitions of key grammatical structures needed to make the eventual reading of the authentic works accessible to TPRS students. She continued her description by pointing out that it was created by an educator, Blaine Ray, and although it was previously considered effective but not conventional, TPRS has become a valued methodology among foreign language teachers as a common and successful method that promotes fluency in speaking and writing. TPRS has evolved, but the main principle was always a way to provide comprehensible input, with the goals of developing proficiency in listening, reading, writing, and speaking (paraphrased introduction, p. 1).

Welch (2014) listed the keys to achieve those competencies, which included that: (1) the language has to be comprehensible, (2) the students should receive sufficient auditory comprehensible input to be able to acquire the language and then to be able to express it orally, (3) the oral language has to maintain the student's interest, (4) students must express themselves in their own ways, not through memorized phrases, (5) the class should take place mostly in the second language, (6) the atmosphere should be only a little stressful so that students participate in a relaxed manner, and (7) the teacher's expectations must be high (Welch, 2014, pp. 1-2).

To paraphrase Welch's (2014) description, in order to accomplish those keys to competency, or essential elements and principles of TPRS, the method had three steps. Before the oral and written story, the first step was to 'establish meaning' so that the students understood the targeted vocabulary, grammatical structure, and phrases they were studying. That could have been done through gestures, pictures, props, translations, videos, or by using only words and structures that the students already knew (by staying in bounds). One essential TPRS technique was to limit vocabulary to high-frequency words and verb structures, meaning the ones most commonly used in the language. Another essential technique was to assess whether each student was understanding everything that the teacher said through frequent comprehension checks. Grammar explanations were simple, very brief, lasting only a few seconds, and focused primarily on the meaning, not the form of an utterance. Complicated metalinguistic terms were generally not used much, if at all, in TPRS classrooms. Cognates, or words that looked or sounded similar to English words, were used often in TPRS and translated if students did not recognize them.

According to Welch (2014), one of the most used and most essential elements in TPRS teaching has been personalization and what Waltz (2015) called customization, or tailoring the lesson to student interests. Including student interests often has been accomplished through Personalized Questions and Answers (PQA), before, during or after a story. The questioning has been done in different ways to individualize or differentiate instruction to meet each particular learner's needs and interests. Welch (2014) noticed and cited the connection of PQA with Marzano, Pickering, and Heflebower's (2011) research because, in her opinion, PQA was an effective way of interesting or engaging the students, by connecting the TPRS stories, vocabulary, and targeted grammar structures to the students' lives. Welch (2014) observed and discussed other connections between Marzano's (et al., 2011) reported educational research and

TPRS, pointing out that TPRS incorporated many the 'best practices' advocated by Marzano and his research group. Among those included kinesthetic movement, using gestures, acting stories out, and actively engaging students through multisensory input. Both Marzano (et al., 2011) and TPRS have encouraged the use of humor to engage students, even using ridiculous but happy details in stories. According to Welch (2014), perhaps the strongest connection was by tailoring instruction to students' interests and their background knowledge (p. 9). PQA was a way to learn more about each individual student. Welch (2014) went on to describe the storytelling and reading parts of TPRS and the questioning method known as "circling" (p. 6) used by most TPRS teachers. Of interest to Welch was reading and discussing the readings since she wanted to use TPRS to make authentic writings accessible to Spanish students at various proficiency levels. For Welch (2014), the learning accomplished through the oral and reading activities used in TPRS would be transferred from the first language to the second language to enable learners to read authentic literature and texts.

For the above-mentioned reasons, Welch (2014) decided to bring together TPRS and authentic literature, which she defined as writing by and for speakers of the language, in this case Spanish. She used TPRS to build bridges or scaffolds between what students knew, could do, and understand to what they needed to be able to do, such as read and understand authentic stories without a dictionary. Among the materials she initially prepared were seven stories, two poems, and a work of theater in her study, taken from a variety of authentic sources from different Spanish-speaking countries. She did this by pre-reading the authentic piece and then designing instruction consistent with the TPRS keys to achieve competencies, essential elements, and principles of TPRS described in her study to achieve her goals, and encouraged others to do the same.

Welch (2014) included in her study suggested activities with the shortened TPRS stories, embedded readings, extended stories, and other materials to help guide students toward authentic resources and the reading of authentic texts. Welch (2014) cited Ray (2012) as the source of a review of thirteen TPRS research studies as evidence to support Welch's position that TPRS was, and is, an effective method. However, that research review was in fact put together by Lichtman (2012a), which Ray and Seely (2012) published in the sixth edition of their book, *Fluency through TPR Storytelling*. Since then, Lichtman (2015, 2016) has continued to add studies to her reviews of TPRS research. Informed by support from research, Welch (2014) perceived and concluded that, with TPRS and access to authentic readings, students would not only acquire a second language in a classroom, but that they would also learn about other cultures in a positive classroom environment (p. 60).

Teaching Latin through TPRS.

Patrick (2015a) had a descriptive article published in a peer-reviewed journal primarily to report on the growing use and the effectiveness of using of comprehensible-input strategies among teachers of classical languages, such as Latin and Greek. He also encouraged more teachers to adopt the approach in order to invigorate their programs. He cited Ray and Seely's (2008) book on TPRS as he described his comprehensible-input approach to teaching Latin which he reported using successfully in the middle and high schools, with adults, and at the university level. His practical and theoretical orientations were informed by Krashen's (1982, 1985, 2009) five hypotheses of language acquisition, the importance of reading (Krashen, 1994, 2004, 2011a), and Patrick's (2015a) approach was influenced by Van Patten's (2014, 2015) discussions on comprehensible input and the role of comprehensible output in language learning (Swain, 1985, 2005a, 2005b).

Rather than use full immersion, Patrick (2015a) followed several TPRS teachers' online blogs which led him to establish an "immersive" (p. 111) or near-immersion goal of using Latin 90% of the time to deliver interesting, comprehensible messages in a low-stress classroom atmosphere. Patrick used English to briefly establish meaning and for some comprehension checks and TPR to practice new vocabulary, but he and his students mostly communicated in Latin. Patrick used stories, humor, props and personalization strategies to obtain and retain student interest, encouraging learners to "give full attention to the discussion" (p. 113). Patrick explained that his students gave choral and individual responses to various types of teacher questions, suggested story details interactively, and learned four words thoroughly for retention each class. He limited vocabulary to words students already knew, plus four, (see Krashen's [2009], i+1) to review and focus on a few words repetitively in various contexts so they could later read in Latin without using dictionaries. All this happened without doing drills or homework, but rather through teacher-student classroom communication. Patrick perceived that these strategies worked "with every student, all the time" (p. 115) in his experience and that within four years of study in interactive comprehensible-input (CI) classrooms students typically achieved a middle-to-high intermediate level of proficiency on the ACTFL (2012) scale.

Patrick (2015a) explained that "CI teaching is intense, demanding, and exciting work. It not only allows, but demands, that the Latin teacher be the expert in all things pertaining to Latin" (p. 116), especially grammar. Patrick (2015a) reported finding measurable gains on standardized proficiency tests over time superior to previous methods, raised enrollments, increased student retention rates for four levels of Latin, and he was developing an AP course. Special education students also succeeded in his department's program when "taught only with CI approaches" (p. 117) in which the teacher's focus was on "delivering understandable messages in Latin... in repetitive, yet engaging ways" (p. 119) and Patrick emphasized that the "conversations must be compelling" (p. 120). The student's "job was to have fun and remain in Latin" (p. 119). Teachers used embedded readings (see Clarcq, 2015) to build scaffolds that enabled students to eventually read classical Latin works of literature that the teachers used for summative assessments of reading and writing. Influenced by Truscott's (1996, 1999, 2007) research on the futility of error correction, Patrick's (2015a) students developed their 'writing fluency' by doing freewrites, timed writings (see V. Ray, 2015), and relaxed writings without receiving any error correction at all, but rather only through the positive evidence of well-formed utterances provided through oral and written input.

Where Patrick (2015a) deviated somewhat from a pure CI approach was in teaching some direct, but short explicit grammar lessons. However, he limited those lessons to a few focused and principled applications (see Krashen, 1978, 1992, 1993) such as for purposes of editing for grammatical accuracy, noticing formal features, synthesizing their learning and meta-cognition, and assessing whether the grammar they were taught incidentally through CI helped with student understanding. Patrick (2015a) acknowledged that a CI approach would "place its demands on teachers who very likely did not learn Latin in this way" (p. 129), but he perceived the approach to be effective and encouraged others to employ it to "create Latin programs that are strong and sustainable" (p. 109). After writing this article, Patrick and 45 of his Latin teacher colleagues attended the 2015 national TPRS conference. Then, he wrote the following article for another online, peer-reviewed journal, extending his readership beyond the teachers of classical languages to modern world languages.

Patrick (2015b) reported that the number of Latin teachers who attended a weeklong NTPRS conference grew from three in 2012 to 46 in 2015. Previously, they had attended the weeklong Latin immersion experience offered in West Virginia by The North American Institute of Living Latin Studies. However, faced with falling student enrollments, Patrick and some colleagues turned to training teachers in CI strategies to invigorate their Latin classes and they developed a program called Pedagogy-Rusticatio. Patrick and TPRS trainer Jason Fritze delivered the first presentation at the American Classical League (ACL, 2015). The Latin Best Practices listserv has grown to over 1300 collaborators who have been sharing experiences, ideas, best practices, and resources. His public school has been offering CI workshops and continuing education as well.

Patrick (2015b) discussed the growing numbers of Latin teachers who have moved from a grammar translation approach to teaching with TPRS and using comprehensible input strategies, the challenges (especially considering the Latin language's high number of inflectional suffixes), and the many student successes that TPRS ad CI teaching has brought to their Latin language programs. Some people may have wondered why these educators would bother teaching and developing speaking proficiency skills for what has been called a dead language, to which Patrick (2015b) replied that "all kinds of students can acquire the language when we deliver understandable messages in the target language and we deliver those in two ways: by speaking and by reading" (p. 53).

Teaching Mandarin Chinese through TPRS.

The notion from language acquisition theory of providing comprehensible input also was emphasized by Neubauer (2015). In a descriptive article, Neubauer discussed her experiences of when she first began using the TPRS method and CI strategies for making messages understood to her high school students in Mandarin Chinese. She recalled, "That first year, I had some significant pushback, especially from students who excelled at rote memory of vocabulary and from those who believed language class should revolve around competitive, output-based games" (p. 47). In addition to student pushback, she received resistance from parents who had expected a different type of instruction. In order to defend her educational practices, to show that her teaching reflected the current thinking in the field, and was grounded in sound theory and research, Neubauer began using quotes from second language acquisition (SLA) theory such as Krashen (2013), research (Truscott, 1996, 2007), and from a book (Nuttall, 1996) that advocated the same techniques that she used in class. She also posted the SLA quotes on bulletin boards in her classroom. Neubauer (2015) encouraged others to do the same if they met with resistance to their teaching method or pushback from students or parents.

Infant Education Using TPRS.

Marimon Gil (her last name) (2015) studied younger children, ages four to five, to determine whether TPRS was appropriate for an infant education program. Marimon Gil (2015) examined the different needs of 24 English learners in Spain of 15 girls and 9 boys, ages 4-5, attending a charter school. One student had Asperger's syndrome, five were gifted, four required extra tutoring, and all 24 spoke Spanish and Catalan, so they were learning English as an additional language. The students had completed their first year of English; Marimon Gil's task was to prepare a 'teaching proposal' for their second year of English study. Cooperative learning was the "most used approach in the school" (p. 11) and working together in groups was required in each of the school's academic programs. The group work was a vehicle for promoting moral values such as "responsibility, communication, collaboration" (p. 11), and learning through social interaction and peaceful cooperation. In addition, the teachers were expected to use a program called Information and Communication Technologies (ICT), but other than that guidance, she (2015) was allowed some academic freedom in developing the instructional program. Marimon Gil (2015) reviewed the literature on language acquisition theory and research which led her to consider the TPRS method.

Marimon Gil (2015) surmised that there was "general agreement among all the scholars regarding the importance of input exposure to acquire" (p. 18) language, so she accepted Krashen's (1982) comprehensible input hypothesis, but she also accepted Swain's (2005a) argument that learner output also played an important role in language learning. The teaching proposal and curricular plan that Marimon Gil (2015) put together contained activities for providing input and for encouraging output too. Her plan was influenced by Ray and Seely's (2012) statement that "making the class 100% comprehensible is the key for the success of TPRS" (p. 51) and she noticed that TPRS did not use textbooks. She also was interested in Asher's (2009) TPR technique of using commands to encourage students to play "an active role by doing movements, gestures, [and] actions" (p. 29) in their own learning. The materials that Marimon Gil (2015) developed reflected those influences and the three steps of TPRS. The reader should note that Marimon Gil is her last name.

Marimon Gil (2015) explained that TPRS first established meaning which consisted of being intentional about "introducing the structures and the vocabulary of the story before reading it or at the same time" (p. 30). In her opinion, the second step of asking a story was the most important part of TPRS and "the most important part of the storytelling is [was] to develop the story asking the students some questions" (p. 31). After developing the story together through social interaction, reading was the "last step of the TPRS approach" (p. 32), followed by discussion, translation, and other follow-up activities. Marimon Gil (2015) synthesized the influences above and included them in her teaching proposal and curricular plan, which she adapted to fit the young learners' needs and abilities in a story about a caterpillar who was very hungry.

In providing the rationale for using the TPRS method in her planning framework, Marimon Gil (2015) cited Lichtman's (2012a) first review of the early research on TPRS which consistently showed that TPRS-taught students did as well or better than those taught through other methods. Lichtman's review included "over 1672 students enrolled in 107 different classes, taught by 47 different teachers in 21 different schools, so the results cannot be attributed to a particular class or teacher" (Lichtman, 2012a, p. 310). Armed with supporting research, Marimon Gil (2015) concluded by answering the question raised in the title of her thesis: Is TPRS an efficient methodology for infant education students? "Yes, it is" (p. 89) was her answer and she submitted her teaching proposal. However, she adapted TPRS and TPR to fit her particular educational setting where they were required to use cooperative learning, technology, and output activities.

Three Teachers' Experiences Using TPRS in One School District.

Espinoza (2015) studied what three teachers experienced using TPRS in one school district. In Espinoza's (2015) qualitative case study, he identified the experiences of three teachers when using the TPRS method in class and in curriculum development, plus their perceptions of the method's impact on students' language acquisition. Participants were selected who met specific criteria. Participants had to be high school teachers with his school district who were trained in TPRS, taught using it, and "were recommended because of their expertise with using the TPRS teaching method" (p. 32). The convenience, yet purposeful sample, was obtained from the school district Espinoza had attended as a student, did his student teaching, and where he currently taught. He asked open-ended questions in three semi-structured, face-to-face, individual interviews of about 30 minutes each in each teacher's classroom. In the first interview, the researcher asked about their background and TPRS training, in the second about their experiences using TPRS, and in the third interview they reviewed and discussed the accuracy of the transcriptions, using member checking to establish the content validity of the data to increase the confidence, credibility, and trustworthiness of the findings.

Espinoza (2015) interviewed only three TPRS teachers. His findings included that they used TPR, comprehensible input, PQA, and that they perceived the students did acquire the target language through TPRS. The teachers sometimes modified or deviated from the three TPRS steps, they wanted additional professional development to improve their TPRS teaching skills, and they sometimes experienced a lack of support. That lack of support was from not having sufficient TPRS materials and from having some teacher colleagues who were unsupportive and did not approve of their efforts to use TPRS. All three TPRS teachers "expressed that their teacher preparation programs were heavily grammar and textbook-based" (p. 64) and did not include lessons specifically on how to provide comprehensible input to students. According to Espinoza (2015), his findings suggested that language teachers "should be open to learning and implementing different teaching methodologies with their classes" (p. 65). Since two of the three teacher participants, before finding TPRS, had "expressed not feeling satisfied with their teaching practices" (p. 67) and with students' ability to speak the target language (p. 53), the researcher recommended that a study of TPRS teacher job satisfaction be conducted for comparison purposes. Espinoza (2015) concluded that TPRS increased "students' motivation for learning and teachers' motivation for teaching" (p. 68).

Elementary School Boys and TPRS / Student Engagement.

Espinoza (2015) interviewed teachers, as did Campbell. For Campbell's (2016) phenomenological dissertation, she studied teacher perceptions of student engagement with third-grade boys when using TPRS in world language classes. All three TPRS teacher participants were trained in the method and each one taught in a different school within the same school district, where Campbell also worked. To study their experiences with her central phenomenon (student engagement) during TPRS lessons, multiple data sources were used. She transcribed and analyzed interviews with teachers and focus groups, used questionnaires, made classroom observations, gave pre- and post-unit tests, and read electronic teacher-reflection journals. The study lasted four weeks, including a planning week followed by a three-week TPRS unit treatment.

Campbell's (2016) literature review established that boys in general tended not to do as well in school compared with girls their age (Gurian & Stephens, 2004, 2006;

Whitehead, 2006; Schwabe, McElvany, & Trendtel, 2015). For that reason, some researchers, such as Campbell, have been searching for more boy-friendly teaching strategies to help close the gender gap. According to King and Gurian (2006) boys have preferred kinesthetic and visual learning styles. Physical and hands-on activities, along with visuals, have appealed to boys. "Ensuring students are engaged in a lesson reduces the chances of drifting, boredom, and potentially undesirable behaviors" (Markelz, 2016, p. 1). Humor and physical movement also have been used as instructional tools to help engage and motivate boys to read (Senn, 2012). After reading about the TPRS method (in Ray & Seely, 2008) and attending a TPRS workshop, Campbell (2016) defined TPRS as a "method with a significant amount of visual and kinesthetic elements" (p. 20).

In her own TPRS teaching experience, Campbell (2016) had "witnessed students experiencing success" (p. 44), a bias she admitted, but she attempted to bracket out (set aside) her own experiences with TPRS from her study. She tried to remain objective and to stay focused on the experiences of her study's teacher participants, not hers, in her data collection and analyses. Campbell used multiple data sources and member checking to increase the trustworthiness and of the data collected, the credibility of her findings, and the dependability of her conclusions. Whether TPRS would foster student engagement had not been explored much in the professional literature, but there was some evidence that highly 'engaged' learners who actively participated in class tended to achieve greater academic success (AMLE, 2010; Bryson & Hand, 2007; Chen & Looi, 2011) than others.

Campbell (2016) was interested in studying whether TPRS could "arouse and hold" student interest and engagement or enhance academic achievement. She analyzed teacher "perceptions of student engagement" (p. 14) when they used TPRS. "The data obtained from all the data sources [listed above] validate TPRS as a method that fosters student engagement" (p. 86). Eighteen out of twenty students in Campbell's (2016) study mastered all the targeted vocabulary, establishing a positive link between student engagement and academic achievement. Campbell (2016) concluded that TPRS cultivated an "environment of active engagement" (p. 84) and that TPRS provided a "foundation for students to build connections" (p. 85). Teacher perceptions supported the notion that the kinesthetic and visual components of TPRS complemented the learning styles of male students and had a positive impact on student engagement.

Despite the evidence from a growing body of empirical research on TPRS that has shown its effectiveness, teachers using the method have sometimes met with resistance from people opposed to its use. The following section discussed resistance from people and some of the other obstacles to using the method which appeared in TPRS studies.

Obstacles and Resistance to TPRS.

There was some evidence in the literature that TPRS teachers encountered obstacles and resistance. Safdarian (2013) discussed some of them. From his perspective, storytelling required more learning time than other methods. Regarding tests, he noticed that TPRS teachers preferred proficiency exams to discrete point grammar tests. Safdarian (2013) mentioned some difficulties teachers faced in aligning TPRS lessons with textbook grammar and prescribed curricula. Espinoza (2015) found not having sufficient TPRS materials was an obstacle and having unsupportive colleagues was a source of resistance to using TPRS. Whaley (2009) found few graded readers were available in Russian, she had few colleagues to collaborate with, and sometimes the TPRS 'dance' (her analogy) flowed better for her than at other times. When that happened, she appreciated the need for mutual encouragement. Neubauer (2015) experienced student pushback, especially from the high-achieving students who had been successful with the previous traditional approach and did not want to change. Garczynski (2003) observed resistant and skeptical teachers who openly challenged the TPRS workshop presenter and the ideals of TPRS. One teacher got up and walked out over the issue of not using textbooks.

Some of the literature reviewed for this study mentioned issues involving curriculum and textbooks. For example, Slavic (2008) observed that no textbook can deliver comprehensible input to students" (p. 10). The following studies produced evidence that using TPRS was more effective than using a textbook. Kariuki and Bush's (2008) empirical study found that students taught using TPRS were more engaged and significantly outscored a textbook-taught group on both translation and vocabulary tests. Dziedzic (2012) found the TPRS-taught group scored significantly higher that the textbook-taught group for both the speaking and writing skills on the Denver Public Schools Proficiency Assessments. The English learners in Cubukcu's (2014) study who were taught using TPRS significantly outperformed the textbook-taught students on vocabulary tests. Pippins and Krashen (2016) studied students who had taken five years of Spanish, with levels 2, 3, and 4 all having been taught through TPRS, with no textbook. Eighty-four percent of those students scored 3 or higher on the Advanced Placement (AP) Exam in Spanish, earning college credits. Pippins and Krashen (2016) concluded that studying grammar from a textbook was not necessary. Davidheiser (2002) found that TPRS students received more comprehensible input that textbook-taught students. Spangler (2009) found that teachers were dissatisfied with the progress students made through textbooks. Garczynski (2003) found that students did significantly better on listening and reading comprehension tests when taught through TPRS than when taught through a textbook. A survey revealed the students preferred the TPRS lessons. After reviewing SLA research, Wong and VanPatten (2003) declared that the evidence showed and that mechanical textbook grammar drills were ineffective. Wenck's (2010) own language learning story reflected that after working hard doing textbook drills for six years and mastering the grammar, and despite being highly motivated to learn the language, she reported that she "could not speak a full sentence" (p. 6) in German.

Marimon Gil (2015) read Ray and Seely's (2012) book on TPRS and noticed that they did not advocate the use of textbooks. The three teachers Espinoza (2015) interviewed for his study were all disappointed that their university teacher preparation programs had all been grammar-based. They learned TPRS after college. Kirby (2012), a principal and former Spanish teacher, was surprised that ACTFL did not endorse any one textbook. He believed that a textbook could help teachers teach to the standards. In his study, he found that teachers who thought they were teaching to the standards were not. Ironically, the lone TPRS teacher in his study, who Kirby (2012) referred to as Don Quixote, did not claim to be teaching to the ACTFL standards, but through multiple data collection sources Kirby concluded that he did, despite his adamant refusal to use a textbook. Don Quixote spoke more in the target language than the other teachers in Kirby's study and his students were highly engaged. Yet, Kirby still considered Don Quixote's absolute unwillingness to use a textbook problematic, despite not having cited a single source that any textbook approach had been proven effective, even in his own study.

Oliver (2013) pointed out that obstacles for her included curriculum and textbook choice when she began her college teaching. Previously, she had used a variety of methods as a high school teacher that reflected the beginnings of the Teaching for Proficiency movement (Kramsch, 1987; Liskin-Gasparro, 2000; Omaggio-Hadley, 1986). She wanted to align her teaching with the developing Communicative Language Teaching (CLT) movement (Allwright, 1977; Breen & Candlin, 1980; Canale & Swain, 1980; Johnson, 1982; Yalden, 1983). She wanted to incorporate the national foreign language standards (ACTFL 1999, 2012) that stressed communication about meaningful topics. However, Oliver (2013) was surprised to discover that the prescribed college curriculum for her classes was a traditional grammar textbook, typical of older methods.

Oliver (2013) knew about TPR and TPRS use in high school, but she felt that the methodological strategies "had slid backward at the university" (p. 141) and that students "learning to *speak* [emphasis in original] Spanish was not a priority" (p. 145) at her university. Her Spanish program language coordinator insisted that she follow the "textbook vocabulary and grammar" (p. 149), but Oliver was allowed some academic freedom in method choice. Oliver coped by opting for a mixed-methods approach (Grammar-Translation, plus TPRS) that she called "modified" TPRS. She found, when she switched from storytelling back to the grammar explanations and textbook exercises, that her students "lost interest" (p. 154). However, Oliver observed that during story time students were more "animated, creative, and engaged [so] discipline was hardly ever an issue" (p. 154) when using TPRS. Oliver's (2013) situation was described at length because other teachers trying to use TPRS and teach for proficiency in various school contexts also have met with similar resistance from colleagues or supervisors. Whether there was good reason for resisting certain aspects of TPRS was an interesting question to explore, as well as identifying areas for potential growth or improving the method.

ACTFL and Room for Growth in the TPRS Method.

Oliver (2013) described her high school and university experiences teaching with seven methods over five decades, to include using TPRS. As she searched for the "optimal method" (p. 183), she viewed the process as linear, moving gradually toward developing an "increased communicative ability in students" (p. 183). The seven methods included Grammar-Translation, Audio-lingual, Individualized Instruction, Direct, Natural, TPR, and TPRS. She wrote that TPRS was useful for promoting proficiency development and for addressing the standards published by the American Council on the Teaching of Foreign Languages (ACTFL, 1999, 2000, 2012).

While much of the professional literature reviewed above has documented the positive aspects and effectiveness of TPRS, there have been works negatively critical of the method. These studies, articles, and analyses pointed out areas of potential growth and recommended modifications or improvements for the TPRS method. For example, Rapstine (2003) had noticed the growing popularity of TPRS in high schools and colleges and he wanted to know its advantages and disadvantages. He did not conduct an empirical research study, but he analyzed the method to identify the strengths and weaknesses of an early variation of TPRS, as he saw them, years before Alley and Overfield (2008) and Taulbee (2008) conducted their critical analyses of TPRS.

Rapstine (2003) examined TPRS through the lens of the ACTFL (1999, 2000) national standards for world language instruction, before Sievek (2009) later recommended modifications to better alignment with those standards. Rapstine (2003) contributed a critical perspective that has influenced the direction and questions studied in the growing body of research on TPRS which has been conducted primarily by teachers. The ACTFL standards of interest to Rapstine (2003) included communication, cultures, connections with other disciplines, comparisons of language and cultures, and participating in communities. Those five standards were published in the National Standards in Foreign Language Education Project (1999) and have continued to inform language teaching practices ever since.

Among the advantages for TPRS that Rapstine (2003) found was that TPRS was able "to include all types of learners" (p. 57), which reflected the philosophy within the ACTFL standards that everyone can learn languages. This notion was supported in the reports of teachers that enrollments had increased through using TPRS (Davidheiser, 2002; Webster, 2003), that TPRS-taught students were successful on standardized tests (Marsh 1998), and students preferred TPRS to traditional teaching (Garczynski, 2003). Storytelling reflected the ACTFL communication standard since the TPRS teacher and students jointly developed stories together, by interacting in a classroom context made learner-centered through using Personalized Questions and Answers (PQA).

Among the disadvantages was Rapstine's (2003) perception that "TPRS requires a lot of work on the teacher's part and a TPRS classroom depends a lot on the teacher's personality" (p. 59). Rapstine (2003) expressed that TPRS fell short in teaching culture and that "students in a TPRS classroom may not be receiving enough comprehensible reading material" (p. 61) and authentic texts. Rapstine (2003) concluded that "further research of both a practical and theoretical nature is required to validate a method that appears to hold promise" (p. 65). However, since Rapstine's (2003) initial analysis, much research on TPRS has been conducted, plus additional analyses of the method.

Alley and Overfield (2008) questioned the "value of TPRS" (p. 22) and concluded from their analysis of literature that "TPRS has more in common with older language teaching methods than with current standards-based instruction" (p. 13). They situated their study by establishing the method's popularity by quoting internet sources of TPRS teachers who praised the method online. The researchers cited the second edition of Ray and Seely's (1998) descriptions of the TPRS method and then Alley and Overfield (2008) wrote their perceptions of how TPRS failed to measure up with "current beliefs about effective language teaching" (p. 14), learning theory, and second language acquisition (SLA) research. However, since the researchers chose to use Ray and Seely's 1998 second edition rather than the third (2002, 2003), fourth (2004, 2005), or the 2008 fifth edition, Alley and Overfield (2008) failed to analyze the 2008 TPRS method. Therefore, the changes and developments that had occurred in TPRS between 1998 and 2008 were not taken into account, so the validity of their data was suspect along with any findings or conclusions drawn. Gaab's (2006) article on how TPRS was an evolving method was not reviewed, so Alley and Overfield (2008) may have been unaware that TPRS was (and is) a continually-evolving method (Gaab, 2006; Ray, 2013; Ray & Seely, 2012, 2015).

Alley and Overfield (2008) declared that "there is little research to support the effusive claims of increased student motivation and achievement that practitioners of TPRS make and that there is a similar lack of qualitative data" (p. 22) to support them.

Perhaps they were unaware of the following studies, articles, and theses: Marsh (1998), Cantoni (1999), Webster (2003), Garczynski (2003), Rapstine (2003), Brune (2004), Kaufmann (2005), Braunstein (2006), Gaab (2006), Perna (2007), Armstrong (2008), Decker (2008), Kariuki and Bush (2008), and Taulbee (2008). Alley and Overfield may have been correct in their 2008 observation that no study had been published yet on the construction of teacher identity, but since then Black (2012) has filled that gap with his dissertation study on how TPRS teachers have developed their professional identities through dialogic interaction online. The gap in the method, that Alley and Overfield (2008) identified, that TPRS did not include "authentic folktales or children's stories from the target culture" (p.19) was filled recently by Cartford, Holter Kittok, and Lichtman (2015) with their empirical study on content-based storytelling (CBS).

After Alley and Overfield's (2008) analysis, in a similar fashion, Taulbee (2008) analyzed TPRS to identify the possible positive and negative aspects of the method. Before doing so, she attended workshops with TPRS presenters Susie Gross and Von Ray, and she read Ray and Seely's (2004, 2005) fourth edition of *Fluency through TPR Storytelling* book and had experienced success using TPRS with her students. Taulbee (2008) found herself suddenly receiving criticism from colleagues because she was, in her words, "the sole TPRS teacher in a district where other teachers followed a traditional model for teaching language" (p. 207). In reaction to those experiences, she designed her master's thesis. Taulbee (2008) needed to decide whether to use TPRS or not, so she set out to identify the pluses and minuses of the method for herself and because other TPRS teachers also had "often met with skepticism from colleagues and administrators" (p. v).

Taulbee (2008) did not design a rigorous research study for her thesis. Instead, she reviewed the literature to identify the advantages and disadvantages of using TPRS and decided that she saw value in both teaching grammar and in using TPRS. After developing twenty lessons for teaching Spanish which covered the textbook grammar and vocabulary within a TPRS framework, she then tried out the materials in her own classes and elicited student feedback on the effectiveness of the instruction they received.

From her literature review analysis and her own direct experiences using the method and materials, Taulbee (2008) found that advantages of TPRS included "long-term retention of vocabulary, enhanced listening skills, enhanced speaking skills, and reported higher retention rates in programs across the country" (p. 1). Teachers reported positive student attitudes and feeling empowered through TPRS. She found that the method taught grammar in context and that teachers who used TPR and TPRS "have reported positive results in student retention and interest in foreign language" (p. 7). Guided by the belief that comprehensible input was essential for language acquisition, TPRS proponents "developed a series of steps to ensure that all language learners understand the language at all times" (p. 15), which lowered their affective filter. Students felt "ownership of the story" (p. 18) when it was personalized or customized to their interests and the teacher accepted their suggested details. They found them to be more engaging especially when the details were humorous, exaggerated, or even bizarre. Advantages included students being actively involved through dramatizing stories, feeling included in class, improving their writing fluency, and eventually gaining the "confidence to speak" (p. 22). To achieve those results, instructors were expected to make all input comprehensible. If students did not understand, they sometimes felt "frustrated and eventually shut down" (p. 19).

Among the disadvantages, Taulbee (2008) found that TPRS teachers were often "in the minority among their colleagues" (p. 22) and that TPRS often was "not met without critics" (p. 206). Working within a foreign language department was challenging when teachers who did not use TPRS received "students in the next level who [did] not understand what certain grammatical terms [were] called" (p. 26). TPRS-taught students did not normally hear long grammar explanations in English or metalinguistic terms. Some people complained that TPRS students were not taught all five of the ACTFL standards because the primary focus on communication left little time for other topics. For new TPRS instructors, it was often difficult to learn all the complex TPRS teaching skills and strategies. They reported that teaching with TPRS took high energy and was "very taxing" (p. 27) on the teacher, but it was worthwhile to help students acquire.

After weighing the advantages and disadvantages of TPRS, Taulbee (2008) developed materials designed "to provide teachers with a way to incorporate contextual grammar exercises while still using TPRS" (p. v). While she personally had been reluctant to use TPRS because of the resistance she received from colleagues, Taulbee decided to create materials for combining a grammar focus within a TPRS approach. She did this because she believed both were important, grammar and TPRS, and because her school district required the use of a particular textbook series. Taulbee hoped to promote acquisition through TPRS and simultaneously an "awareness of linguistic features" (p. 3). With these two goals in mind, Taulbee's (2008) research question became: "How could TPRS be adapted into a traditional, grammar-based curriculum?" (p. 3).

Taulbee (2008) created enough materials within a TPRS story framework to last a semester, to include three units, six lessons, and three themes. Each lesson had targeted vocabulary, plus communication, grammar, and cultural learning objectives. She provided story scripts for the teacher, readings, extended readings, and internet links for extra practice or homework. The lessons were designed for easy implementation and she encouraged brief explanations of grammar so that most of class time could be spent on the oral interaction of stories. The teacher-researcher implemented the semester-long program and elicited student feedback to evaluate its effectiveness. Taulbee (2008) reported that her experience "revealed what she had anticipated: students reacted positively to storytelling" (p. 209). Nearly all students chose stories as their favorite learning activity. However, when asked about grammar, the range of student responses indicated they only "somewhat understood it to fully understood the grammar" (p. 210). Based on student feedback, Taulbee (2008) deduced that "grammar, when taught alongside TPRS curriculum [held] little meaning for the students. The researcher found repeatedly that student involvement in the stories held the most class interest" (p. 211). Taulbee perceived that students did acquire Spanish, but were unable to apply the grammar rules that they learned through explicit instruction in their writing. In the end, Taulbee (2008) concluded that students preferred storytelling to grammar instruction.

Noting that in TPRS, there has been a primary concern on developing language proficiency, Sievek (2009) shared similar concerns with Rapstine (2003) over TPRS and world language standards. Sievek (2009) recommended that teachers modify TPRS, as he had done, to better align their teaching practices to comply with the ACTFL (2000) standards. Sievek (2009) encouraged TPRS teachers to include all five standards in their instruction: Communication, Culture, Connections to other academic disciplines, Comparisons of first and target languages, and Communities. Additionally, Sievek (2009) encouraged an additional emphasis on grammar teaching, but without losing the primary TPRS focus on providing comprehensible input to students through storytelling. Besides Rapstine (2003) and Sievek (2009), Kirby (2012) found that the world language teachers in his study fell short in teaching to the five ACTFL (2000, 2012) standards.

Kirby (2012) was a former Spanish teacher and current high school administrator with twelve years of experience. He conducted a case study, with both quantitative and qualitative data, to study how world language teachers perceived the ACTFL (2000) standards, and whether the standards were implemented in their classrooms, as well as the methods, approaches, and materials they used for teaching to the standards. Kirby (2012) was interested in finding out whether there was a disconnect between teacher perceptions and their actual classroom teaching practices. The teacher participants were five level two Spanish teachers, all from different high schools. The data were collected from one questionnaire, four 60-minute classroom observations using Eisner's (1985) evaluation protocol, a disclosure document, textbooks, classroom materials, handouts, and structured interviews. To address the concerns for trustworthiness and credibility (validity and reliability), member checking was used and university professors checked the audit trail, did an inter-rater reliability check, and provided feedback to the researcher. Pseudonyms were used to protect the confidentiality of study participants, with Don Quixote being the study's only TPRS instructor.

After a cross-case analysis and synthesis of the five cases, Kirby (2012) found that teacher perceptions did not always match what he observed in the data. For example, three out of five teacher participants reported that they understood the ACTFL standards, but Kirby (2012) discovered they were "unfamiliar with the proper definitions of each" (p. 157) standard. They thought the 'connections' standard meant connections with the students, but it actually referred to making connections of foreign language class with other academic disciplines in the curriculum. Kirby recommended mandatory in-service training to correct that disconnect. The teachers believed they were "sufficiently implementing the standards in the classroom" (p. 158), but Kirby and the panel of three professors who served as "inter-rater consultants" (p. 160) all determined that the teachers were not. Kirby found that grammar-translation was used most of the time, but Kirby concluded that "observation contradicts the best practices which suggest a balanced approach employing equal use of varied teaching methods" (p. 158). Kirby failed to cite any empirical study to support that best-practice view.

Kirby (2012) was surprised to discover that the ACTFL did not endorse any one textbook or method as being the best for teaching to the standards. Kirby wrote, "If we knew what methods aligned with the standards, it could help move the adoption of ACTFL standards forward" (p. 147). Kirby determined that teachers did not include each of the five standards regularly in their instruction. Instead, the following percentages were observed in the classroom observations made: Communication 90%, cultures 45%, comparisons 20%, communities 10%, and connections 10%. The numbers did not add up to 100% because teachers sometimes addressed more than one standard in a class period.

Overall, Kirby (2012) found that his group cohort of five teachers was "50.3% consistent comparing what the teachers perceive they are doing and what they actually did. There was a disconnect across all analyzed areas" (p. 159). His conclusion was that his study supported a personal communication from the director of education at the ACTFL, that "there is both a lack of knowledge and an unwillingness at multiple levels to implement the mandated ACTFL five Cs" (p. 178). The five Cs referred to the standards of communication, cultures, connections, comparisons, and communities (ACTFL, 2012).

Kirby (2012) and his inter-rater consultants noticed that Don Quixote said his favorite teaching method was "TPRS, without question" (p. 111), but the classroom observations of his teaching indicated that he used TPRS only 37.5% of the time, Grammar-Translation 33.3%, the Natural Approach 16.7%, the Cognitive Approach 8.3%, the Audio-lingual Method 4.2% of class time, and TPR and the Silent Way not at all. Don Quixote was unaware that he was really mixing the methods. An interrater consultant noted that Quixote had an "almost hostile attitude toward every method but what he has learned about Krashen's ideas… He has completely bought in to Blaine Ray's version of TPRS" (p. 121). Another interrater consultant observed that Quixote said he based his teaching on TPRS, "although he does not seem to know much about it" (p. 122). On the other hand, perhaps he did and the professors may have misunderstood.

In Kirby's (2012) study, Don Quixote described his own style of teaching by saying, "My class is almost 100% communicative in that I'm speaking and the kids are speaking. I'm asking questions and they're answering my questions" (p. 113). He went on to stress how important it was for him to connect his lessons with the students' lives to engage their interests. Quixote added, "Storytelling is a way to take them out of the classroom and transport to another adventure" (p. 114). He mentioned using five target phrases repetitively per class and making them comprehensible. Quixote said that the TPRS method allowed him to use his personality. He added, "I'm kind of a ham so I can be emotional. I can act and it is fun for the kids. The more energy they give me, the more I give back to them" (p. 209). In 2003, Quixote observed someone telling a story, asking lots of questions about it, and "put it together with a classroom management program" (p. 210). Since then, he has continued to use his variation of TPRS because, as he said, "The kids have to answer in Spanish. It's effective" (p. 212). Quixote explained, "I use TPRS because it allows me to be me in the classroom. It allows me to connect with the kids" (p. 214). Quixote added, "Blaine Ray has written some stupid little stories and they're so nutty they remember them" (p. 218). Those descriptions did reflect the TPRS principles and he reported using the method at all levels, beginning through AP.

On a scale of 1-10, Quixote rated himself only at only a 'two' in how aware of the ACTFL standards he was, despite Kirby's observation that he in fact implemented the standards regularly in his teaching. Kirby also noticed that Quixote spoke more than the other teachers in the target language and he noticed that Quixote was fluent in Spanish. In his first observation, Kirby (2012) wrote, "This was an interesting teaching method; however, it requires a lot of teacher energy and the teacher needs to have a good command of the language" (p. 239) to make it work. In his four classroom visits, Kirby observed that Don Quixote did in fact teach to the standards, especially communication, connections, and cultures, but he fell short in comparisons and communities.

An area of Don Quixote's teaching that caused Kirby (2012) much concern was his unwillingness to use a textbook. Kirby reported, "He refuses to use a textbook, which I found professionally problematic. His mastery of TPRS is excellent, but his teaching could be well enhanced by including other teaching methods" (p. 119). Kirby (2012) claimed that "authoritative colleagues were employed to help reduce the possibility of researcher bias" (p. 40), yet he made that unsubstantiated remark without any reference to any research supporting the superiority of adopting an eclectic approach.

The word 'textbook' appeared in Kirby's (2012) dissertation 77 times, to include remarks made by his expert panel of authoritative colleagues whose role also included providing for inter-rater reliability. However, their remarks were similar to Kirby's. One interrater consultant said, "My belief is that students need to have a text in order to review grammar structure, verbs, and conjugations" (p. 120). No research study was cited to support that belief. However, there was at least one study reviewed for this dissertation which refuted that position by showing that students successfully acquired Spanish, making gains equivalent to first language grade-level expectations in writing fluency, through content-based instruction with no direct, explicit, grammar teaching at all (Cartford, Holter, Kittock, and Lichtman, 2015). A second inter-rater consultant in Kirby's (2012) study commented that Quixote's "disregard of any kind of textbook is worrisome" (p. 122). A third consultant remarked, "A standardized textbook which incorporates and promotes the five Cs should be adopted statewide" (p. 165). He suggested that districts reassign teachers for not "maintaining a basic sense of foreign language professionalism such as using a good textbook" (p. 166). Again, those remarks did not come accompanied by any findings from empirical research showing the superiority of a textbook approach. On the other hand, the interrater consultants may not have been consistent in their values for using a textbook approach since one negatively criticized Carlos Fuentes for focusing on grammar and being too textbook driven.

In short, Rapstine (2003) and Alley and Overfield (2008) were critical of the TPRS method, noting its positive and negative aspects, from their perspectives. Taulbee

(2008) did the same and tried out twenty lessons for integrating grammar and TPRS. Sievek (2009), like Rapstine (2003), observed that TPRS did not attempt to cover all five of the ACTFL (2000, 2012) standards, focusing more on the Communication standard, which Ray and Seely (2002) had admitted to earlier, believing that activities not leading to developing proficiency would "steal valuable class time" (Ray & Seely, 2012, p. xix). However, Ray and Seely (2012) did concede that it was "fine to include the other four [standards] within communication, but it is counterproductive to work on any of them in class time without… mainly focusing on the development of communicative proficiency" (p. xx). Kirby (2012) regarded the disregard for the standards by the TPRS teacher in his study as unprofessional and polarizing.

The notion of polarization was extended to teachers who otherwise might have considered using TPRS if not for some specific concerns in other areas. Lichtman (2014, 2015) discussed how concerns over TPRS' use of translations rather than employing a full immersion approach, limiting or even excluding an emphasis on direct grammar instruction, and not always including learning about cultures caused some teachers to steer away from using the method. Lichtman (2015) recommended teaching culture incidentally and purposefully through the context of using TPRS stories. Also, Lichtman (2012b) had found in her own research that both children and adults could learn language through both implicit and explicit instruction in classroom settings.

In the classroom, Oliver (2013) was required to include grammar instruction, but otherwise was permitted to use TPRS. To comply with her supervisor's wishes to follow prescribed curricular guidelines, Oliver (2013) had tried out a modified form of TPRS in her own teaching, but soon discovered that she was not satisfied with students' results when not using the TPRS method. Other modifications, adaptations, or variations to TPRS in practice may have affected or influenced in some ways how the method has been changing and evolving.

Changes and Evolution of the TPRS Method.

Gaab (2006) raised the question as to whether the changes and variations in TPRS happened due to evolution or creation. She discussed the collaborative interaction that was responsible for many changes. The seven editions of Ray and Seely's book on TPRS, *Fluency through TPR Storytelling*, provided one source for viewing the changes from 1997 to 2015 which were discussed above in the section on the development of the method.

Ray (2013) discussed and reviewed some of what he considered the main changes that have occurred in the TPRS method over time and mentioned that he expected that "we will continue to see TPRS evolve" (p. 42). Through research, the creativity of some of its practitioners, collaborative interaction, following student results, making data-driven decisions, trying out new strategies, discovering new effective techniques, and by teachers sharing their lived experiences using TPRS with each other, the method has continued to evolve.

Summary and Organization of the Study

Chapter II opened by briefly reorienting the reader to the introduction and background of the problem, followed by a discussion on the theoretical foundations and conceptual frameworks which situated the study overall. Then, there was a thorough review of the professional literature on the TPRS method of world language instruction. The early beginnings of TPRS were discussed, along with the early focus on student achievement data. The development of and changes in the method were traced over time, from Ray and Seely's (1997) seminal work up until the present day, along with the myriads of teacher skills which have been added over time to a methodology which has been continually evolving, never remaining stagnant. Empirical research was discussed which included comparing TPRS with other methods, examining studies with no control groups on TPRS alone, and descriptive TPRS studies.

Some of the topics discussed in those studies and in this literature review included teacher experiences using TPRS, researchers who mentioned obstacles and resistance to using the method that they encountered while conducting their studies, and studies which examined the method through a critical lens. By closely examining the advantages and disadvantages of TPRS and by comparing the principles and practices with the ACTFL guidelines and standards, areas for potential growth were identified in the literature. Reflecting on TPRS from the perspective of ACTFL, the professional association of world language educators, had potential for modifying or improving the method which has been changing and evolving since its beginnings. Some of those changes and developments that have occurred over time were made visible in the seven editions of Ray and Seely's (1997, 1998, 2002, 2004, 2008, 2012, and 2015) book on TPRS and in Ray's (2013) reflections on some of the major changes.

The literature review set up this study by situating it both within theoretical foundations and related research. Despite mentioning some experiences that teachers who used TPRS had in their studies (Black, 2012; Campbell, 2016; Davidheiser, 2002; Espinoza, 2015; Lichtman, 2014; Neubauer, 2015; Oliver, 2013; Welch, 2014; Wenck; Whaley, 2009), no other researchers interviewed as many TPRS teachers in depth about their common lived experiences as did this study. In addition, other research studies did not focus on why some teachers who were trained in TPRS decided not to use the method and what they considered obstacles to its use. Beyond the phenomenological portion of identifying TPRS teacher experiences, this study collected data from traditional teachers on their perceptions of what worked well, in their non-TPRS classrooms. That data enabled TPRS teachers to consider adding new effective teaching techniques and best practices to the method as it continues to evolve into the future.

Chapter I of this dissertation introduced the study and Chapter II reported the literature which situated this study. Despite the growing professional body of work on TPRS, a gap was identified from this literature review that the researcher designed a study to fill, as discussed in Chapter III. Chapter III explains the research methodology, design, and procedures for carrying out the study. Chapter IV presents the data analysis and results of the study. Chapter V summarizes the study, discusses implications, makes recommendations for further research, and draws conclusions.

CHAPTER III

METHODOLOGY

Introduction

This qualitative study using a quasi-phenomenological approach described the common lived classroom experiences of high school, grades 9-12, teachers who used the Teaching Proficiency through Reading and Storytelling (TPRS) method of world language instruction. The study explained why some teachers trained in TPRS abandoned using the method and what they perceived as obstacles to its use. The study also identified the techniques perceived as effective by traditional teachers for promoting student success in comprehending and producing the target language.

The TPRS method required no textbook or grammar syllabus and focused on providing students with comprehensible, repetitive, and interesting input of fluency structures within the context of a story. For this study, a traditional approach included a textbook, a grammar syllabus, and production-based communicative classroom learning activities. A purposeful sample included ten teachers who used TPRS in their classes, ten teachers trained in TPRS who discontinued its use, and ten teachers not trained in TPRS who used a traditional approach, who had no experience with the TPRS methodology.

Data were collected through face to face, in-person, open-ended, semi-structured interviews. A categorical model of TPRS teacher experience was beginning to emerge reflecting nine categories of experience, but it was unclear how they interacted. The results of the data analysis identified sixteen common lived experiences and twelve obstacles faced by teachers when using TPRS, plus four recommendations to consider incorporating into the changing and evolving method of world language instruction.

Statement of the Problem

A growing body of research documented the effectiveness of the TPRS method in a variety of classroom contexts (Beyer, 2008; Braunstein, 2006; Bustamante, 2009; Castro, 2010; Davidheiser, 2001, 2002; Dziedzic, 2012; Garczynski, 2003; Jennings, 2009; Kaufmann, 2005; Miller, 2011; Oliver, 2012, 2013; Roberts & Thomas, 2014, 2015; Spangler, 2009; Varguez, 2009; Watson, 2009; Wenck, 2010). Those studies, among other benefits, showed that students taught using the TPRS method did learn to speak and write in the target language. After taking training in a language they were unfamiliar with at a TPRS workshop, many teachers have learned from first-hand experience that the method could work, according to teacher testimonials in Ray & Seely (2012, 2015). Despite knowing that the method could be effective, many teachers newly trained in TPRS were either reluctant to use the method, or have abandoned its use in their classrooms; part of that reluctance was over the issue of grammar. Kaufmann (2005) argued that there was a place for explicit grammar instruction and discussed how some educators worried whether the TPRS method could be applied in a school district that required using an approved textbook. Despite the research that documented the effectiveness of the method, some TPRS teachers have encountered resistance to using TPRS from students, non-TPRS instructor colleagues, parents, and administrators (Black, 2012; Espinoza, 2015; Oliver, 2013; Neubauer, 2015; Taulbee, 2008; Whaley, 2009).

There has been little phenomenological research that identified, described, or interpreted the common lived experiences of teachers using the TPRS method. Therefore, those trained but reluctant users may have had little knowledge of how the possible challenges, obstacles, and resistance they experienced may have been overcome by other TPRS teachers. In addition to reluctant teachers, department heads, parents, students, administrators, and other school community stakeholders, the readers of this study could become better informed to make decisions about language teaching in their own schools once they know about the common lived experiences of TPRS teachers.

This chapter stated the problem and purpose of this study and the gap in the research that the study was designed to fill. This chapter also discussed the selection of study participants, the role of the researcher, data collection, and the data analysis procedures that were used to answer the following research questions for the study.

Research Questions

The following research questions guided this qualitative dissertation study.

1. What were high school teachers' common lived experiences using the Teaching Proficiency through Reading and Storytelling (TPRS) method to teach modern world languages?

2. What did high school teachers trained in TPRS, who decided not to use the TPRS method in their language classrooms, perceive as obstacles to its use?

3. What techniques did high school language teachers using a traditional approach perceive as effective for promoting student success in learning to comprehend and speak the language being taught?

Research Methodology

A qualitative methodology was more appropriate than a quantitative methodology to answer the type of questions asked in this study, in part due to the subjective nature of human experience. To directly discover people's perceptions of their experiences it was logical to ask those who had lived those experiences. Another way might have been to observe them, but interviews had the advantage of getting at a person's perceptions, thoughts, feelings, and beliefs about their experiences. Interviews offered an opportunity to ask what happened and they felt about those experiences. A quantitative study may have viewed reality as objective, but a qualitative methodology allowed for a subjective perspective of reality from a personal perspective of living through it (Merriam, 2009). The researcher knew very little about using TPRS beforehand, but throughout the course of the study, his perspective was affected by those learning experiences. However, it was not his experience that he wished to understand. The goal was to discover and to explore the 'common' experiences lived by several teachers using TPRS. Each teacher study participant's experience was expected to be different, and influenced by local context, but some commonalities were anticipated, shared by all, which helped to identify the essence of using TPRS, the central phenomenon under study. A search through books on research methodologies (Corbin & Straus, 2015; Merriam, 2009; Miles & Huberman, 2009; Moustakas, 1994; Richards, 2011; Richards & Morse, 2013; van Manen, 1990; Vogt, Gardner, Haeffele, 2012) and on how to conduct interviews (Brinkmann & Kvale, 2015) led to a quasi-phenomenological research methodology and design as the best fit for answering this study's primary research question and for addressing its purpose.

The purpose of this qualitative study using a quasi-phenomenological approach was to identify and describe the common lived experiences by language teachers using the TPRS method of world language instruction in classrooms and why some teachers decided not to use it. Understanding those common experiences supplied educational leaders with information to inform their decision making. A qualitative study, using a quasi-phenomenological approach, was appropriate because it provided the informational data necessary for answering the research questions on common lived experiences (Merriam, 2009; Richards, 2011; Richards & Morse, 2013). The nature of the qualitative study using quasi-phenomenological approach and its procedures served to elicit the recalled experiences of teachers who had experienced the phenomenon first-hand or could answer questions about their perceptions (Moustakas, 1994; van Manen, 1990). The primary focus was to elicit the perceptions about those experiences from study participants who had lived them (Hycner, 1985) to better understand the essence of using TPRS, the central phenomenon of the study. A secondary focus was identifying the obstacles to using TPRS. A third focus was on obtaining information on what traditional teachers perceived to be effective techniques which could potentially improve the method. The qualitative design allowed for obtaining the data needed for these foci.

Research Design

This qualitative study using a quasi-phenomenological approach had thirty study participants who were all high school world language teachers. A qualitative design was used because the researcher decided that interview data would provide the information needed to answer the research questions. Group A teachers were asked questions to elicit their perceptions of the experiences they had using the TPRS method of world language instruction. They were interviewed to discover the common lived experiences of TPRS teachers. Group B teachers were trained in TPRS and tried out the method, but for their own reasons decided to reject it as their primary method of teaching. Group B teachers were interviewed to discover what they perceived the obstacles to using TPRS were. Group C teachers had no training or experience using TPRS. Group C study participants provided information on which teaching techniques they perceived as effective for promoting comprehension and production of the language being studied. That information was then considered when the researcher analyzed the data to decide which teaching techniques, activities, strategies, applications, or approaches to recommend for incorporation into the always changing and evolving TPRS method.

The question of how many study participants were needed arose early in the design decision phase. The number ten was arrived at after reviewing the professional literature to see how many study participants had been used in phenomenological studies. The suggested ranges varied by different authors, from three or four to 10-15 (Creswell, 2013), three to ten (Dukes, 1984), five to 25 (Polkinghorne, 1989), and ten (Riemen, 1986). In identifying how many interviews were enough, it would logically be at the point where there was little or no new information being obtained from additional interviewees. For Miles (2014), that saturation point was reached at ten participants. It was determined that three groups of ten, or 30 total participants, were adequate for this study because the data obtained were sufficient to answer the research questions.

Population and Sample Selection / Selection of Participants.

Study Participant Demographics.

There were three groups of ten teachers, with 30 study participants total in the study of 18 women and 12 men. The average age was 39, ranging from 25 to 58 years old. Their experience teaching ranged from three to 36, with an average of 14 years of total teaching experience. Group A was composed of TPRS teachers whose experience using the TPRS method ranged from two to 19 years, for an average of eight years of TPRS teaching experience. There were five women and five men in Group A. There were six women and four men in Group B and seven women and three men in Group C.

The 30 study participants taught five different languages, including Spanish, French, German, Mandarin Chinese, and English. Twenty-three taught in public and seven in private high schools. They taught in 12 states, including Utah, Pennsylvania, Delaware, New Jersey, Illinois, Indiana, Missouri, Idaho, Wyoming, Colorado, California, and Arizona. Additional demographic data was not collected.

Participant Selection Criteria.

A purposeful, criterion-referenced, sampling was used. All study participants had taught a language at the high school level for at least one year and they all had three or more years of total teaching experience. There were three groups of 10 teachers each, for a total of 30 total participants in the study. In the first two groups, all teachers had attended at least one TPRS training workshop or conference, to ensure the fidelity of method delivery, and they had tried teaching using the method at least once.

Group A consisted of ten teacher participants who considered themselves to be primarily TPRS teachers and they were selected for participation in the study to answer research question one. Group B teachers did not consider themselves to be primarily TPRS teachers. They had received TPRS training and tried out the method, but later decided either to limit or reject its use entirely in their classrooms. Group B teachers were selected to answer the second research question. Group C teachers had no training or experience using the method as part of the purposeful criteria for their selection. They were included in the study to address the third research question. With no experience or training in TPRS, they provided an outsider's view of what they perceived to be effective teaching techniques. The researcher used their data to compare with TPRS principles to determine which techniques to consider recommending for incorporation into the evolving method.

Signed consent was obtained from three local superintendents to recruit study participants from their school districts, if needed. The Group A study participants and some Group B participants were interviewed at a national TPRS teacher's conference. After telling a few people about the study, the word spread and there was enough interest that volunteers approached the researcher and signed consent forms to be interviewed for the study. The remaining study participants were identified after the conference through personal contacts, snowballing, referral, or by word of mouth and were accepted provided they met the study selection criteria. Vogt et al. (2012) considered snowballing an acceptable way of identifying participants provided they fit the study's selection criteria. No one who met the selection criteria was turned down who wished to participate.

The study participants were interviewed at places of agreed-upon convenience where it was quiet enough for the audio recorder to pick up the sound, which included conference and public library rooms, or the homes of those interviewed if they preferred. The first dozen interviews were practice interviews, and were not included in the data analysis, so that the researcher could develop his interview skills. Practice was needed to increase reliability because the interviewer in a qualitative quasi-phenomenological study was considered the primary data collection instrument. Merriam (2009) pointed out that "the human instrument can become more reliable through training and practice" (p. 222).

Instrumentation.

See appendices A, B, and C for the semi-structured interview protocol questions that were asked to groups A, B, and C respectively for this study. The questions were developed after reading the books on qualitative research cited in this paper and were approved by the researcher's former chairperson who had prior experience conducting interviews for research purposes. The semi-structured interview questions were asked face-to-face and in-person, were audio-recorded, and later transcribed verbatim for a subsequent quasi-phenomenological analysis of interview data adapted from Hycner's (1985) guidelines. To increase the accuracy, credibility, trustworthiness, and confidence of the data and analysis, four verification strategies were used in this study. The strategies included first ensuring the interview was conducted effectively to obtain rich information from the participant and then describing that data thoroughly, staying true to the participant's own words. The researcher tried to capture each teacher participant's complete perceptions and lived experiences with using TPRS. In addition to first providing a thorough description, the second strategy was member checking. After the transcription was done, it was sent to the person who was interviewed to have it checked for accuracy. The third and fourth strategies included peer review of the data analyses for all three groups, and bracketing which were both discussed below in more detail under validity and reliability. The peer reviewers included two educators with earned doctorates and one doctoral candidate.

The interviewer was the primary data collection instrument, as mentioned above. The researcher was also the interviewer. Among the skills needed were how to elicit information without guiding the interview to the point of leading the participants. The interviewer needed to be neutral on all issues, to the extent possible, and accepting of whatever the teacher participant shared, not being judgmental in any way. As discussed above, Hycner (1985) considered bracketing, or setting aside one's own experiences with the phenomenon, an essential strategy for addressing concerns of validity and reliability.

Validity and Reliability.

Validity. Validity and reliability have been terms more often associated with quantitative rather than qualitative research. The findings for studies were valid only if the data were credible and trustworthy. In qualitative research and for this study, rather than discuss issues of validity, the relevant terms were considered the integrity of the data, authenticity, credibility, confirmability, dependability, and transferability. While the term validity has not always been used by qualitative researchers, Hycner (1985) did use it when discussing his phenomenological research, but for this study the researcher preferred to use trustworthiness and credibility rather than internal validity and the term transferability rather than external validity, following Merriam (2009).

In this study, the validation strategy of member checking or "respondent validation" (Merriam, 2009, p. 217) was used to verify or validate the transcription of the interview with each person interviewed to ensure that the information was true and correct, what the teacher participant in the study intended to say, and reflected the perceptions of the experiences lived. Hycner (1985) added that when follow-up interviews were done, it was an additional "validity check" (p. 291). When the researcher in this study was unclear or uncertain about any statement that appeared in a transcription, he contacted the study participant to ask for clarification. In analyzing and reporting the data, the researcher attempted, in Hycner's (1985) words, to stay "as true as possible to the phenomenon" (p. 300) by staying "quite true to the literal statements and meanings given by the participant" (p. 301) to increase the credibility of the data.

Reliability. Merriam (2009) pointed out some differences in the assumptions behind the issue of reliability. To her, reliability in quantitative research generally reflected whether the study could be replicated and whether repeated observations yielded the same results. However, in qualitative research in the social sciences, "researchers seek to describe and explain the world as those in the world experience it" (p. 220). Merriam (2009) explained that human behavior was not always consistent and "never static, nor is what many experienced necessarily more reliable than what one person experiences" (p. 221). Given that perspective, an issue of reliability was whether the results were consistent with the data.

The researcher in this study was careful and aware of the importance not interpreting or drawing conclusions that were not supported by the data. To address the issue of credibility and to increase the trustworthiness, dependability, and transferability of the data analysis, a panel of three peer reviewers were used for peer examination of the researcher's analysis to check for consistency. Merriam (2009) had explained that the examination or review could "be conducted by a colleague either familiar with the research or one new to the topic" (p. 220).

There were three colleagues, individuals that the researcher had attended doctoral classes with, who agreed to participate in the peer review process. Two of those reviewers held earned doctorates and one was a doctoral candidate at the dissertation phase. They were asked to code ten transcripts each to highlight what Hycner (1985) called "units of relevant meaning" (p. 284). This was a critical point in the data analysis because those statements where relevant to the research questions. Over 95% intercoder agreement, between the researcher and each of the three peer reviewers, was found when coded separately. The second phase was to discuss any areas of disagreement. Nearly one hundred percent agreement was reached through discussion. The few initial disagreements involved whether the statement from the transcript was a unit of 'relevant' meaning or a unit of 'general meaning' which indicated something important but not relevant to the research question. The credibility of the data analysis was confirmed through the consistency of the peer review.

In this study, the issues of trustworthiness and credibility were addressed through four strategies which included a thorough description of the data, member checking, peer review, and critical self-reflection. The latter was accomplished through, in Hycner's (1985) words, "suspending (bracketing) as much as possible the researcher's meanings and interpretations and entering into the world of the unique individual who was interviewed" (p. 281). A colleague interviewed the researcher twice and they then discussed the importance of bracketing. The two interviews and his feedback were all three audio-taped and the researcher listened to them on repeated occasions to remind himself just how important bracketing was in a phenomenology, which focused on the study participants' experiences. The researcher was intentional about ensuring that the study participants' experiences were captured in the data and not his own. Merriam (2009) had listed eight strategies for "promoting validity and reliability" (p. 229) which she recommended for both quantitative and qualitative studies. The four strategies used in this study appeared on her list.

Data Collection and Management.

The step-by-step procedures followed in conducting this study were adapted from Hycner's (1985) guidelines for collecting and analyzing interview data using his phenomenological approach. Study participants were selected using the purposeful, criterion-referenced, sampling described for the three groups above and in the Selection of Participants section below. Interview questions (see Appendices A, B, C) were prepared to elicit the data required to address each of the research questions. The researcher took steps to set aside his own biases regarding the central phenomenon, as discussed below, both during the data collection and data analysis phases. The interviews were conducted, verbatim transcriptions were prepared by the researcher, and the data were organized and analyzed, as described below.

Permission to conduct the study was obtained from the Neumann University Institutional Review Board (IRB). The data were collected through interviews. Three groups of ten study participants each were interviewed. Groups A and B both had training and experience using TPRS, which provided an emic or insider's perspective on TPRS as they provided data on the experiences they had and obstacles encountered. Group C was selected for its etic perspective and that data were used to address the third research question on which techniques teachers with no experience with TPRS perceived as effective which may not have been incorporated into the method yet. The semi-structured interview questions appeared in the appendices (see Appendix A, B, C).

Electronic documents have been stored on the researcher's password-protected home computer. The transcriptions, audio-tapes, and other materials have been stored in a locked closet at an undisclosed location when not being used and will be destroyed by shredding papers, deleting electronic documents and erasing tapes three years after the study has been completed. The data gathered through the interviews with each participant were transcribed verbatim by the researcher and written transcriptions prepared for the systematic data analysis adapted from Hycner (1985). The accuracy, trustworthiness, dependability, and credibility were increased by member checking of interview transcripts (Hycner, 1985; Johnson & Christensen, 2012; Moustakas, 1994).

Data Analysis Procedure.

The data were analyzed to answer the following three research questions.

1. What were high school teachers' common lived experiences using the Teaching Proficiency through Reading and Storytelling (TPRS) method to teach modern world languages?

2. What did high school teachers trained in TPRS, who decided not to use the TPRS method in their language classrooms, perceive as obstacles to its use?

3. What techniques did high school language teachers using a traditional approach perceive as effective for promoting student success in learning to comprehend and speak the language being taught?

Procedures.

Adapting Hycner's (1985) approach, the analysis of the interview data began with listening to the taped interviews and reading the transcriptions repeatedly to "get a sense of the whole interview" (p. 281) before systematically reducing that data to manageable units. The researcher attempted to bracket out, or set aside, his own experiences with the central phenomenon of using the TPRS method and get a sense of the whole experience the teacher participant had using TPRS, unbiased by his own interpretation. The researcher, following Hycner's (1985) guidance, attempted to "bracket interpretations and biases while trying to stay as true to the interviewee's meaning as much as possible" (p. 281). This postponing of making any premature interpretations of the data may have differed from other qualitative approaches, but it was followed to ensure or increase the likelihood that the data collected were credible (internal validity), transferable (external validity), and trustworthy and dependable (reliable). Issues of validity and reliability were further discussed below.

To identify and describe the teachers' common lived experiences, there were steps taken to reduce the data down to manageable units for answering the research questions, but without losing sight of each individual study participant's entire experience of using TPRS. To avoid losing the sense of the whole interview and the study participant's entire reported experience of the central phenomenon, Hycner's (1985) "explicitation" (p. 300) process was followed, going from the whole, to the part, and back to the whole interview again. To explicate (or explicitate) the data, the researcher listened to the entire interview after each "phenomenological reduction" (p. 280) of the data set to maintain a sense of the whole, yet stay "true to the literal statements and meanings given by the participant" (p. 301). The data were reduced to two units of meaning, both general and relevant.

The researcher transcribed the interviews and then identified the 'general' units of meaning, or the many different ideas the study participant said. Hycner (1985) defined a unit of 'general' meaning as the words, phrases, or sentences that expressed a "unique and coherent meaning (irrespective of the research question) clearly differentiated from that which precedes and follows" (p. 282). The researcher eliminated the redundancies by deleting the units repeated in the transcription. Those general units of meaning were analyzed to discover which ones were relevant to the research questions. Identifying "units of relevant meaning" (p. 284) further reduced the total data set, making the amount of data more manageable for the researcher.

After eliminating the redundancies of repeated units, clusters of meaning that were relevant to the research questions were highlighted and then grouped together into themes. The researcher wrote a summary of each study participant's experience who used or tried out the TPRS method. Those summaries were compared and composite summaries were written for Group A and for Group B data. Comparisons were made and sixteen common lived experiences, and twelve obstacles to using TPRS were identified, along with nine themes. Those themes were not developed into an experiential model because the data did not reveal how the thematic elements interacted with each other.

Group A interviews were conducted to answer the first research question and sixteen common lived experiences were identified and described. Group B interviews were conducted to answer the second research, and twelve obstacles to using TPRS were identified and discussed. Group C teachers were interviewed to answer the third research question, and four recommendations were made for adding techniques to the method.

Ethical Considerations

No potential threats or harm to human subjects were anticipated or experienced in the conduct of this study. All study participants were adults with high school teaching experience. Their personal data were not reported to protect their anonymity and because they were not needed to answer the specific research questions for this dissertation study.

The researcher explained to the study participants that the nature of the study was to ask them questions about their teaching experiences and techniques they perceived were effective. The researcher assured the participants that their identities would be protected and their input kept confidential, private, and anonymous. In the data, each participant was given a designation such as "B1" which indicated a person from group B.

There were three groups of ten teacher participants in each group. The study participants were told that their participation was voluntary and that they could drop out of the study at any time with no negative consequences of any kind. Each participant was given an opportunity to ask questions and each one signed a consent form of which they were given a copy. The Institutional Review Board of Neumann University approved the project. No humans or animals were harmed from their participation in this study.

Limitations and Delimitations

Limitations. The study findings were not generalizable beyond the purposeful sample of study participants. The common and differing experiences of teachers varied, depending upon differences in local school contexts. The data obtained from the experienced teachers who participated in this study may not have been representative of all TPRS teachers or those who had less experience or no experience with the method. Some variability in teacher experiences was expected. Experiences with the central phenomenon were not studied as they were being lived, but rather through recollections, which was an acceptable practice in phenomenological studies (Hycner, 1985; Merriam, 2009). In phenomenological studies, the data were generally accepted as trustworthy and credible, provided that data validation strategies were used as they were in this study.

Delimitations. The study design involved collecting data through in-person, open-ended, semi-structured interviews. While four validation strategies were used, the triangulation of multiple data sources was not, which some reviewers may have regarded as a delimitation of this study. The researcher also served as the interviewer for this study, but he was not a professional interviewer, which delimited the study. The interviewer was the primary data collection instrument. Not using other types of data or data collection instruments allowed only for limited quantitative measures.

Assumptions. This qualitative study using a quasi-phenomenological approach assumed that the recalled experiences of selected participants produced trustworthy and dependable information. This study also assumed that participants told the truth, with integrity, and that they gave authentic and accurate answers to questions. It was further assumed that the common lived experiences could reveal useful information and trustworthy data from which credible and transferable findings could be drawn. An underlying assumption was that the primary data collection method, conducting personal interviews, followed by a quasi-phenomenological analysis of interview data (adapted from Hycner, 1985) enabled the researcher to answer the research questions accurately, confidently, with credibility, and that the findings derived from the data analysis were credible, dependable, trustworthy, and transferable (Merriam, 2009; Vogt, et al., 2012).

Summary and Organization of the Study

The first chapter of this dissertation introduced the study. The second chapter provided a review of related professional literature and research studies that situated and informed the study. A gap in the literature was identified; this study was designed to fill that gap. The third chapter described the research design and procedures for carrying out the study. Next, the fourth chapter reports the results of the data analysis and the study. After the fourth chapter, the summary, conclusions, and recommendations follow in the fifth and final chapter of this dissertation.

CHAPTER IV

DATA ANALYSIS AND RESULTS

The purpose of this qualitative study using a quasi-phenomenological approach was to describe the common classroom experiences lived by TPRS teachers, to identify the obstacles to the method's use, and to discover techniques for improving the method. That approach helped the researcher uncover the essence of teachers' experiences using TPRS to teach world languages and provided data for interpreting those experiences. Exploring those common lived experiences provided insight into the phenomenon of using TPRS. The study focused on discovering why some teachers used TPRS, why others did not, and made recommendations for possible additions to the method.

Interview data were collected from a purposeful sample of thirty teachers through in-person, open-ended, semi-structured interviews. There were ten teachers each selected for three groups who met specific criteria for participation in the study. Group A teachers were those who used TPRS as their primary teaching method (and were attending a weeklong national TPRS conference). Group A teachers were interviewed to identify the common lived 'experiences' of TPRS teachers who used TPRS. Group B instructors had been trained in TPRS, but decided not to use the method predominantly in their teaching. Group B study participants were identified by the researcher by attending workshops, meeting teachers, referrals, and following up by email and phone calls to see who met the criteria and were willing to participate in the study. Group B instructors were interviewed to identify what they perceived as obstacles to using TPRS.

The interview data gathered from Group A and Group B formed the corpus of the phenomenological portion of the study because those two groups had lived experiences with using the TPRS method. They had been trained in the method and either used the method in their teaching or at least tried it out in their classrooms. However, a phenomenological analysis of Group C data was not possible because Group C teachers, by the design of the study, had no experience using the TPRS method at all. For that reason, this was not a pure phenomenological study since one group of participants had not experience using the method. For that reason, this was a qualitative study using a quasi-phenomenological approach.

Group C participants, identified through individual referrals (snowballing), had no training or experience at all with the TPRS method. Therefore, their input could not be considered when making comparisons among and between TPRS users. The findings of Group C data appeared after comparisons were made between Groups A and B in this chapter. Group C participants were included in the study only to identify what they perceived as effective techniques as Group C provided a point of view entirely outside of TPRS experience. Group C input could only be used to address research question 3 since those study participants had no training and no experience using TPRS. Group C study participants were determined to be the best suited to answer research question 3. The teaching 'techniques' that these outsiders from Group C (teachers unfamiliar with TPRS) perceived as effective were examined only as possible recommendations to consider incorporating into the TPRS method. For this study, the word 'techniques' was defined in a broad sense to identify several possible ways to improve the method.

The data analysis uncovered sixteen common lived experiences (out of 31 units of relevant meaning) from Group A interviews to answer the first research question. Twelve obstacles to using the TPRS method were identified from the interview data from

Group B. In addition, four categories of recommendations to consider adding to the TPRS method emerged from Group C informant data.

In the following data reporting sections, in order to protect their confidentiality, the ten Group A teacher participants (TPRS users) were identified as A1, A2, A3, A4, A5, A6, A7, A8, A9, and A10. Similarly, the ten Group B teachers (TPRS rejecters) were identified as B1, B2, B3, B4, B5, B6, B7, B8, B9, and B10. The same naming pattern was applied for Group C participants (interviewees untrained in TPRS) who had no experience using the TPRS method as C1, C2, C3, C4, C5, C6, C7, C8, C9, and C10.

Frequency counts for the experiences discussed below were qualified as follows: 10 = all, 9 = nearly all, 7-8 = many, 6 = over half, 5 = half, 3-4 = some, and 1-2 = few. For example, "common to all" meant that all ten Group A TPRS teachers had that same experience. Experiences that were common to all ten teachers who were interviewed for this study from Group A were considered common lived experiences of TPRS teachers.

Group A Interview Results

Group A participants addressed the first research question of this study: What were high school teachers' common lived experiences using the TPRS method to teach modern world languages? Sixteen experiences were common to all ten of these TPRS teachers, as follows. Table 4.A.1. below listed the first eight of those sixteen.

Table 4.A.1. Common Lived TPRS Teacher Experiences, part 1.

All 10	Were unsatisfied with student results before TPRS.	
10	Attended a TPRS workshop.	
10	Attended follow-up training after first workshop.	9 ongoing training.
10	Attended a one-week national TPRS conference.	

10	Used gestures in their teaching.	
10	Reported improving upon their beginning skills.	9 had early difficulty.
10	Discussed feeling confident or in the zone with TPRS.	
10	Collected anecdotal data, student success with TPRS.	9 increased retention.

Experiences 'Common to All' 10 Group A Participants (TPRS users).

1. All ten were unsatisfied with student results before TPRS.

What were the common lived experiences of TPRS teachers? Sixteen common lived experiences, from 31 categories, emerged from the interviews of all ten (Group A) teachers interviewed who used TPRS as their primary method in their high school world language classrooms. Group A teachers considered themselves to be primarily TPRS teachers. All ten were unsatisfied with the previous results attained by students who were taught through other methodologies. All ten teachers mentioned anecdotal data that supported their perceptions that TPRS was effective.

For example, one teacher (who mixed the methods) concluded through direct observation and in-class writing assessment evidence that her students "did not improve after book work [and] TPRS is better for the students" (A4). She noticed that when she departed from the exclusive use of the TPRS method and taught grammar explicitly, rather than through an implicit approach (pop-up grammar) consistent with TPRS principles, that her students' number counts on freewrites, timed writings, and fluency writings decreased. However, when A4 incidentally covered grammar in context, or when she did not teach grammar at all, student number counts rose on 5-10 minute timed writings, a measure of writing fluency.

Another teacher who had been disappointed not only with her students' performance before she found TPRS, but also with her own language learning experiences in secondary school said, "I wish TPRS had been around so that I could've learned this way in school" (A8). "TPRS is a vehicle for language acquisition. It works for every subcategory of students" (A10). A related remark typical of Group A participants on student performance with TPRS was, "There is nothing that gets you better results with students [than using TPRS]. When the parents, teachers, and community all recognize it, then you can't deny the results" (A9).

2. *All ten attended at least one TPRS workshop.*

3. *All ten attended some follow-up training after their first workshop.*

4. *All ten attended at least one weeklong national TPRS conference.*

Each Group A teacher interviewed engaged in both beginning skills training and in continued professional development. They all attended at least one (1-3 day) TPRS workshop, at least one weeklong national TPRS conference, and some type of follow-up support training either online or through professional learning communities (PLCs).

5. *All ten reported using gestures in their teaching.*

6. *All ten reported improving upon their beginning skills.*

7. *All ten discussed feeling confident or in the zone with TPRS.*

8. *All ten collected anecdotal data of student success with TPRS.*

A skill used by all Group A participants was the use of gestures in their teaching. All ten reported improving their TPRS skills to the point of feeling in the zone and confident, and nearly all (9 of 10) have continued with ongoing training. A10 expressed, "You never know everything. I'm still learning. I want to know everything I can."

Above, Table 4.A.1, part 1, listed eight common lived experiences. The following table listed eight more experiences common to all, as described below.

Table 4.A.2. Common Lived TPRS Teacher Experiences, part 2.

All 10	9.	Knew about and discussed language acquisition theory.
10	10.	Perceived providing "comprehensible input" as important.
10	11.	Discussed Brain Research as supporting TPRS.
10	12.	Talked about Teaching for Mastery as part of TPRS.
10	13.	Reported experiencing support and success from students.
10	14.	Reported experiencing support from parents.
10	15.	Reported experiencing support from administrators.
10	16.	Encountered obstacles or resistance when using TPRS.

Paradigm Shift, Input, Acquisition, Brain Research, and Teaching for Mastery.

All ten TPRS teachers experienced a philosophical paradigm shift and discussed the underlying language acquisition theory, brain research, mastery learning, and the notion that providing students with comprehensible input all informed the principles and practices of TPRS. All ten teachers employed multi-sensory input which included using gestures and movement to help establish meaning, teach for retention and promote long-term memory. Taken together, this paradigm or "philosophy shift" (A3), from learning to acquisition, contrasted with the "Skill-Building Hypothesis" (Krashen, 2015, p. 168). Krashen explained that the Skill-Building Hypothesis always informed traditional second language teaching and assumed that the conscious learning of grammar rules with a focus on output and production practice was necessary for language learning to occur.

However, TPRS rejected the "Skill-Building Hypothesis in favor of the "Comprehension Hypothesis" (Krashen, 2015, p. 168), which assumed that language was acquired subconsciously by understanding meaningful messages in the language through input made comprehensible and compelling. Commenting on this paradigm shift, A5 explained that in his experience, "There are people who don't understand TPRS or who have a different philosophical base and sometimes there have been interactions with some of them that, on a professional level, might be seen as problems." Stressing those differences, another teacher reflected on and described TPRS as being more of an 'attitude' or 'mindset' about education or a philosophy "centered on students and respect and love for the students, honoring them, their time, how they learn, and everything else grows out of that" (A7). Group A participants were not saying that other teachers or approaches did not positively regard students, but they did describe using TPRS as requiring a fundamental theoretical paradigm shift, philosophical orientation, and belief system that informed their decision making.

Support from Parents and Administrators.

All ten TPRS teachers received support from parents and administrators when using the method. A few examples followed. "My administrators, they always support me" (A8). "I was recommended the method by a principal [who] used to be a language teacher. Now, I am currently very, very supported by administrators" (A1). "I am very fortunate to be in a school where my entire department has been trained in TPRS and my administrators have attended conferences as well" (A2).

Teacher Success and Student Success with TPRS.

All ten participants discussed experiencing success as a teacher when using TPRS. For example, A7 started an Advanced Placement (AP) program in his school which began with ten students who all scored well on the exam the first year and grew to

35 students (with 90% scoring 3 or higher on the AP Spanish Exam) in three years. In those same three years, A7's school went from four to 50 students in level 3. A8 said, "I increased my enrollment by 50% [and my] failure rate went way down" in French.

Nearly all (9 out of 10) of the TPRS teachers in Group A improved their student retention rates and they perceived that more students succeeded after they implemented TPRS into their own language classrooms. Since using TPRS, A5 reported seeing in his students "a much better facility in the language. They are able to use the language in a far better way." With TPRS, some of A5's German students placed into upper-level university language classes by testing or placed out of a language requirement entirely after receiving TPRS instruction in high school.

Obstacles, Resistance, Persistence, and Student Success Data.

All TPRS teachers (in Group A) interviewed encountered obstacles, problems, issues, challenges, or resistance from people, when using TPRS, yet they persisted until each one experienced success in class using the method. For example, A8 declared, "Other foreign language teachers is [sic] the number one obstacle." A10 pointed out her need to persist when she said, "I had to convince people and there were roadblocks. I just kept working at it. I knew I had to stick to it because I could see that the kids were learning a lot more."

All ten Group A participants collected some anecdotal evidence of student progress and some (3 out of 10) TPRS teachers used standardized test scores to provide empirical evidence in support of their data-driven decisions to use the method. "Data can silence the voices of opposition and resistance. It basically shows that we can have kids as good as or better than kids who are learning with the traditional approach" (A1). "I've tracked data on common assessments that we used across our department. That empirical evidence has been powerful and it also protects me from being different" (A9).

Experiences Common to "Nearly All" Group A Participants (TPRS users).

Beginning with TPRS. Early Difficulties.

Nearly all (9 out of 10) TPRS teachers interviewed experienced initial difficulty learning the skills and strategies of the method and they received ongoing additional training to improve their instructional skills, which all ten Group A participants were able to do. Among those skills, was using gestures. As one TPRS teacher explained, "A lot of teachers abandon the method because it's so difficult at the beginning. It has to be a long-term goal for the teacher, [but] after five years, it feels like second nature" (A1). Another teacher said, "In my first year of teaching with TPRS, it was really hard to do, [but] after three years a lot of things that were difficult are not" (A6).

Student Engagement.

Part of the method's effectiveness depended upon the instructor's perceived ability to engage students. For example, A10 said that one way to engage students was to "talk about them" and topics they find interesting. A5 said, "I talk about my students' interests and develop relationships." A8 also encouraged relationship building through French and she said, "Students say mine is the only class where they know everyone's name." A2 discussed personalizing the lessons and make them more meaningful in order to increase student engagement. She said, "We asked students to tell their stories about their childhoods and I was blown away by what they were able to come up with." A7 stated that in his experience, "With TPRS, they [students] have to be more engaged."

Student Success, Retention, and Increased Enrollment.

Nearly all (9 out of 10) TPRS teachers reported having increased their student retention rates, with their students moving up to higher level classes. "I have the very pleasant experience of having students for four years; I see gains" (A5). A7 saw retention increases in his school's Spanish program, to include boys and special needs students in the higher-level classes. A7 explained, "I have ADD [attention deficit disorder] boys who do okay in my class because we don't sit that long. We get them up and moving." Other teachers also noticed a more diverse group of students in the upper levels than before using TPRS. One teacher said, "What I thought was really interesting is I didn't have necessarily just the people who excelled in other classes continuing on with the language; [but] an interesting mix of abilities" (A3). To describe this situation, A6 explained, "One of the things we call TPRS is, it's immersion with a difference and no child left behind… [because] you don't let any kid just get lost."

According to A4 and A10, even at-risk minority children from low-income families who previously failed foreign language classes have done well with a TPRS approach. Per A9, "Everybody and anybody can learn a language." Other TPRS teachers perceived that special education students experienced success from TPRS and in A10's large urban public school district they had empirical test data to support that contention, but their study has not yet been published.

Experiences Common to "Many" (7-8 out of 10) Group A Participants.

Many TPRS teachers who were interviewed for this study experienced resistance from some students and from other foreign language teacher colleagues, but they also received their support. For example, A10 mentioned both students and colleagues:

Kids are overwhelmingly positive, but there are a few that still want to know the [grammar] rules, the four percent. The biggest obstacle that I face is people who have been out there for many years teaching and have resistance to change. Who embraces [TPRS] are the younger teachers, but the older ones who try it are probably the most heartwarming stories (A10).

A9 emphasized his difficulties with colleagues who misunderstood the paradigm shift:

My biggest obstacle has been my closest work friends, colleagues who have turned their backs on me. The biggest obstacle was to go from misunderstanding, on their part, to understanding, because to me you can't just tell someone about TPRS, they have to experience it (A9).

A4 decided to use TPRS more despite the resistance from colleagues. She said, "I will be doing more TPRS next year, even if it causes ripples in the department [because] the more instruction I do in TPRS, the better their [student] performance." A4 did increase her use of TPRS in class the following year, but later retired to open her own language school where she did not face resistant colleagues.

Sustaining TPRS, Collaborative Colleagues, and the TPRS Community.

Many (7-8 out of 10) TPRS teachers had both collaborative colleagues and successful students. "What this TPRS community is good at is sharing ideas" (A9). Another teacher added that the TPRS community is always "searching for different ways to do it better. We're all in this thing together and we're all helping each other" (A7). There were examples in the interview data of mentorship, collaboration, success, and efforts to sustain TPRS use. For example, A2 reflected upon her experiences:

My first year teaching I had a mentor who had been using TPRS for five years who helped me. I have found that, with TPRS, students are able to score more consistently and consistently better. My students are more successful [than before TPRS]. They acquire more when they're having fun, so it doesn't feel like they're learning. The learning takes place naturally. I have not had resistance. We're a very fortunate school system to have the support that we do (A2).

As another TPRS teacher explained, "Our whole department has committed to using TPRS. Administrators have been supportive. Having other people to talk to and coming to these conferences is really the key. You can't just learn it and then go do it. You need to continue to be connected" (A6).

Reluctant to Change.

Many (7 out of 10) TPRS teachers were reluctant to use the method initially or were (self) resistant, until they decided to accept (or buy into) the paradigm shift from production-based to comprehension-based instruction, from explicit to implicit grammar acquisition, and from the learning to acquisition model which all informed pedagogic choices in TPRS classrooms. As A10 explained the TPRS view on grammar:

> Grammar is a meaty part of language, but teaching the rules about grammar is not how we acquire. Grammar is acquired through context. Acquisition happens in the brain subconsciously. I quit talking about grammar. You learn to speak through listening and you learn to write through reading (A10).

For some teachers, making this paradigm shift was difficult. For example, A5 was not impressed when he first heard about the method and he originally said that it "did not seem to make sense or be something that would work." For him, his adoption of TPRS was a "rather gradual process" (A5). "What we seek to do is optimize immersion. The comprehensible input theory drives our instruction" (A9). As A10 explained the TPRS paradigm goals for memory, vocabulary and verb tense development, acquiring natural language, and the need for repetition:

> We are working on long-term memory, not short term. That's why we limit and shelter vocabulary, but we never shelter grammar. It has to include present, past, and future time, which is natural language. You have to have a lot of repetition for acquisition [to occur] in context (A10).

Classroom Management.

Many (7 out of 10) TPRS teachers reported that their classroom management improved when using the TPRS method, whereas some (3 out of 10) found classroom management more difficult. "I had much less [trouble] because the kids weren't bored" (A4). As A7 explained why classroom management can be challenging with TPRS:

> With TPRS, they have to be more engaged. Because TPRS is more free form, more open, students get a sense of more permission to talk, act, emote, and all hell breaks loose. Now my discipline has to be based more on human interaction, relationship building, awareness of where my students are, reading their body language, of proximity, body positioning, and arrangement of the classroom. I have to have more tricks in my bag to keep discipline now. Now, in every single presentation that I do, I have an element of classroom management (A7).

Experiences Common to "Over Half" (6 out of 10) Group A Participants.

Over half of those TPRS teachers interviewed experienced resistance from parents. For example, A10 pointed out her initial problems with parents:

The obstacles at first were parents. They didn't understand. They felt as if we were just playing games, having fun, and the kids were loving it, but not learning. Mind you, these are parents who suffered through their own experiences in foreign language classrooms, who didn't learn how to speak, but who felt that learning grammar was important. I had to learn how to speak to them (A10).

While A10 discussed her experiences of speaking to parents to directly address concerns, another approach was to earn acceptance for TPRS through student achievement results gradually over time. A7 explained, "I've tried to convince people slowly over the years or by results."

Experiences Common to "Half" (5 out of 10) Group A Participants.

Administrators.

Half of those interviewed experienced some resistance from administrators. For example, A10 pointed out her experience with different administrators:

The administrators that supported TPRS would walk into the classroom and see engagement. For them, that was powerful. But then, administrators who didn't really know if it was working or not would come in and they didn't see grammar instruction. We would have many more discussions. We, as a department, just didn't give up (A10).

Experiences Common to "Some" (3-4 out of 10) Group A Participants.

Pre-workshop Teaching, Administrator Training, and Standardized Testing.

Some (3 out of 10) TPRS teachers tried out the method before receiving training (A4, A8, A9); some had administrators who attended TPRS training (A2, A8, A10); and some collected standardized test data (A1, A7, A10) on their students.

One teacher's students' performance data on the National Spanish Exam "has now validated my using TPRS" (A1). He had 51/75 students score at or above the 75th percentile, with 11 of those scoring at or above the 95th percentile nationally. Out of 19 prize winners, 11 were his students, to include 7 out of the top 8. "It basically shows that with this method, we can have kids 'as good as or better than' kids who are learning with the traditional approach" (A1). Another teacher had ten students pass the AP exam in the first year of his program with those numbers rising to 35 in three years with a 90% pass rate (A7). A third informant from Group A reported:

> I have a district of data, of over 100 teachers, and thousands of kids taking our [proficiency-based] common assessments. The data have shown that TPRS is superior in terms of listening, reading, writing, and speaking. The data are overwhelmingly in favor of TPRS (A10).

Group B Interview Results

Group B participants addressed the second research question of this study: What do secondary level teachers trained in TPRS, who decide not to use the TPRS method in their language classrooms, perceive as obstacles to its use? In other words, why did Group B teachers trained in TPRS reject the method? What were their experiences with TPRS?

Twelve obstacles emerged from an analysis of Group B interview data. The twelve obstacles included insufficient training, underdeveloped TPRS teaching skills, classroom management difficulties, resistance from people, curriculum concerns, wanting to cover a broader vocabulary, textbook grammar, a lack of appropriate prepared materials, issues over first language use, teacher confidence, planning time, and the high energy demands of TPRS storytelling. Those obstacles were discussed below.

Table 4.B.1. Obstacles, part 1.

Attended workshop	Follow-up	Weeklong conference	Ongoing training	Beginning skills hard	Skills improved	Classroom management difficult	Class mgt improved
All 10	6	3	0	9	3	9	0

All ten Group B study participants (TPRS rejecters) encountered what they perceived as obstacles to using TPRS. One perceived 'obstacle' was a lack of skill improvement or insufficient training. While all ten Group B study participants interviewed attended a TPRS workshop and observed student success when using or trying out the method, only three Group B teachers attended a weeklong national TPRS conference, and none of them participated in ongoing professional development to sustain or improve their skills.

Managing the Classroom and Resistance.

Despite nearly all (9 out of 10) of the Group B teacher participants experiencing early difficulty learning to use their new TPRS teaching skills, only three (3/10) reported that they improved them. Similarly, nearly all (9 out of 10) said that for them classroom management was more difficult when using TPRS than when they used more traditional methods of teaching, yet none of those nine reported working to improve their classroom management skills. Two reported feeling confident or in the zone when using TPRS.

Many (6 out of 10) Group B study participants also reported resistance from people (students, colleagues, administrators) as an obstacle to using TPRS. Self-resistance appeared when teachers new to TPRS did not accept the paradigm shift discussed above. Some students resisted directly, as did some colleagues and administrators, but teachers trying out TPRS also experienced some support from others, as follows.

Table 4.B.2. Obstacles, part 2. Resistance.

Self-resistance	Student resistance	Colleague resists	Administrator
6	6	6	2

Table 4.B.3. Obstacles, part 3. Support.

Student support	Parent support	Colleague support	Administrator went to a workshop
All 10	1	3	4

Resistance from Others.

People were mentioned and perceived as 'obstacles' to using TPRS by over half of the Group B participants, to include self-resistance (6 out of 10) and not knowing the brain research (6 of 10) that supported using the method. Over half of Group B reported experiencing resistance from some of their students and from their foreign-language teaching colleagues when they used TPRS. A few (2 out of 10) experienced direct resistance from administrators, many (6 of 10) had a lack of support from administrators, and no Group B principals attended a TPRS workshop, despite the fee being waived (free) for administrators. Only four teachers from Group B received active support from their colleagues and even fewer (1 of 10) experienced support from parents.

While resistance from people was considered an obstacle in some cases, there were other types of obstacles that all or nearly all the teachers who tried out or used TPRS encountered. The following obstacles arose directly from the different theoretical and philosophical paradigms behind the TPRS method a traditional grammar-based textbook curriculum which are discussed elsewhere in this paper.

Table 4.B.4. Obstacles, part 4.

Curriculum concerns	Wanted broader vocabulary covered	Covering textbook and explicit grammar	Needed teaching materials and ancillaries	Issues of 1st and 2nd language use
All 10	10	10	9	10

Obstacles encountered by all ten Group B participants were perceived to include being required to teach a preset curriculum, cover vocabulary and grammar from an approved textbook, and respond to issues on first language or target language use in class. B1 took issue with not following the "curriculum that is approved" by the school board. B2 was required to cover textbook grammar and a "much more broad vocabulary base" than she thought TPRS would allow due to its principle of limiting vocabulary to high-frequent fluency structures.

If B3 could have changed TPRS, she said that would have added some direct, explicit grammar instruction. However, people using TPRS covered grammar incidentally as it arose in context rather than intentionally planning explicit grammar lessons. The two philosophical or theoretical paradigms were different. B4 only used TPRS "a little because the grammar curriculum is a big obstacle" and there is pressure on her to cover it all. With common assessments that tested the grammar features from the textbook, B5 was "strongly recommended not to use" TPRS by an administrator who had previously chaired the world language department. B6 said that some of the out-of-context textbook grammar drills seemed, in her word, "bizarre" and that she preferred the TPRS methodological approach because through TPRS the "grammar wasn't separate," but rather presented within the context of stories, in personalized teacher-student interactions, and in the classroom readings.

Curriculum and Vocabulary.

A criticism was that the TPRS curriculum was not well-spelled out, as it was by the grammar syllabus in traditional textbooks, which B7 said could be "threatening and uncertain to a lot of people" who did not know where TPRS might take them as teachers. B5 said, "Some days I had trouble figuring out where was I going with this" and B5 also wondered whether TPRS-taught students could cover as much vocabulary. B7 perceived that covering a broader vocabulary, while following TPRS principles, was "something a lot of people are looking for and a lot of other teachers who may get these students at later levels are looking for too."

Proficiency Goals and Textbook Concerns.

B9 recommended that TPRS clearly set its student proficiency goals at 'Advanced Low' on the American Council on the Teaching of Foreign Languages (ACTFL) scale. From that perspective, she doubted "whether all of the Advanced Low grammatical constructs could be done through TPRS" (B9), so she opted for a mixed-methods approach in her own classroom. B10's language department was in the process of adopting the TPRS method and he realized that he "was using a method that was not helpful to [students] by going the traditional textbook route," as he reflected that he was still linked to the textbook in some ways. B10 said he had not completely accepted the TPRS philosophical paradigm shift away from traditional explicit grammar teaching.

Some teachers, to include B8, never saw TPRS as "completely replacing the textbook" and said that they did not intend to use the method exclusively in their classrooms. As B1 said, "You don't find your text materials or your curriculum laid out for you in a TPRS mode." None of the Group B participants used TPRS exclusively in their teaching and they all used a traditional textbook to teach grammar explicitly. In other words, Group B teachers who tried out TPRS in their classrooms did not completely accept the paradigm shift from traditional teaching to TPRS.

Language Use and Meeting ACTFL Guidelines.

The question of finding an appropriate combination of first and second language use in the classroom emerged in interviews with both Group A and Group B. In the former, A10 had pointed out that full immersion program advocates had disagreed with using any English (first language) translations, but in the TPRS method quick translations were used to establish meaning of new target vocabulary (for less than 10% of class time). However, Group B participants argued for a greater use of first language use (English) than TPRS principles and ACTFL guidelines would allow. For example, rather than follow the TPRS principle (and ACTFL guideline) of providing comprehensible input in the target language 90% of the time in class, B8 said that a "real language teacher needs to explain conjugation" and answer questions about grammar and culture, in English (first language use), even if lengthy explanations were given.

Both B1 and B10 said they sometimes allowed for social classroom chat in English to lower the affective filter and to make students feel more comfortable. B2 allowed English use when students played computer translation games on *Scatter* and *Quizlet*. B3 taught explicit grammar lessons in French class using mostly English. Some administrators expected to observe explicit grammar lessons, as B4 explained:

I can't risk too many bad visits and evaluations. If I give a whole English class about direct object pronouns, my observer is going to be delighted and if I just talk all Spanish, they're not going to see the point (B4).

On the other hand, B5 wanted to use more TPRS to increase the target language use in her classroom for both herself and her students. She perceived that her students would not acquire the language without hearing plentiful amounts of repetitive, interesting, and comprehensible input. B6 reflected on her own teaching and said, "When I don't use TPRS, I do use a lot more English and that's not what I want to be doing."

In addition to the above-mentioned nine obstacles, three other problems emerged from the Group B interviews when those participants were explaining why they rejected using TPRS exclusively in their classrooms. Three emergent topics included the perceptions of many and nearly all TPRS rejecters that confidence, planning time, and high energy were among the demands of using the TPRS method.

Table 4.B.5. Obstacles, part 5.

Teacher confidence	Planning time	High energy
9	9	8

Confidence Building, Planning Time, and High Energy Demands.

Nearly all (9 of 10) of the Group B interviewees perceived the following topics as obstacles to using TPRS. Nearly all reported experiencing problems with their own confidence in using the method, a need for planning time, and a lack of pre-prepared TPRS materials with easy-to-use ancillaries. Only attending one workshop was not enough for B3 to feel confident in using the method. B4 cited 'personality' factors as lowering her confidence in using the method. She explained:

I'm not a fun girl and that is a weakness. I find my weakness is in story asking; it just falls flat. I cannot seem to get that cute. The best TPRS teachers have a little bit of 'cute' going for them. They are clever and can see an odd side to it and it's funny (B4).

Another teacher had trouble being confident in her planning, saying "I always felt lost with what I was doing, week to week" (B5). A lack of confidence made it difficult for her to lead, plan, and coordinate the curriculum both vertically and horizontally with colleagues. After attending four TPRS workshops, a French teacher explained, "I'm still learning TPRS. I'm not yet a good storyteller" (B8). As it took her some time to become confident in using TPRS, an upper level Spanish teacher gave into the "tendency to fall back on what's easier" (B9). A Chinese teacher perceived the biggest obstacle to gaining confidence to use TPRS was insufficient training and low skills development, saying "TPRS is not something that you can learn overnight" (B7).

Time Requirements.

Nearly all (9/10) perceived 'time' as an obstacle to using TPRS. B1 mentioned the time and energy required for TPRS teacher skill and materials development, planning, story writing, ongoing training, and problems with curriculum alignment and coverage. B2 took the time to type up stories that she and her students had co-constructed in class to personalize the stories. B4 discussed how teaching explicit grammar took time away from storytelling, making time an obstacle to using TPRS in that sense. B5 mentioned the additional time requirements needed if there were TPRS proficiency tests given in addition to departmental common assessments.

B8 stated that he needed more time to explore TPRS and to improve his skills. B9 discussed how students needed to hear fluency structures repeated, using the TPRS method, "hundreds of times" to acquire them. Per B10, in the beginning there was more planning time required than after a teacher's TPRS skills improved, but he also did not want to throw out existing lessons that he had already put a lot of planning time into. B6 lamented over the lack of TPRS Chinese materials and the time needed to prepare her own. B7 hoped that something could be done to improve materials because now using TPRS "takes a lot of preparation [time] and that's intimidating to people."

Many (8 out of 10) Group B teachers perceived 'energy level' to be an obstacle to using the method. TPRS "can be exhausting [and it] takes a certain type of energy" (B1). B2, who mixed the methods, said that when she used TPRS every day that she "found that exhausting." B4 said that TPRS takes "a little bit of personality to pull it off… it's hard, takes high energy, [and] can be exhausting." One Chinese teacher reported that she had not rejected the method, but that she had not "had the time and energy to implement it [and] to get better at it [because] it is so much effort to write stories" (B6).

In the sections above, Group A and Group B experiences were identified. The following section contained comparisons of the groups who have used TPRS. These comparisons revealed both common and different experiences between groups.

Comparisons of Group A and B

Initial Teacher Training, Early Student Success, and Decision Making.

All twenty participants (A=10, B=10) attended at least one TPRS workshop and saw their students succeed after teaching them through the TPRS method. Group A teachers decided to use TPRS as their primary method of instruction, but Group B did not. Group B teachers decided to teach textbook grammar through a traditional approach.

Table 4.AB.1. Comparing Groups A and B, part 1.

Group A	Group B	Experience
10	6	Were unsatisfied with student results before TPRS.
10	10	Attended a TPRS teacher-training workshop.
10	10	Saw students succeed with TPRS method.
10	0	Used TPRS as their primary method of instruction.

There were ten participants in each of the two groups who had experience with TPRS and there were both common experiences and different experiences between the two groups. All ten Group A teachers attended follow-up workshop training, compared to six from Group B. In addition to attending TPRS workshops, all ten teachers in Group A also attended a weeklong national TPRS conference (NTPRS), compared to three from Group B. Nearly all the Group A teachers continued with ongoing training and professional development to sustain or improve their skills (A=9, B=0), but Group B study participants did not.

Nearly all (A=9, B=9) of the teachers with TPRS experience reported that learning the TPRS teaching skills was difficult, especially in the beginning. Nine teachers from both groups had that same experience. All ten Group A teachers reported having improved their skills (A=10, B=3), but only three Group B participants reported improvement. All ten Group A teachers said that they felt successful, in the zone, or in the flow (Csikszentmihalyi, 1990, 1997; Krashen, 2015) when teaching using TPRS (A=10, B=2), compared to only two from Group B.

Part 2 comparisons follow, as presented in Table 4.AB.2 with discussion below.

Table 4.AB.2. Comparing Groups A and B, part 2.

Group A	Group B	Experience
10	6	Attended follow-up workshop training.
10	3	Attended a weeklong national TPRS conference (NTPRS).
9	0	Continued ongoing training and professional development.
9	9	Reported that learning TPRS skills was difficult, especially at beginning.
10	3	Reported having improved upon their beginning TPRS teaching skills.
10	2	Said they felt confident, successful, in the zone, or in the flow using TPRS.

Some Group A teachers found classroom management difficult at first, but nearly all Group B teachers did (A=4, B=9). Many Group A teachers reported that they improved their classroom management skills, but Group B teachers did not (A=7, B=0). Group A teachers experienced support from parents (A=10, B=1) and some support from administrators (A=10, B=4), but Group B participants received less support. Both groups encountered obstacles and resistance when using or trying out the TPRS method.

Table 4.AB.3. Comparing Groups A and B, part 3.

Group A	Group B	Experience
4	9	Found classroom management more difficult when using TPRS.
7	0	Improved their TPRS classroom management skills.
10	1	Received support from parents when using TPRS.
10	4	Received support from administrators when using TPRS.
10	10	Encountered obstacles and resistance when using TPRS.

Thus far, in this chapter, the experiences of teachers who were trained in the TPRS method were described. Group A teachers (TPRS users) decided to use TPRS as their main method when teaching foreign languages. Group B study participants (TPRS rejecters) decided to base their teaching on a traditional textbook approach and cover a grammatical syllabus taught through explicit instruction. Both groups had training and experience using TPRS. Their common and different experiences were described above.

Obstacles, Resistance, and Challenges.

Obstacles were faced by teachers when using TPRS. As discussed above, these obstacles included people who resisted TPRS, to include: self, students, parents, colleagues, and administrators. Also, the obstacles included concerns over curriculum, textbooks, grammar, vocabulary coverage, problems with confidence, planning time, teaching materials, first and target language use, the high-energy demands of the method, skill difficulty, and classroom management challenges. Group B participants provided what they perceived as obstacles to using TPRS which led those teachers to either reject using the TPRS method or limit its use. However, Group A teachers continued to use TPRS undeterred.

Below, comments were noted from Group A participants who continued to use TPRS as their primary methodology despite encountering obstacles, resistance, and challenges. For example, when A10 saw teachers who "started to fail in their practice of TPRS," she worked to provide and improve teacher training in her district. A10 did not give up. When A9 received resistance from colleagues, by patiently sharing more about what he was doing, he was able to lead them from "misunderstanding to understanding" and gradually earn their acceptance, which took over two years to accomplish.

Another Group A teacher perceived that "other foreign language teachers is [are] the number one obstacle" (A8). She coped with them trying to get her fired (because her students did not do well on discrete point, out of context, isolated grammar tests) by accepting a job offer in a different school where TPRS was more accepted. A8 decided that changing jobs was easier than trying to convince her school to change to more of a standards-based proficiency testing model more in line with ACTFL guidelines.

A7 had thought he needed to talk all the time, but when he started to lose his voice he added more TPRS reading activities, which were also a part of the method and another way to provide input that was comprehensible beyond storytelling, to cope with his difficulties. To help other colleagues deal with classroom management concerns, A7 included techniques as part every presentation he gave at conferences and he provided information on his website for teachers on improving TPRS classroom management.

Challenges also have been internally encountered through reflective practices pertaining to challenges teachers have faced. For example, A6 directly dealt with her own concerns over curriculum, textbooks, materials, vocabulary and grammar coverage, planning, and developing her school's program in sync with TPRS principles and national standards through professional development. She attended conferences and received support and encouragement through online discussions with other TPRS practitioners working through similar challenges and concerns.

Even experienced TPRS instructors have had problems mastering the teaching skills of TPRS. A5 said that obstacles, problems, and challenges for him were generally of his own making. At times, he overestimated what students had acquired, had gone through the material too fast, or realized through assessment that he may not have laid the groundwork or adequately prepared students for what he was asking them to do. A5 would, in those cases, go back and review, slow down, or practice more with students.

A4 addressed the high-energy demands of teaching with TPRS by first limiting its use, but she decided that approach was unacceptable. After seeing how her students' performance went down when she used other methods, she went to receive more training at a national TPRS conference (NTPRS) to discover additional ways of providing comprehensible input that were consistent with TPRS principles. By using TPRS activities such as Total Physical Response (TPR), embedded readings, novels, and MovieTalk, A4 was able to avoid mixing the methods and used TPRS exclusively.

How TPRS teachers coped with resistance and obstacles varied, but what they had in common was perseverance in finding ways to use the TPRS method. Some examples follow. A4 responded to external colleague resistance by first obtaining permission to use TPRS more often, but after that year A4 quit her job and opened a language school of her own where she was not required to coordinate with colleagues who resisted TPRS.

A3 found that he could reduce his planning time by improving his own TPRS teaching skills because he co-constructed stories with his students in class. Among A3's guiding principles for storytelling were to teach for proficiency, speak slowly and clearly to allow students time to process information, ask many questions, elicit student input, and assess their comprehension of the story. Using a multi-sensory approach, A3 taught from bell to bell in class, and he looked for ways to provide a variety of repetitive, comprehensible input of high-frequency vocabulary and verb structures, using topics that he hoped would be compelling to hold his students' attention. A3 tried to make students feel comfortable, touch their emotions, see smiles on student faces, enjoy his work, and not leave any student behind.

There were other ways of coping with resistance and obstacles that TPRS teachers faced. For example, A2 said that she experienced days when she felt "flat," and the story just did not work. The students were not always fully engaged or interested and not every session could be a "homerun" lesson. Rather than abandon the method, on those days, she would branch off to an alternative strategy for providing comprehensible input, such as an embedded reading. When A1 faced resistance from colleagues and from administrators because he used TPRS, he collected data by having his students take the nationally normed and standardized National Spanish Exam. Their high scores both validated his methodology and earned him the support of his administrators.

Study participants from both groups, A and B, encountered similar obstacles, problems, issues, and resistance when trying out or using TPRS in their respective classrooms. However, their responses and decisions differed when faced with such roadblocks and adversity. Whereas Group B teachers rejected using the method, Group A teachers found ways to cope with these challenges and to continue using TPRS until they found what they perceived as success, for both themselves and for their students.

Group B participants faced obstacles and resistance. For example, nearly all (9) of the ten interviewed as Group B participants found learning the TPRS teaching skills difficult to master especially early on, experienced problems with self confidence in mastering the method, and encountered obstacles to using the method. These obstacles or problems, among others, included the imposed need to cover a grammar-driven textbook curriculum with a prescribed broad vocabulary, difficulties with planning or coordinating lessons, a shortage of appropriate materials for providing comprehensible input, issues related to first or second language use, and classroom management challenges.

Many (7-8 out of 10) Group B study participants found the high-energy demands of the method exhausting for teachers trying TPRS out. Over half (6 of 10) met with resistance from people, to include internally grappling with a paradigm shift to TPRS as well as meeting resistance from students and colleagues. Some (3 of 10) experienced some support from colleagues or administrators, but none in Group B had administrators who attended a TPRS workshop. Half were isolated, and all alone, when trying out the method, some (3 of 10) discussed how brain research supports using TPRS or improved their TPRS teaching skills, and none reported improving their classroom management skills. A few (3 of 10) attended NTPRS, discussed feeling confident in teaching using TPRS, and only one mentioned having experienced support from parents. Despite the obstacles, both teacher groups experienced success when using TPRS.

Group C Interview Results

Group C participants were interviewed to address research question 3 of this study: What techniques do secondary language teachers using a traditional approach perceive as effective for promoting student success in learning to comprehend and speak the language being taught? This question was asked to identify, from an etic point of view completely outside of TPRS training and experience, what techniques they believed were effective for language learning and acquisition. Those identified techniques were then considered as possible recommendations to be added to the TPRS method.

The techniques mentioned by Group C participants fell into three basic categories. These categories included: (1) techniques which did not fall within the TPRS theoretical paradigm, (2) techniques which were already part of TPRS, and (3) techniques which did fit within the TPRS paradigm. The techniques consistent with TPRS principles that fell within the philosophical paradigm would be the obvious candidates for possible TPRS method inclusion.

However, determining whether a given technique fit within the TPRS paradigm depended upon how the technique was delivered. For example, even using a 'story' could fall outside the paradigm if TPRS principles were not applied correctly when using the technique. If the story failed to provide interesting, repetitive, comprehensible input in context, then that story would fall outside the TPRS paradigm. Therefore, when reading the following section, techniques must comply with the TPRS guidance and principles found in Ray and Seely (2015) in order to qualify for possible inclusion in the TPRS method. On the other hand, if a convincing rationale were provided, then a given technique might be added to the method even if that technique did not fall strictly within the TPRS paradigm. Regarding the fidelity of method delivery issue, only correctly applied techniques should be considered for recommendation to become part of the TPRS methodology. In the case of TPRS any possible upcoming certification, the people who will have prescribed that certification will likely have decided what techniques were included, or not included, when delivering the TPRS method with a high degree of fidelity. In addition, logically, techniques identified which were already part of TPRS did not need to be added.

In the end, it was left for each individual TPRS teacher to decide which techniques to use in class. However, the following techniques, strategies, activities, and approaches emerged from Group C study participant interviews who considered them effective for learning to comprehend and produce the target language. The researcher's four recommendations that follow were made only after analyzing each technique for whether it fit within the TPRS principles, paradigm, and was informed by second language acquisition research.

Techniques Outside the TPRS Paradigm.

Normally, techniques which did not fit inside the TPRS theoretical paradigm would not be considered for inclusion unless they were applied using TPRS principles or have a detailed, persuasive rationale for consideration. The following techniques, for the most part, were perceived as being 'outside' the TPRS paradigm and therefore were therefore 'not' recommended for method inclusion.

Those techniques included explicitly taught grammar drills and exercises from textbooks or worksheets, verb conjugation charts, dictionary use, taking class notes, rote memorization, memorizing vocabulary or dialogs, memory tricks, extensive contrastive analysis (in the first language), games, puzzles, Spanglish (or non-standard language use), forced output (writing and speaking) before learners are developmentally ready, listen and repeat drills for pronunciation, homework beyond the student's abilities unless comprehensible, prizes, competitions, research reports in the first language, student transcriptions unless done by the teacher, project-based teaching, and output-based or other production-based activities beyond the student's developmental readiness level.

Other non-TPRS activities mentioned included flipped classrooms, the correction of students' errors, think-pair-share (unless brief), discussion about culture or grammar in the first language, discussing curriculum learning maps extensively in the first language, and lengthy explicit grammar explanations in the first language. Taking students out of their comfort zone, or raising the affective filter, was not considered to be part of TPRS.

Cooperative learning was considered to lie outside of the TPRS paradigm if the interactions involved forced output beyond the students' readiness levels. Taking class time away from acquisition-rich activities to prepare students for tests of out-of-context, isolated, discrete grammar points was outside the TPRS paradigm. Over 10% of class time was considered too much non-target language use, so most TPRS instructors have limited their first-language use to 'establishing meaning' for new target vocabulary, new fluency structures, and for doing story comprehension checks.

After identifying whether a given technique that was considered effective by Group C teachers fell within the TPRS paradigm or not, the next step of analysis was to identify which of those techniques were already part of the TPRS method. Logically speaking, there would have been no need to add any technique that was already included in the TPRS method.

Techniques Already Part of TPRS.

The techniques already part of TPRS did not need to be added to the method. Group C participants did mention some techniques that were already part of the TPRS method, but since Group C informants had no training or experience with the method, then they likely could not have known that.

Those techniques included critical thinking, using realia, teaching culture (if in the target language), target culture activities, authentic materials, and reading skills such as skimming and scanning, the chunking of information, reading translation activities to assess comprehension, including 'pop-up' grammar in cultural situations, images, pictures, cartoons, skits, acting out scenes, arts, artists, painting, crafts, drawing, interviews, conversations, inductive and deductive reasoning with brief explanations. Brainstorming, brief warm-ups, QSR (Quick Start Review), story reviews, modeling, variety, descriptions, seeding vocabulary, manipulatives, little balls, props, stuffed animals, establishing discipline and rapport, and setting clear expectations were also mentioned by Group C study participants.

Other activities already part of the TPRS method included mixing domains such as psycho-motor, cognitive, social, and affective, in a multi-sensory approach. Those included listening to slower speech presentations, graphic organizers, TPR, gestures, movement, hands-on tasks, music, jingles, raps, proficiency-based activities, combining elementary and secondary approaches, scaffolding, promoting a growth rather than fixed mindset, alternative assessments, using activities appropriate to the students' age group and cognitive development levels, and differentiating instruction with an awareness of each student's specific needs.

Additional activities already part of the TPRS method included using teacher-created materials from the internet, if comprehensible, allowing students wait time or time to think when answering questions, discussing topics interesting to students, role playing, allowing for some student choice, establishing a safe climate conducive to learning and respect for others, lowering the affective filter, reflecting deeply and often on how to improve, encouraging students to always do their best and modeling that behavior for them, leading by example, promoting bilingualism and multilingualism, and taking pleasure in the teacher's job.

Techniques Within the TPRS Paradigm.

The techniques which Group C informants perceived as effective could be considered for method inclusion provided they fall within the TPRS paradigm, if properly applied, reflected the TPRS principles described in Ray and Seely (2015), and had the potential to promote professionalism within the field and TPRS use. The following techniques were mentioned and each one should be considered on its own merits for possible inclusion or recommendation to become part of, or used with, the TPRS method.

Recommendations for Teachers to Consider Using with TPRS.

There were four categories of consideration for recommendations.

1. These included adding activities specifically for aligning with the three modes of learning promoted by ACTFL: interpretive, interpersonal, and presentational. TPRS teachers generally have included more activities in the interpretive and interpersonal modes than presentational. Interpretive tasks involved listening and reading to comprehend input. TPRS has placed less emphasis on the presentational mode because it involved production, to include speaking and writing. TPRS practices have delayed or postponed forced production before comprehension-based have been accomplished.

2. Another area of professional input was to consider additional ways to teach more to the five ACTFL standards: communication, cultures, connections, comparisons, and communities. TPRS has stressed comprehension and communication primarily with a secondary focus on infusing culture into stories, but has fallen short in making connections to other disciplines, comparing the ways the first and second language are the same or different, and community programs and projects have received the least attention.

3. A third category of techniques involved the recommended and extended use of technology, in cases where that those applications can provide input to the students in context that is interesting or compelling, repetitive, and can be made comprehensible through the technology. Some individual teachers have

used technology extensively, but many have not. Perhaps more sharing among professionals could bring about improved learning in this area.

4. A fourth suggested category was to incorporate 'some' focused error correction, within certain constraints. Among the approaches considered could perhaps include trying out an approach similar to the Collins Writing System (Collins, 2008) which one study participant described in an interview. In that system, only a limited number and types of mistakes would be corrected, so as not to overwhelm the students. It is recommended that any error correction be done with the caveat that those corrections be provided within a meaningful, communicative context, and not violate the 90% target language use goal of TPRS and ACTFL. In other words, no more than 10% total non-target language use should be included in TPRS classrooms for them to remain acquisition-rich environments.

A Question on Research Design: Why was Group C included in the Study?

Much of the 'resistance' that TPRS teachers experienced involved professional interaction with teachers who had no training, knowledge or experience with the method. They fit Group C study participant criteria. By collecting data directly from Group C informants, concerning what techniques they believed were effective, and possibly incorporating some of those new techniques into the method, there was potential for TPRS to evolve in directions more acceptable to traditional, mainstream, language professionals.

Another reason for finding out what Group C teachers believed to be effective was to identify places where those techniques were 'already part' of TPRS or consistent with its principles. That data could potentially bring TPRS teachers and non-TPRS instructors together on common ground where they could agree. A final reason for including Group C in this study was to identify techniques which might 'improve' the method. TPRS has evolved over the years (Ray, 2013) and that continued evolution depends upon being aware of the current thinking in the field of language teaching which Group C informants provided for this study.

Upon reflection, this researcher had originally proposed only interviewing teachers from groups A and B because phenomenologists study lived experiences. It was only through discussion with professors and dissertation committee members that the third research question was added to this study and Group C participants were identified as the informants best suited to answer that third research question. Bringing in Group C changed the original study design because asking that third research question was outside of a pure phenomenology since those study participants had 'no' experience with using the TPRS method. However, under 'lessons learned' from the project, this researcher will likely include both an insider viewpoint and an outsider perspective in the design of future related studies, for the reasons mentioned above.

Summary and Organization of the Study

Chapter IV presented the results of the data analyses for this study. Two groups of participants provided insights into the common classroom experiences lived by TPRS teachers who used or tried out the method. Group A study participants were teachers who used the TPRS method of foreign language instruction as their primary method. Group B teachers were trained in TPRS, but rejected its primary usage in their language classrooms.

A third group, Group C teacher informants, who had no training or experience using TPRS, provided their perceptions of effective language teaching for learning to comprehend and produce the target language. The techniques the latter group perceived as effective were considered for possible inclusion into the TPRS method, provided they fall with the TPRS theoretical paradigm and that those techniques reflect TPRS teaching principles. Chapter V includes a summary of the study, a discussion of the findings, implications for practice, recommendations for further research, and conclusions.

CHAPTER V

SUMMARY, CONCLUSIONS AND RECOMMENDATIONS

Summary of the Study

This qualitative study using a quasi-phenomenological approach described the common lived classroom experiences of secondary level, grades 9-12, teachers who used the Teaching Proficiency through Reading and Storytelling (TPRS) method of world language instruction, identified obstacles to its use, and elicited information on effective teaching techniques which had the potential for improving the method. The study focused on why some teachers used TPRS and others did not after having been trained in the method and trying it out. explained why some teachers trained in TPRS abandoned the method and what they perceived as obstacles to its use. The study also identified the techniques perceived as effective by traditional teachers for promoting student success in comprehending and producing the target language as well as the modes and standards encouraged by ACTFL for best practices in world language education. The results of the study identified sixteen common lived experiences and twelve obstacles faced by teachers when using TPRS, plus four recommendations to consider incorporating into the evolving method.

Discussion of the Findings

The findings of the study were discussed below for the three research questions. There sixteen common experiences lived by TPRS teachers answered the first research question. The twelve obstacles to using the method addressed the second research questions. The four recommendations that were made to consider adding to the method answered the third research question. Following the discussion of the findings below were the implications of the study for future practice, recommendations for further research, and the conclusions drawn. The discussion began below with the first research question.

The findings of the study were listed in Chapter IV, but they were further discussed in this chapter. Following the structural guidance of Lunenberg and Irby (2008, p. 229) for writing Chapter V, each result or study finding (TPRS teacher experience) was discussed below referencing the previous professional literature which either supported or refuted each finding. None of the names used in this study referred to any of the study participants. The names cited below were the names of researchers.

Research Question 1

What were high school teachers' common lived experiences using the Teaching Proficiency through Reading and Storytelling (TPRS) method to teach world languages?

There were sixteen common experiences lived by teachers using TPRS. In this study, all ten TPRS teachers from Group A had the following 16 experiences (bolded) in common. The teacher participants currently using TPRS in Group A of this study had the following experiences in common. All ten of them:

Experience 1: Were unsatisfied with student results before TPRS.

All Group A teachers were unsatisfied with student results in language class before they were taught using the TPRS method, so they were willing to try a new approach. By comparison, six out of the ten teachers in Group B were unsatisfied. Since 40% of the teachers in Group B were satisfied with student performance, there may have been less motivation for them to change the ways they were teaching. In the professional literature, in support of this finding, Ray (in Ray & Seely, 1998, 2004) related that before creating the TPRS method, he had been unsatisfied with student recall. Espinoza (2015) found that two of the three teachers he interviewed had not been satisfied with their own teaching or with their students' inability to speak the target language before TPRS.

As the researcher, I have tried to bracket out my own experiences and opinions during the data collection, data analysis, and reporting of the findings. However, at this point, it is time to interpret the data and the findings, using my own voice. By comparing the difference between Group A and B, it is not surprising that all ten who decided to use TPRS as their primary method of instruction were previously unsatisfied with student results. Since they were unsatisfied, they were likely looking for a more effective method and willing to make a change. With more than half of Group B teachers being satisfied (6 of 10), those teachers may not have been as eager to make a change in the way they taught. Therefore, that finding was not a surprise to this researcher.

Experience 2: Attended a TPRS workshop.

All study participants in Groups A and B attended a workshop, but their reactions varied. After Whaley (2009) first attended a TPRS workshop, she decided not to retire from teaching because her students improved so much when she changed to TPRS and she received an award for excellence in teaching. Similarly, Lichtman (2014) changed the way she taught after attending a TPRS workshop as she perceived that her students retained more structures and vocabulary when they were acquired in context through storytelling. Lichtman (2012a, 2012b, 2015, 2016) has continued to review and participate in ongoing TPRS research. Taulbee (2008) and other researchers attended more than one workshop. While attending a workshop, Garczynski (2003) was surprised to hear some teachers openly arguing against using the method partly because Ray and Seely (2002) did not endorse or encourage the use of textbooks in TPRS. However, in the data for this study, several teachers reported that they attended multiple workshops.

Not only did all Group A and B study participants attend a workshop, they all tried the method out in their classroom and all 20 saw students succeed with TPRS. That raises the question as to why, after seeing students succeed, why would a teacher reject using the method? The data on the number of obstacles faced by Group B and the amount of support the teacher received, or did not receive, may help explain their choices. All 20 encountered some obstacles and resistance when using TPRS. All ten TPRS users received some support from parents and administrators compared to only one and four of the rejecters. Without support, some teachers may have given up.

Experience 3: Attended follow-up training after the first workshop.

Four of the ten Group B teachers did not attend a follow-up workshop, but all Group A participants did. Black (2012) mentioned that the TPRS teachers whose interactions he studied in an online professional learning community (PLC) were enthusiastic and frequent workshop attenders working to improve their craft through ongoing professional development.

All Group A TPRS users attended a follow-up workshop, a national conference, and worked to improve their TPRS teaching skills, compared to Group B rejecters who had six attend a follow-up workshop, three a national conference, and none reported having improved upon their beginning skills. In short, the users attended more training. Nine users continued with ongoing training, but no rejecters did.

Experience 4: Attended a one-week national TPRS conference.

Jody Klopp organized the first weeklong national conference (NTPRS) in 2001 and they have continued each July ever since, drawing over 200 teachers annually from the United States and other countries (Ray & Seely, 2004, 2015). For example, Patrick (2015b) wrote about the growing interest in TPRS in the language he taught, reporting that the number of Latin teachers who attended an NTPRS conference grew from three in 2012 to 46 in 2015. While all ten Group A teachers attended at least one national conference, only three from Group B did. This researcher attended the last five NTPRS conferences and noticed that several sessions involved TPRS teaching skill development, to include using gestures to help establish the meaning and recall of new vocabulary.

In the interviews, Group A teachers spoke openly about the professional friendships they formed at the national conferences. The weeklong conferences provided opportunities to practice teaching and receive coaching, attend a variety of sessions on TPRS, and experience the method as a student as well. I have now attended five national conferences in the last five years. Without the conference experience, it may be more difficult to sustain the use of the method. Some called it summer camp.

Experience 5: Used gestures in their teaching.

Asher (1965, 1996, 2009) concluded from his early research that using gestures was an effective strategy for teaching languages because their use resulted in long-term retention of vocabulary. Ray and Gross (1998) published a book on using gestures with TPRS. Seely and Romijn (2006) discussed Ray's contribution of adding stories to Asher's Total Physical Response (TPR) language acquisition strategy. McKay (2000) had incorporated gestures into his version of TPR Storytelling. Armstrong (2008) perceived that her elementary school children enjoyed the gestures, but worried that older children might not. However, Armstrong's student survey revealed that the middle school children liked the gestures too.

Oliver (2012) used gestures when teaching university students and adults, as did Davidheiser (2001, 2002). Kariuki and Bush (2008) observed that students appeared more engaged when using gestures. Welch (2014) cited the research of Marzano, Pickering, and Heflebower (2011) who found that using gestures and actively engaging students through multisensory input were among the best practices in education. Waltz (2015) created and taught teachers how to use directional gestures to help their students acquire the tones of Mandarin, which previously had been more challenging before that improvement in teaching Chinese was advanced.

All Group A users reported using gestures and TPR in their teaching despite TPR being dropped from the workshops a few years ago. They said they use them because they work and they believe students retain vocabulary longer through multisensory input.

Experience 6: Reported improving upon their beginning skills.

Seely and Romijn (2006) described TPRS as a complex method. Despite its complexity, all ten Group A teachers reported improving upon their beginning skills, but none from Group B did. Slavic (2007) identified 49 skills to master and many focused on engaging students. Bryson and Hand (2007) discussed the need to engage students in their own learning. Rowan (2013) and Marzano (et al., 2011) described activities intended to increase student engagement in class. Hedstrom (2012, 2014, 2015) offered suggestions for engaging students through TPRS strategies, especially through personalization and classroom interaction. Pippins (2015) advocated using names and personalized questions to improve the teacher's interactive TPRS skills with students. Confidence came to the TPRS teachers in this study who improved their teaching skills.

Simply put, the data revealed that 18 out of 20 reported that learning the TPRS teaching skills was difficult, especially in the beginning, and most people require about five years before they feel very confident in them to the point of being in the flow. Improvement comes with training and practice. This comment explains the point below.

Experience 7: Discussed feeling confident or in the zone (flow) with TPRS.

While all Group A teachers eventually felt confident and in the zone when they were using TPRS, only two Group B teachers reported feeling that confident. Clarcq (2015) discussed the journey of becoming more confident through the acquisition of TPRS teaching skills to the point of feeling in the flow (Csikszentmihalyi, 1990, 1997). Slavic (2015) mentioned that his own confidence grew as he developed his skills.

Several people have said that before your skills are highly developed that you are too worried with yourself to adequately read and respond to the students. Those who have not yet learned to co-construct stories with their students comfortably rarely reach the level of confidence where they feel in the flow and it may not happen every day. Some said that being a confident TPRS teacher requires a certain personality, but a study is needed to support or refute that belief. Anyone can provide comprehensible input.

Experience 8: Collected anecdotal data of student success from TPRS.

Braunstein (2006) elicited anecdotal evidence in the form of student attitude surveys. They reflected the students' perceptions that TPRS helped them to remember vocabulary, to understand the language, and to feel interested and not bored. The adult English language learners were not embarrassed in TPRS class. Webster (2003) relied on anecdotal data to support his perceptions that TPRS had increased student retention and lowered student attrition in his school. A more rigorous study design perhaps may have shown whether those changes happened because of TPRS and that there were no other potentially confounding variables to explain the changes or were due to chance alone.

In the workshops, they generally do five-minute timed writings after instruction to assess whether attendees are picking up the language. Many teachers, afterwards, continue to have their students demonstrate their writing fluency in that way. Other teachers collect evidence such as attitude surveys, test scores, or active questioning but most TPRS teachers tend to assess whether students are mastering what they teach. Many TPRS teachers say they use the method because it works, so they collect evidence.

Experience 9: Knew about and discussed language acquisition theory.

Ten Group A teachers and eight Group B teachers discussed second language acquisition theory in their interviews. The writings of Asher (1988, 1996), Krashen (1981, 1982), and Krashen and Terrell (1983) had explained second language acquisition theory. Ray and Seeley's (1997) first edition of their book on TPRS reflected those theoretical foundations from the early beginnings of the method up to the present day, through seven editions of *Fluency Through TPR Storytelling: Achieving Real Language Acquisition in School*. There were five hypotheses described in those early books, but recently Krashen (2015) has been referring to them collectively as the Comprehension Hypothesis, writing that "language acquisition is the result of understanding messages, or receiving comprehensible input" (p. 168) in his theory.

Not only are language acquisition theory and brain research findings in the TPRS workshops, but during the interview process I noticed that the majority of TPRS teachers have received additional training and have knowledge, both practical and theoretical, which informs their teaching practices, but few Group C study participants were aware of the thinking behind the methods they use. Group A teachers were the most informed.

Experience 10: Perceived providing comprehensible input as important.

Ten Group A teachers and eight Group B teachers perceived comprehensible input was important. Krashen (1985) had described comprehensible input as the one essential element for language acquisition. Over time, Krashen (1989, 2004, 2011a) placed an increasing amount of emphasis on reading. He changed the name of the input hypothesis (Krashen, 1985) to the compelling input hypothesis (Krashen, 2011b). Compelling input was more than just interesting. Citing Csikszentmihalyi's (1990, 1997) concept of being in the flow, Krashen (2015) wrote that "optimal language acquisition puts the language acquirer in a state of flow, a state of mind in which only the activity exists" (p. 169) and readers forgot it was a foreign language while wrapped up in a compelling story. Those ideas were incorporated into the evolving TPRS methodology as well (Ray & Seely, 2015), plus brain-friendly instruction.

As I mentioned above, experienced TPRS teachers are generally aware of theory.

Experience 11: Discussed brain research as supporting TPRS.

While all ten Group A teachers discussed brain research as being supportive of TPRS, only three Group B teachers did. Tate (2016) had pointed out in her book by the title of *Worksheets Don't Grow Dendrites* that filling in worksheets, a typical activity in traditional legacy classrooms, was not an effective strategy for engaging the brain. TPRS workshop handouts used by Coxon (2017), Ray (2015), and Tatum-Johns (2010), among others included some practical teaching applications derived from brain research studies that informed the TPRS methodology (Asher, 2012; Jensen & Snider, 2013; Medina, 2014; Sousa, 2017; Tate, 2016; Zadina, 2014).

When I first attended a TPRS workshop six years ago, I had very little knowledge of brain research. However, many TPRS teachers appeared to have training and knowledge well beyond the TPRS workshop and conference coverage.

Experience 12: Talked about teaching for mastery as part of TPRS.

All ten Group A participants discussed 'mastery' in TPRS as being the daily goal of instruction. That contrasted with different from the bell-shaped curve concept where the bulk of scores were expected to fall in the middle, only a few students were expected to excel, and others are expected to fail. Ray (2016) discussed his application of teaching for mastery, one sentence at a time, and not moving on until everyone who was trying to learn it did. In TPRS, the teacher set a pace that everyone could keep up with without leaving others behind. Ray (2016) said he was influenced by Hunter's (1982) book on *Mastery Teaching* and Hunter cited Bloom's (1968, 1971) ideas on mastery learning.

Blaine Ray, the founder of TPRS, was heavily influenced by teaching for mastery and its principles are evident in daily TPRS lessons. Teachers are encouraged to teach one sentence at a time, with repetitive questioning, review, dramatization, fun, and constant formative assessment to check that all students are understanding nearly every statement made in the target language. The emphasis is not on covering or finishing anything but rather on comprehending messages in context through the target language.

Experience 13: Reported experiencing support from students.

Both study participant groups of teachers reported receiving support from students. Whaley (2009) described her own experiences using TPRS which included receiving support from her students who were learning Russian in class. She also received support from colleagues online. Neubauer (2015) experienced some 'pushback' from resistant students, but reported that she worked to earn their support.

The research and interviews indicated that all students can learn through TPRS, but every moment in class counts. There is an effort not to waste any time at all, so ironically the students who have tended to resist TPRS the most have been the previous top students. They have been successful by learning the day's objectives but have rarely engaged from bell to bell. TPRS students are taught to respond to every statement or question the teacher makes. Students who have not worked that hard in class before often resist. TPRS people talk about the 4 percenters, those students who were successful in school and received good grades, but they may not have had to pay attention all the time. Most of the students, however, engage with TPRS if the instruction interests them.

Experience 14: Reported experiencing support from parents.

In this study, all ten teachers in Group A experienced some support from parents, but only one Group B study participant mentioned receiving any parental support when using TPRS. Eight Group A TPRS teachers also met with resistance from parents. In the literature, Whaley (2009) wrote that she received support from parents.

Resistance or complaints from parents can cause teachers concern, but support can be very encouraging. Many TPRS teachers appreciated the supportive parents.

Experience 15: Reported experiencing support from administrators.

Ten teachers from Group A experienced some support from administrators compared to four in Group B and two recalled receiving direct administrator resistance. Three administrators with Group A went to a TPRS workshop, but none did from the other group in this study. From the literature, Taulbee (2008) mentioned that some teachers had skeptical administrators who were sometimes resistant to TPRS. Kirby (2012), who was a principal conducting a research project, observed one TPRS teacher in his study and reported mixed, but mostly positive reactions to what he observed in class.

I believe that administrators may not always be aware of the impact they have on teachers. Since TPRS has been a bottom-up, grass roots movement, the method may be more likely to have entered a school by a teacher attending a workshop than by an administrator introducing a new methodology. If not all the teachers are on board with TPRS, and if there is a set curriculum with closely articulated lockstep curricula in place, TPRS may never get off the ground. It fares better when there is academic freedom or active administrator support, but few participants' administrators attended a workshop. Administrators may need to know about the TPRS paradigm when evaluating teachers. A document has been sent to Charlotte Danielson by TPRS teachers for her perusal.

Experience 16: Encountered obstacles or resistance when using TPRS.

All participants in this study from both Groups A and B encountered obstacles and met with some resistance to TPRS. Seven Group A teachers and six from Group B were somewhat self-resistant (did not buy in) in that they struggled with whether to accept the philosophical paradigm shift from what Krashen (2015) called the Skill-Building Hypothesis to the Comprehension Hypothesis. Watson (2009) had heard disagreements among colleagues about the method, so she conducted her own empirical research study to compare the effectiveness of a traditional approach with TPRS. She found evidence to support that TPRS was effective at the beginner level. Pippins heard resistant colleagues doubt whether the method was effective with upper levels or for long periods of time, so Pippins and Krashen (2016) did a longitudinal study of TPRS use culminating in an AP course and found that TPRS students did as well or better than the national average, without receiving any grammar instruction for three years.

As noted above, all 20 Group A and B study participants encountered obstacles and resistance, but some decided to use TPRS while others rejected it. It is difficult to say definitively why that is the case because so much depends upon a few people in any given educational setting and whether they support or resist TPRS. Teachers who are not required to coordinate their teaching with others may be more free to teach as they like, but without supportive colleagues to work with, TPRS teaching may be difficult to sustain. Many TPRS teachers join online PLCs and regard those members who may be like-minded more as their colleagues than they do other world language teachers in their own schools.

My own TPRS story may not be a common one. I have been learning about TPRS for seven years now, trying to study other people's experiences with the method, remain neutral on the issues, and refrain from judging others. I am a lone wolf in my own public school district, where I am the only TPRS teacher. I have attended several workshops and conferences, purchased many materials and DVDs of people teaching using the method, and I attend a PLC that meets once a month at different schools in a tristate area, plus the trainings they provide. Most TPRS teachers have a support system of some type to encourage one another, share materials, and offer moral support or else they eventually stop using the method. Some teachers leave the method and return to it when their circumstances change. I wonder whether TPRS will be more accepted if educators, both teachers and administrators, become aware of the research that supports the TPRS method, knowledgeable of second language acquisition research, and more administrators buy in. In this age of internet communication, TPRS has become more available to people with computers. At the most recent workshop I attended, about half of the teachers there said they first heard about TPRS online, and their curiosity brought them to a workshop. Whether that results in more or less resistance remains to be seen.

Research Question 2

What did high school teachers trained in TPRS, who decided not to use the method in their language classrooms, perceive as obstacles to its use? Teachers perceived that there were 12 obstacles to using TPRS. The obstacles included:

Obstacle 1: Insufficient training.

Taulbee (2008) discussed how difficult it was to learn all the TPRS skills. Slavic (2007, 2008, 2014, 2015) and Waltz (2015 wrote books to help teachers learn more about TPRS beyond the first workshop. Taulbee (2008) perceived that one workshop was just not enough for most teachers new to the method to master it. However, only three Group B teachers, out of ten, attended a weeklong national conference, and no Group B teachers reported receiving ongoing training. Group B participants perceived their TPRS teaching skills remained underdeveloped.

I agree that insufficient training is an obstacle. Since the TPRS skills are many, they take time and training to learn.

Obstacle 2: Underdeveloped TPRS teaching skills.

Nine of the ten Group B teachers found the TPRS teaching skills were difficult to learn in the beginning, yet only three reported working to improve those skills. Oliver (2012) mentioned that she had difficulty learning all the skills at first and that they were underdeveloped at the time she conducted her college TPRS study. One skill some teachers found challenging was maintaining class management when using TPRS.

While some people learn the TPRS skills faster than others, some have said it takes up to five years to fully develop them.

Obstacle 3: Classroom management difficulties.

Nine out of ten in Group B found classroom management more difficult when using TPRS, yet none of them reported that they were working to improve their classroom management skills. Roof and Kreutter (2010) reported having discipline difficulties in middle school when using TPRS during the interactive story sessions due to disruptive student responses and highly-engaged students, so they modified their TPRS approach. In his book on TPRS strategies, Slavic (2015) discussed eight classroom management techniques. Ray and Seely (2010) added an appendix on classroom management with suggestions from four TPRS teachers included in their book.

Four Group A teachers perceived classroom management was more difficult when using TPRS compared to nine in Group B. One French teacher said it was much easier to manage class because the students were never bored with TPRS, but others have said that since the method encourages active engagement that some students never calm down. As in any class, clear expectations must be established and there must be techniques in place to bring the students back from loud, active, engagement.

Obstacle 4: Resistance from other people.

Six teachers from Group B experienced some resistance from students when they used or tried out the TPRS method. Six teachers from Group B encountered resistance from other world language teaching colleagues. Two Group B study participants met with direct resistance from administrators. No Group B teachers reported any parental discord. At least five studies, articles, or books from the literature review for this study mentioned that teachers had encountered obstacles or met with resistance from people (Black, 2012; Espinoza, 2015; Oliver, 2013; Neubauer, 2015; Slavic, 2015).

People can get in the way of TPRS use, especially those unfamiliar with the method, its philosophical foundations, second language acquisition research, brain research, and people unfamiliar with the ACTFL standards and guidance.

Obstacle 5: Curriculum concerns.

All ten Group B teachers cited curriculum as an obstacle to using TPRS. Lichtman (2015) pointed out that among the concerns that kept some teachers from using TPRS were curricular issues. Some traditional teachers wanted to see a larger role for grammar and culture study and immersion program instructors preferred a smaller role for translation. Lichtman (2015) recommended adding more culture into the stories. The TPRS goal for first language use was 10% or lower because 90% (ACTFL, 2012) target language use reflected in the TPRS goal to provide comprehensible input in the language. Webster (2003) developed TPRS curricula and Espinoza (2015) asked three TPRS teachers about their experiences developing curricula consistent with TPRS principles.

Move away from academic freedom and the need to articulate curricula both vertically and horizontally have blocked many would be TPRS teachers from using the method. As one Group B teacher said, "Go along to get along." On the other hand, if an entire department moves toward TPRS together, there is a greater chance for success. TPRS has a different approach to curriculum development than many school districts do. Most schools tend to equate a curriculum with a textbook, but TPRS focuses on teaching high frequency vocabulary and fluency structures, so textbooks are not needed. That logic was refuted by Kirby (2012) who felt that it was unprofessional not to use a text.

Obstacle 6: Wanting to cover a broader vocabulary.

All ten Group B teachers were concerned that TPRS limited vocabulary exposure in favor of covering fewer vocabulary for longer retention rather than cover the longer lists of words found in traditional textbooks. Informed by different philosophical frameworks or paradigms (Krashen, 2015), TPRS sheltered vocabulary, but not grammar. In traditional teaching, textbooks took the opposite approach by limiting grammar exposure but not vocabulary. A review of textbooks used in most language classrooms showed that typically first-year courses limit verbs to the present tense, but in TPRS classrooms all tenses were used as they naturally came up in conversations. Since Ray and Seely's (1998) second edition of their book on TPRS, the method has limited the number of new vocabulary in each lesson or used what they at that time called 'guide words' (Joe Neilson's terminology) that TPRS teachers would ensure were repeated often in multiple contexts to guide students toward long-term retention. The traditional teachers tended to use the vocabulary published by the textbook companies which were thematic or topical, whereas TPRS taught high-frequency vocabulary based on Davies' (2006) research which produced a list of the words most often used in spoken and written contexts in the real world of the language being studied.

The differences in philosophy and approach regarding the teaching of vocabulary, whether broad or narrow, shallow or deep, and where the words were obtained, resurfaced as an issue often in the interview data, as did disagreements regarding textbooks and grammar. In short, TPRS limits the number of vocabulary words taught, but does not shelter grammar or verb tenses. In contexts where a huge number of low frequency vocabulary are required for teachers to cover, TPRS may not survive.

Obstacle 7: Textbook grammar.

As mentioned above, an obstacle to TPRS use was grammar. Group B study participants reported that they were required to teach grammar and from a prescribed textbook. TPRS teachers generally did not use a textbook or limit the grammar used in class. All ten Group B study participants mentioned that textbooks and grammar were both obstacles to using TPRS for them. Kirby (2012) was surprised that the TPRS teacher in the group of teachers he studied did not use a textbook at all, yet Kirby's observations were that the TPRS-taught students were highly engaged, and he perceived they were learning. However, as a principal, Kirby found it unacceptable there was no textbook being used, and there was no direct explicit grammar instruction in TPRS.

There simply are not any studies that have demonstrated that grammar is acquired in the order it is presented in any textbook, yet many teachers are required to teach the grammar from a textbook. On the other hand, ACTFL has not endorsed any textbook.

Obstacle 8: A lack of appropriate prepared materials.

Nine out of ten Group B study participants mentioned the lack or shortage of appropriate materials was an obstacle for them to use TPRS. B9 pointed out that in her situation, the teachers in the world language department decided on which textbook series to use largely based on the number of ancillaries that came with the textbook because they lacked preparation time. Highly-skilled TPRS teachers do not always require any materials at all, but rather based their lessons on classroom interactions with students in the target language (Hedstrom, 2012, 2014, 2015; Rowan, 2013; Slavic, 2015). There were teachers who said they wanted to use TPRS and they wanted pre-prepared materials created with TPRS principles in mind that they could use with minimal preparation time.

Since time is the enemy because there never seems to be enough of it, for many people, lack of time to prepare lessons results in teachers wanting to pull prepared materials off the shelf. For those people, a lack of appropriate materials can be a devastating obstacle. On the other hand, several experienced TPRS teachers have taught their best lessons with no materials. They taught one sentence at a time, involved their students in an engaging or compelling topic, and made the input comprehensible.

Obstacle 9: Issues over first language use.

All Group B participants had some issue about the proper amount of usage of the first language in TPRS, either too little or too much. Grammar-oriented teachers sometimes may have spoken too much first language, but immersion program teachers advocated no first language use, wherever possible. Lichtman (2014) mentioned that some teachers had concerns over how much translation was being used in TPRS classes. If the first language was used too often, then the target language would not have acquired, per Krashen's (1985, 2006) Comprehensible Input Hypothesis.

Given that only comprehended messages (intake) in the target language trigger acquisition processes, most of the talk heard in class should be in the language being taught, if teaching for proficiency is the goal. However, some translation may be helpful for establishing meaning or checking for comprehension or else the student may only be hearing noise. Immersion under those circumstances is really more like submersion. To me, the ACTFL (2012) guideline of 90% target language use is probably about right for most students who hope to acquire a language in a classroom setting. Too much first language use cannot create an acquisition-rich environment. Of course, the teacher must have a command of the target language to be able to speak 90% of the time in it and be skilled in making the input comprehensible, repetitive, and interesting to students.

Obstacle 10: Teacher confidence.

Nine of ten Group B participants perceived teacher confidence was an obstacle to TPRS use and that the skills were difficult to master in the beginning. Only three said they improved their TPRS teaching skills in part due to only six of them attending any follow-up training beyond the first workshop and none of them reported they received ongoing professional development in TPRS. Two Group B teachers did say they felt in the 'flow' (Csikszentmihalyi, 1997) at least once when trying out the method with their students in class, but did not feel they could sustain that confident feeling over time. Clarcq (2015) described the TPRS journey as one of growing confidence along the way.

Having at least enough confidence in oneself to provide comprehensible input to the students is definitely a requirement for language to be acquired. Confidence in one's TPRS skills allows the instructor to pay more attention to student needs interpersonally.

Obstacle 11: Planning time.

Nine Group B teachers said the lack of adequate planning time was an obstacle to using TPRS. Slavic (2014) provided six skills for getting started in providing input that students could comprehend and ten activities to do before attempting storytelling, or story asking, to address the challenges of early skill development and a lack of planning time. Ray and Seely (2015) listed publishers who had TPRS materials and resources available for purchase to address the challenge of limited planning time for lesson development.

The amount of planning time varies from person to person. One teacher who conducts TPRS workshops spends his planning period learning another language. He teaches in the high school during the day, college classes at night, is active in his family's home life, and serves on several professional committees. He plans very little, but it took him five years, he said, to improve his TPRS teaching skills to the point where teaching was not like work to him, but more like play. He co-constructs his TPRS stories with his students, so that they feel some ownership. He said he's in the flow every single class now. Moat people probably need more planning time than that, but it is not an absolute.

Obstacle 12: High energy demands of storytelling.

Eight of ten Group B study participants perceived that there were high energy demands for storytelling and they were an obstacle to its use. In a mixed-methods study, Watson (2008) compared a TPRS teacher with a highly-regarded teacher who taught from a textbook. Among the data sources were classroom observations. Watson found that the TPRS teacher asked between four and eight questions per minute in Spanish, but the textbook teacher did not ask students any questions at all on the days when Watson observed his classes. The textbook teacher did use book chapter vocabulary eleven times per class period, but not repeatedly. Since Watson's (2008) study, TPRS workshop presenters have encouraged teachers to ask at least 4-8 questions per minute which helped explain why some teachers perceived there were high energy demands of the method. Examples of high energy teaching came in the active TPRS demonstrations given at some workshops (i.e., Coxon, 2017; Ray, 2015, 2016; Tatum-Johns, 2010).

Most of the interviewees agreed that TPRS requires high energy from the teacher, but some people disagree. It depends upon how the individual teacher runs each class.

Research Question 3

What techniques did high school language teachers using a traditional approach perceive as effective for promoting student success in learning to comprehend and speak the language being taught?

Group C study participants were selected and interviewed specifically to provide information used to answer the third research question. The selection criteria included having not been trained in TPRS and having no experience using the method. For the purposes of this study, the word 'techniques' was interpreted in the broad sense. The 'techniques' included activities, approaches, methods, strategies, experiments, computer models, applications, counseling, presentations, and tasks used to teach language in class. There were numerous techniques which traditional teachers perceived to be effective in their classrooms which were reported as results in Chapter IV. It was recommended that teachers consider each 'technique' in terms of what would fit their needs within their own educational contexts and belief systems. However, for this study, the techniques they identified were analyzed in terms of whether they (1) were already part of TPRS, (2) fell philosophically outside of the TPRS paradigm, or (3) fell within the paradigm. Only those techniques that fell within the paradigm were considered for recommendation to be incorporated into the method, provided they were implemented within TPRS principles.

Some of the techniques perceived as effective by traditional teachers which were already part of TPRS, and therefore did not need to be added to the method, included critical thinking, using realia, teaching culture in the target language, authentic materials, reading skills, translations to assess comprehension, brief explanations of grammar and culture, images, pictures, cartoons, skits, acting out scenes, arts, artists, painting, crafts, drawing, interviews, conversations, inductive and deductive reasoning tasks with brief explanations, and brainstorming. Brief warm-ups, Quick Start Review (QSR), story reviews, modeling, variety, descriptions, seeding vocabulary, using manipulatives, little balls, using props, stuffed animals, establishing discipline and rapport, and setting clear expectations were mentioned as effective, but were already part of the TPRS method. Other types of activities and techniques discussed as effective by Group C participants included mixing domains such as psycho-motor, cognitive, social, and affective, in a multi-sensory approach. Those included listening activities, graphic organizers, Total Physical Response (TPR), using gestures to connect words to movements, music, raps, combining elementary and secondary approaches in language class while providing age-appropriate activities, scaffolding, and using alternative assessments. In addition, among others, techniques already part of the TPRS method included differentiated instruction, asking a variety of types of questions, role plays, discussing topics of compelling interest to students, allowing for student choice when possible, and creating an overall classroom climate conducive to learning and acquiring the target language.

Techniques mentioned by Group C teachers which fell outside of the TPRS philosophical paradigm were rejected and not recommended to be part of the method. Among those rejected techniques were out-of-context explicitly taught grammar drills from traditional textbooks or worksheets, the rote memorization of vocabulary lists, memory tricks, and decontextualized grammatical analyses discussed in the first language. Tasks requiring forced output, beyond the learner's developmental stage, were rejected, as were homework assignments beyond the student's ability. Any technique which involved lengthy discussion in the first language which interfered with the TPRS goal of providing comprehensible input in the target language 90% of the time was rejected. Techniques which aimed to prepare students for taking tests of isolated, discrete point grammatical features were considered outside the paradigm and were rejected.

The techniques which Group C study participants perceived as effective were considered for method inclusion, provided they fell within the TPRS paradigm, assuming they were properly applied as informed by TPRS theory (Krashen, 2015) and the TPRS principles described in Ray and Seely (2015). Among those techniques were interpretive meaning-making listening and reading activities, interactional question and answer (Q&A) sessions on a variety of topics, and student presentations provided the language skills required did not exceed the learner's developmental readiness. Those three techniques were examples of the three modes (interpretive, interactional, and presentational) that were promoted by the American Council on the Teaching of Foreign Languages (ACTFL, 2012), a professional organization of world language teachers that developed the standards for world language teaching.

There were techniques and activities perceived as effective by traditional teachers which have not always been included in TPRS classes (Kirby, 2012) included discussions of cultural information, connections with other academic disciplines, contrastive comparisons between languages, and community involvement. Both ACTFL (2012) and some Group C teachers expressed that standards-based instruction was meant to go beyond communication skills.

Group C study participants perceived the potential of using technology to improve world language instruction and they perceived some focused attention and explicit grammar had important roles to play in that instruction. Some of the 'new technologies' teachers perceived as effective included interactive computer programs such as *Duolingo* and *Nearpod*, technology applications such as *Translator* and *Speak and Translate*, and online learning centers such as *Quizlet*. Some traditional teachers in this study perceived the *Collins Writing System* (2008) was an effective tool and technique for providing some focused grammar attention on student written tasks, without overwhelming students.

The following four recommendations below were made to consider incorporating into the method, based on Group C input for the third research question. They could fit within the TPRS paradigm and principles which were discussed throughout this study. Those four recommendations were listed below for consideration for method inclusion.

Recommendation 1.

Consider adding additional techniques for aligning instruction with the three modes of learning promoted by the American Council on the Teaching of Foreign Languages (ACTFL, 2012): Interpretive, interpersonal, and presentational.

Cox (2015) discussed a position statement from her state's Commissioner and Deputy of Education. The statement required that learner assessments in world language were to include the interpretive, interpersonal, and presentation modes of communication. Those three were the modes promoted in the ACTFL (1999, 2000, 2012) literature. TPRS typically included more interpretive and interpersonal modes than presentational because it is a comprehension-based method. However, provided the speaking and writing tasks are at the student's level of proficiency and developmental readiness, there is no problem.

Recommendation 2.

Consider adding more new techniques for teaching to the five ACTFL standards of communication, cultures, connections, comparisons, and communities.

The five standards were first developed in the National Standards in Foreign Language Education Project (1999). They were later published by the ACTFL (1999, 2000, 2012), a professional organization of national and international world language teachers, education specialists, and administrators. Kirby (2012) found a disconnect in the perceptions and practices regarding the standards. All but one of the world language teachers he studied perceived they were teaching to the standards, but he discovered that they "were unfamiliar with the proper definitions" (p. 157). Kirby concluded, through multiple data sources including questionnaires, observations, and interviews, that most of the teachers were not implementing the standards, so he recommended mandatory in-service training to correct that disconnect.

The lone TPRS teacher in Kirby's (2012) study, given the pseudonym of Don Quixote, said that he did not even attempt to teach the standards, but ironically Kirby found through direct observation of Don Quixote's classes that his instruction complied with and was in line with most of the standards, despite his open disdain for them. Kirby's (2012) findings and conclusions from his study supported a personal communication received by Kirby from the director of ACTFL, that there was "both a lack of knowledge and an unwillingness at multiple levels to implement" (p. 178) the five standards. There was additional evidence in the professional literature that the standards were not being met. In an analysis of TPRS through an ACTFL lens, Rapstine (2003) found the method inadequately covered the standard of culture. Sievek (2009) recommended modifying the TPRS method to better align with the five standards.

Ray and Seely (1998) admitted that for them the Communication standard was the most important use of class time. Some TPRS teachers do a better job than others of infusing culture into the stories, but it can be done. With content-based language teaching becoming more popular, there may be innovative ways of teaching academic content while language is acquired. Comparisons between the target and first language can be done, but with the limitation that the total amount of talk time be less than 10%. Where TPRS falls short lies especially in the Community standard. Positive ways to accomplish this should be explored.

Recommendation 3.

Consider applying new technologies for providing comprehensible input in context. Care should be taken to ensure that the input provided to students is interesting or compelling, repetitive, and can be made more comprehensible through the technology.

Black's (2012) study was situated within an interactive socio-cultural theoretical (SCT) framework in which teacher participants repositioned themselves and constructed their changing personal and professional identities as they interacted in an online professional learning community (PLC) video study group. Among the topics they discussed involved looking for ways to learn about and through new technologies about how to provide comprehensible input through online, preferably interactive, student resources. The use of those resources was recommended to be consistent with the Comprehension Hypothesis (Krashen, 2015) theoretical paradigm and TPRS teaching principles (Ray & Seely, 2015).

In my opinion, if there is a failure to use the new developing technologies, teaching languages may prove difficult to sustain. There must be new and unexplored ways to provide repetitive, interesting, and comprehensible input in context using them.

Some Group C study participants generally used several applications to facilitate or supplement their instruction.

Recommendation 4.

Consider 'some focused error correction' and explicit attention to form, at some point in the language program, perhaps for upper-level writing development, within the constraints of the TPRS paradigm and the principles of TPRS. In my opinion, any attention to grammar or form should be provided within a meaningful, communicative context. Teachers should be careful not to raise the student's affective filter and to follow the ACTFL (2012) guideline of at least 90% target language use by both teachers and students to create an acquisition-rich, near immersion experience in the classroom.

There were differing views on error correction in the literature review. Truscott (1996, 1999, 2007) found that students who received feedback on their papers rarely incorporated that feedback into subsequent writings they produced. Pippins and Krashen (2016) did not advocate error correction, but others did. For example, Cantoni (1999) was in favor of some sort of focused error correction for some learners, who may have wanted or needed more explicit feedback than others. Oliver (2012) found that her college students were willing and wanting to correct errors in their written compositions. Nguyen (et al., 2014) provided Chinese learners with clear, corrective feedback on their written work. Davidheiser (1996, 2001, 2002) included grammar study groups at the university in what he considered were student-centered TPRS classrooms. De Vlaming (2013) and others included grammar study and corrective feedback with TPRS.

On the other hand, Krashen (1992, 1993, 2013) pointed out his perception that the effects of corrective feedback and grammar teaching were only peripheral. Krashen

(2015) described the role of conscious learning as limited, but he admitted that it could "be used to occasionally make input more comprehensible" (p. 169). TPRS has always included grammar teaching, but in different ways than in traditional classrooms (Ray, 2005) or in legacy methods. In one of Ray's (1993) early books, *Teaching Grammar Communicatively*, he (1993) described his communicative approach for including grammar through implicit instruction, which has since then been integrated into the story lessons (Ray, 2006; Ray, 2013; Ray and Seely, 2015).

VanPatten (1996, 2002, 2004) discussed how some direct and explicit grammar instruction has been incorporated in processing instruction (PI) while providing input in meaning-based, supportive, classroom interactional contexts. Foster (2011) found positive effects for PI instruction. Even though VanPatten (2016) realized that explicit knowledge could not become implicit knowledge, an incidental focus on form could help learners notice the forms in context and how they affected meaning, as Long (1991) had previously pointed out. In that seminal paper, Long (1991) proposed an incidental 'focus on form' as an instructional design feature within an otherwise communicative approach. Kaufmann (2005), Ellis (2012), and Foster (2011) argued that there was still a place for an explicit focus on form and some focused error correction within today's proficiency-based and communicative classrooms. As VanPatten (2004, 2017) pointed out, the decisions on making corrections or any grammar focus should be highly selective, principled, and well-grounded in second language acquisition (SLA) research.

Summary and Organization of the Study

This dissertation study included five chapters. Chapter I introduced the study, provided the background, defined the terms, and stated the problem and purpose of the study. Chapter II described the theoretical foundations and the conceptual frameworks that informed the study, reviewed the professional literature and related research that situated the study by identifying a gap in the literature that the study was designed to fill. Chapter III explained the research methodology, design, and procedures for carrying out the study. Chapter IV presented the data analysis and results of the study. Chapter V summarized the study, discussed implications, made recommendations for further research, and drew conclusions.

Implications for Practice

The findings of this study had implications for researchers, teachers, and administrators concerned with making decisions informed by second language acquisition theory and grounded in research. The literature review for this study provided evidence from a growing body of research studies that the Teaching Proficiency through Reading and Storytelling (TPRS) method of world language instruction is effective in classrooms at the infant, elementary, secondary, university, and adult levels.

The method was theoretically informed by the Comprehension Hypothesis (Krashen, 2015) which explained that second languages were acquired through understanding messages in the language being studied, which has happened in worlds both outside and inside the classroom. In a sense, TPRS was found to be a method that provided a near-immersion environment within the classroom that mirrored in some ways the natural way people have always acquired languages in the real world. Applying that theoretical foundation to world language classes, the instructor's job has become providing students with comprehensible input at least 90% of the time, in accordance with the national standards of the American Council on the Teaching of Foreign

Languages (ACTFL, 2012), the professional organization of world language teachers. TPRS classrooms have done that through interactive communication in the classroom and by personalizing the lessons to make them more interesting or compelling to students.

The principles of the TPRS method included providing that input through strategies compatible with brain research (Jensen & Snider, 2013; Medina, 2014; Sousa, 2017; Tate, 2016; Zadina, 2014), through multisensory activities that promoted long-term learning (Asher, 2012), and by using highly engaging instructional strategies (Marzano, Pickering, & Heflebower, 2011; Slavic, 2014, 2015) informed by and grounded in second language acquisition research (VanPatten, 2016, 2017).

Being aware of the sixteen common experiences lived by TPRS teachers using the method had implications for making informed decisions regarding world language instruction in schools. Those experiences included being unsatisfied with student achievement before finding TPRS, attending workshops, conferences, and developing new teaching skills, to include using gestures and other skills that teachers new to TPRS reported as being difficult to learn. The implications of these experiences for administrators was for them to support, find funding, and provide time for ongoing professional development and planning. Other experiences included feeling confident after acquiring those new teaching skills and having their students succeed through TPRS. They had anecdotal data of success, but an implication was that additional data be obtained to provide empirical evidence of that success. TPRS teachers that were interviewed for this study knew about and discussed second language acquisition theory, perceived that providing comprehensible input to students was important, and knew some connections between brain research and TPRS. They experienced support and success from students, parents, and administrators. The implication there was for continuing that support and extending it to other teachers learning the methodology. Despite experiencing success, they also encountered obstacles and resistance when using TPRS.

This study found twelve obstacles to using TPRS which resulted in some teachers deciding not to use the method. The implication was since the method was found to be effective, the known obstacles should be eliminated or reduced in their impact. Those obstacles included insufficient training, underdeveloped TPRS teaching skills, classroom management difficulties, resistance from people, curriculum concerns, vocabulary, textbook grammar, a lack of appropriate materials, issues over first language use, low teacher confidence, insufficient planning time, and the high-energy demands of TPRS. The implication of this finding, taken together, was that steps be taken to address each concern with the goal of removing obstacles that get in the way of student learning.

In addition to the above implications derived from the interview data of both TPRS teachers from Group A and TPRS rejecters from Group B, there were also implications derived from the interviews of non-TPRS teachers with no experience or training in TPRS. Among the implications from Group C data was for educators to keep up with changes in the new technologies, to be aware of the professional guidance from language teachers' associations, such as ACTFL (2012), and to provide instruction using techniques in the modes of communication and techniques that fit within the national standards. Four recommendations were made to improve the TPRS method by using techniques and approaches perceived to be effective by non-TPRS teachers, as discussed above. In sum, this study provided insight into the common lived experiences of TPRS teachers, obstacles to the method's use, and techniques recommended to improve the method. These insights enabled educators to make informed decisions in practice.

Recommendations for Further Research

During the conduct of this research study, a model of TPRS teacher experience was beginning to form with nine emerging themes: unsatisfied, training, paradigm, beginning, obstacles, success, sustaining, leadership, and decisions. Interview protocols were not drafted to ask the study participants probing questions about those themes, so the model remained underdeveloped, lacked specified dimensions, and it was unclear how the elements or themes might have interacted with each other. I recommend that a study be designed with the goal of developing a model or some type of lens for viewing TPRS teacher experience.

Black (2012) conducted the first case study viewing TPRS teacher experience through a socio-cultural lens when he studied an online professional learning community (PLC). I recommend that more studies examine successful PLCs and share their findings in that growing area of ongoing professional development and support.

One finding of this study was that all 20 study participants from Groups A and B encountered obstacles, resistance, or challenges when using TPRS. Identifying how those obstacles may have been overcome by some teachers was beyond the scope of this study. I recommend a follow-up study to explore coping strategies.

Some of this study's participants suggested that there may be a TPRS teacher personality. I recommend that a study be designed to explore that notion due to the interest expressed by some teachers. There may be some personalities who find this method appealing, but with practice and training perhaps anyone can provide the contextualized, compelling, repetitive, and comprehensible input needed for students to acquire an additional language in class.

Conclusions

The purpose of this qualitative study using a quasi-phenomenological approach was to describe the common classroom experiences lived by TPRS teachers, to identify the obstacles to the method's use, and to discover possibilities for improving the method. The data analysis uncovered sixteen common lived experiences of high school TPRS teachers, twelve obstacles to the method's use, and four recommendations were made for improving the method. The study filled a gap in the research because few studies had explored teacher experiences using TPRS or asked why some teachers did or did not adopt or adapt TPRS. Those two groups provided an emic, or insider's view, of TPRS use because those teachers had been trained and had either used the method or at least tried it out in their classrooms. Their reflections helped uncover their experiences using the method and what they perceived the obstacles to its use were.

With existing research that showed the method was effective, the implications of this study's findings were to aim at reducing the impact of the obstacles to using the TPRS method and to provide support for those teachers using this method that has been documented as effective. A third group of teachers was interviewed to provide an etic, or outsider's, view. That group had no training or experience using TPRS, but they did provide their perceptions of which teaching techniques were effective. Those could be incorporated into the evolving method, if they fit the TPRS paradigm and the teachers follow TPRS principles. The researcher made four recommendations from their input for TPRS teachers to consider.

From the literature review, the sixteen common lived experiences of TPRS teachers, the twelve obstacles to using TPRS, and the four recommendations made from this study, this researcher drew the following conclusions. The TPRS method was found to be an effective but challenging teaching method, so teachers who decided to use this method in their teaching deserve to be supported, not resisted. The obstacles and resistance that TPRS teachers faced when using the method need to be removed so that supported teachers can provide quality instruction that is informed by theory, grounded in research, and highly engages the acquirers of additional languages in the world language classrooms of today and tomorrow.

REFERENCES

Alley, D., & Overfield, D. (2008). An analysis of the Teaching Proficiency through Reading and Storytelling (TPRS) method. *Dimension*, 2008, 13-25.

Allwright, R. (1977). Language learning through communication practice. *ELT Documents*, *76*(3). London, UK: British Council.

American Classical League, ACL. (2015). CI presentations, offered at the ACL. The ACL, 860 NW Washington, Blvd., Hamilton, OH 45013.

American Council on the Teaching of Foreign Languages. (ACTFL). (1999, 2012). ACTFL standards and proficiency guidelines. Alexandria, VA: Author.

American Council on the Teaching of Foreign Languages. (ACTFL). (2000). *Standards for foreign language learning: Preparing for the 21st century*. Alexandria, VA: Author.

Association for Middle Level Education (AMLE). (2010). *Research and resources in support of This We Believe: Keys to educating young* adolescents. Westerville, OH: AMLE.

Armstrong, A. (2008). Fun and fluency in Spanish through TPRS. *UW-L Journal of Undergraduate Research*, *XI*, 1-6.

Asher, J. (1965). The Total Physical Response approach to second language learning. *The Modern Language Journal, 53*(1), 3-17.

Asher, J. (1966). The learning strategy of the Total Physical Response: A Review. *The Modern Language Journal, 50*(2), 79.

Asher, J. (1969). The total physical response approach to second language learning. *The Modern Language Journal, 53*(1), 3-17.

Asher, J. (1977). *Learning another language through actions: The complete teacher's guidebook* (1st ed.). Los Gatos, CA: Sky Oaks Productions.

Asher, J. (1988). *Brainswitching* (1st ed.). Los Gatos, CA: Sky Oaks Productions.

Asher, J. (1996). *Learning another language through actions*. Los Gatos, CA: Sky Oaks.

Asher, J. (2000). Strategy for second language learning, VHS, discussed in *Learning another language through actions* (6th ed.). Los Gatos, CA: Sky Oaks.

Asher, J. (2009). *Learning another language through actions: The complete teacher's guidebook* (7th ed.). Los Gatos, CA: Sky Oaks Productions.

Asher, J. (2011). A new note about TPR presented to several hundred language instructors at the International Forum on language teaching in Los Alamitos, CA: *The International Journal of Foreign Language Teaching, 6*(1): 34-35.

Asher, J. (2012). *Brainswitching: Learning on the right side of the brain: Fast, stress-free access to languages, mathematics, science, and much, much more!* (2nd ed.). Los Gatos, CA: Sky Oaks Productions.

Asher, J. J., Kusudo, J. A., & De La Torre, R. (1974). Learning a second language through commands: The second language field test. *The Modern Language Journal, 58*(1), 24-32.

Avant Assessment. (2002). The web-based Standards-based Measurement of Proficiency (STAMP) Test of reading, writing, and speaking. Eugene, OR: The University of Oregon's Center for Applied Second Language Studies (CASLS).

Bakhtin, M. M., & Holquist, M. (1981). *The dialogic imagination: Four essays*. Austin, TX: University of Texas Press.

Bakhtin, M. M., Holquist, M., & Emerson, C. (1986). *Speech genres and other late essays* (1st ed.). Austin, TX: University of Austin Press.

Bamberg, M., & Georgakopoulou, A. (2008). Small stories as a new perspective in narrative and identity analysis. *Text & Talk, 28*(3), 377-396.

Beal, D. (2011). *The correlates of storytelling from the TPRS method of foreign language instruction on anxiety, continued enrollment, and academic success in middle and high school students* (Doctoral dissertation). Available from ProQuest Dissertations and Theses database. (UMI No. 3449943)

Bernal Numpaque, N. R., & García Rojas, M. A. (2010, Jan.-June). TPR Storytelling, a key to speak fluently in English. *Cuadernos de Lingüística Hispánica, 15* (enero-junio), 151-162.

Beyer, F. (2008). *Impact of TPR on the preterit tense in Spanish* (Master's thesis). Available from ProQuest Dissertations and Theses database. (UMI No. 1453782)

Black, N. J. (2012). *Developing dialogic teaching identities through online video study groups* (Doctoral dissertation). Available from ProQuest Dissertations and Theses database. (UMI No. 3524133)

Blanton, M. (2015). *The effect of two foreign language teaching approaches, Communicative Language Teaching (CLT) and Teaching Proficiency through Reading and Storytelling (TPRS), on motivation and proficiency for Spanish III students in high school* (Doctoral dissertation). Available from ProQuest Dissertations and Theses database. (UMI No. 3708358)

Bloom, B. (1968). Learning for mastery. *UCLA Evaluation Comment, 1*(2). Center for Evaluation of Instructional Programs.

Bloom, B. (1971). Mastery learning. In J. H. Block (Ed.), *Mastery learning: Theory and practice* (pp. 47-63). New York, NY: Holt, Rinehart, & Winston.

Braunstein, L. (2006). Adult ESL learners' attitudes toward movement (TPR) and drama (TPR Storytelling) in the classroom. *CATESOL, 18*(1), 7-20.

Breen, M., & Candlin, C. N. (1980). The essentials of a communicative curriculum in language teaching. *Applied Linguistics, 1*(2): 89-112.

Brinkmann, S., & Kvale, S. (2015). *Interviews: Learning the craft of qualitative research interviewing* (3rd ed.). Thousand Oaks, CA: Sage.

Brown, J. M., & Palmer, A. S. (1988). *The listening approach: Methods and materials for applying Krashen's input hypothesis*. New York, NY: Longman.

Brune, K. M. (2004). *Total Physical Response Storytelling: An analysis and application* (Bachelor's thesis). Eugene, OR: University of Oregon.

Bryson, C., & Hand, L. (2007). The role of engagement in inspiring teaching and learning. *Innovations in Education and Teaching International, 44*(4), 349-362.

Bustamante, M. (2009). *Measuring the effectiveness of a TPRS pilot course in Spanish at the 100 college level* (Master's thesis). Available from ProQuest Dissertations and Theses database. (UMI No. 1470219)

Campbell, C. (2016). *Teacher perceptions of fostering student engagement through the use of the TPRS world language instructional method* (Doctoral dissertation). Available from ProQuest Dissertations and Theses database. (UMI No. 10127070)

Canale, M., & Swain, M. (1980). Theoretical bases of communicative approaches to second language teaching and testing. *Applied Linguistics, 1*(1), 1-47.

Canion, M., & Gaab, C. (2008). *Piratas*. Chandler, AZ: TPRS Publishing. The publisher's name was changed to Fluency Matters in 2016.

Cantoni, G. (1999). Using TPR Storytelling to develop fluency and literacy in Native American languages. In Reyner, Cantoni, St. Clair, & Yazzie, *Revitalizing Indigenous Languages*. Flagstaff, Arizona: Northern Arizona University.

Carnegie, D. (1981). *How to win friends and influence people* (Rev. ed.). New York, NY: Simon and Schuster.

Cartford, B. A., Holter Kittok, J., & Lichtman, K. (2015, Oct.). Measuring fluency development in content-based storytelling elementary Spanish instruction. *The International Journal of Foreign Language Teaching, 10*(2), 2-9.

Castro, R. (2010). *TPRS for adults in the ESL classroom: A pilot study comparing Total Physical Response Storytelling with the Grammar-Translation teaching strategy to determine their effectiveness in vocabulary acquisition among English as a Second Language adult learners* (Master's thesis). San Rafael, CA: Dominican University of California.

Chang, M., & Chen, J. (2015). A study on the effectiveness of TPR and TPRS in short-term Chinese language training at the beginner level. International Conference on Information Technologies in Education and Learning (ICITEL). Atlantis Press.

Chen, W., & Looi, C. (2011, June 9). Active classroom participation in a Group Scribbles primary science classroom. *British Journal of Educational Technology (BJET), 42*(4), 676-686.

Chomsky, N. (1965). *Aspects of the theory of syntax*. Cambridge, MA: MIT Press.

Clarcq, L. (2015, Feb. 20). *Your CI journey: Getting stronger every day*. A six-hour training workshop in Teaching with Comprehensible Input (TCI), sponsored by TriState TCI, and hosted at William Penn Charter School, in Philadelphia, PA.

Collins, J. J. (2008). *The Collins writing program: Improving student performance through writing and thinking skills across the curriculum*. West Newbury, MA: Collins Education Associates.

Corbin, J., & Straus, A. (2015). *Basics of qualitative research: Techniques and procedures for developing grounded theory* (4th ed.). Thousand Oaks, CA: Sage.

Cox, S. (2015). *The effect of dialog in the comprehensible input Spanish classroom* (Master's thesis). Available from ProQuest Dissertations and Theses database. (UMI No. 1605091)

Coxon, M. (2017, Jan. 23-24). Handout for a TPRS 2-day workshop held in Essington, PA, near Philadelphia. Eagle Mountain, UT: TPRS Books.

Creswell, J. W. (2013). *Qualitative inquiry and research design* (3rd ed.). Thousand Oaks, CA: Sage.

Crouse, D. (2013). Making the connection: 21st century skills and languages. *The Language Educator, 8.* Retrieved from http://www.actfl.org

Csikszentmihalyi, M. (1990). *Flow: The psychology of optimal experience*. New York, NY: Harper Perennial.

Csikszentmihalyi, M. (1997). *Finding flow: The psychology of engagement with everyday life*. New York, NY: Basic Books, Perseus.

Cubukcu, F. (2014). A synergy between storytelling and vocabulary teaching through TPRS. International Association of Research in Foreign Language Education and Applied Linguistics. *ELT Research Journal, 3*(2), 84-90.

Cummins, J. (1989). Language and literacy acquisition in bilingual contexts. *Journal of Multilingual and Multicultural Development, 10*(1), 17-31.

Davidheiser, J. (1996). Grammar groups in the student-centered classroom. *The Foreign Language Annals, 29*(2), 271-278.

Davidheiser, J. (2001). The ABC's of TPR storytelling. *Dimension, 2001*, 45-53.

Davidheiser, J. (2002, Spring). Teaching German with TPRS. *Die Unterrichtspraxis/Teaching German 35*(1), 25-35. Retrieved from ERIC database.

Davies, M. (2006). *A frequency dictionary of Spanish: Core vocabulary for learners.* New York, NY: Routledge, Taylor & Francis.

Decker, B. (2008). *Body language: The effectiveness of Total Physical Response Storytelling in secondary foreign language instruction.* Saint Paul, MN: Macalester College. Available from www.researchgate.net / www.malester.edu

Demir, S., & Cubukcu, F. (2014). To have or not to have TPRS for preschoolers. *Asian Journal of Instruction, 2*(1), 186-197.

De Vlaming, E. M. (2013). *TPRS in de Duitse les: Onderzoek naar effecten van TPRS op het toepassen van grammatical* (TPRS in the German class: Research into the effects of TPRS applying grammar, Master's thesis). Nijmegen, Netherlands: Hogeschool Arnhem Nijmegen.

Dukes, S. (1984). Phenomenological methodology in the human sciences. *Journal of Religion and Health, 23*(3), 197-203.

Dziedzic, J. (2012, March). A comparison of TPRS and traditional instruction, both with SSR. *The International Journal of Foreign Language Teaching, 7*(2), 4-7.

Egan, K. (1986). *Teaching as story telling: An alternative approach to teaching and curriculum in the elementary school.* Chicago, IL: University of Chicago Press.

Egan, K. (2005). *An imaginative approach to teaching.* San Francisco, CA: Jossey-Bass.

Egan, K. (2008). *The future of education: Reimagining our schools from the ground up.* New Haven, CT: Yale University Press.

Ellis, R. (2008). *The study of second language acquisition* (2nd ed.). Oxford, UK: Oxford University Press.

Ellis, R. (2009). Task-based language teaching: Sorting out the misunderstandings. *International Journal of Applied Linguistics, 19*(3), 222-246.

Ellis, R. (2012). *Language teaching research and language pedagogy.* West Sussex, UK: Wiley-Blackwell.

Eisner, E. W. (1985). *The educational imagination: On the design and evaluation of school programs.* New York, NY: Macmillan.

Espinoza, P. L. (2015). *Three teachers' experiences developing and implementing Teaching Proficiency through Reading and Storytelling (TPRS) curriculum in their world language classes* (Master's thesis). Available from ProQuest Dissertations and Theses database. (UMI No.1605751)

Forward, M., & Ogle, S. (1997). *TPR Storytelling extension activities* and instructor's manual. Fort Worth, TX: Forward and Ogle.

Foster, S. (2011). *Processing instruction and teaching proficiency through reading and storytelling: A study of input in the second language classroom* (Master's thesis). Available from ProQuest Dissertations and Theses database. (UMI No. 1504823)

Gaab, C. (2006, Mar.). TPRS: Evolution or creation? *Language Magazine, 5*(7), 1-6. Available from www.languagemagazine.com and fromwww.tprstorytelling.com

Gaab, C. (2011, Apr.). Multistory construction. http://www.languagemagazine.com

Garcia, R. (1988, 2000). *Instructor's notebook: How to apply TPR for best results* (2nd ed.). Los Gatos, CA: Sky Oaks.

Garczynski, M. (2003). *Teaching proficiency through reading and storytelling: Are TPRS students more fluent in second language acquisition than audiolingual students?* (Master's thesis). Available from ProQuest Dissertations and Theses database. (UMI No. EP30485)

Giorgi, A., Fischer, W. F., & von Eckartsberg, R. (1971). *Duquesne studies in phenomenological psychology, 1*. Pittsburgh, PA: Duquesne University Press.

Gross, S. (2012). TPRS saves the day! Plenary address at the NTPRS conference in Las Vegas, NV [DVD]. Eagle Mountain, UT: Blaine Ray Workshops.

Gurian, M., & Stephens, K. (2004). With boys and girls in mind. *Educational Leadership, 62*(3), 21-26.

Gurian, M., & Stephens, K. (2006, Winter). How boys learn: How are the boys doing? *Educational Horizons,* 87-93.

Hastings, A. J. (1995). The focal skills approach: An assessment. In Eckman et al., *Second language acquisition.* Hillsdale, NJ: Lawrence Erlbaum.

Hatch, J. A. (2002). *Doing qualitative research in education settings.* New York, NY: State University of New York Press.

Hedstrom, B. (2012). *Understanding TPRS.* Available from Brycehedstrom.com

Hedstrom, B. (2014). The special person. *The International Journal of Foreign Language Teaching, 9*(1), 29-31.

Hedstrom, B. (2015, Oct.). Make any student the most interesting person in the room. *The International Journal of Foreign Language Teaching, 10*(2), 55-57.

Holleny, L. E. (2012). *The effectiveness of Total Physical Response Storytelling for language learning with special education students* (Master's thesis). Glassboro, NJ: Rowan University.

Horwitz, E. K. (2008). *Becoming a language teacher: A practical guide to second language learning and teaching.* New York NY: Pearson Education.

Horwitz, E., Horwitz, M., & Cope, J. (1986, Summer). Foreign language classroom anxiety. *The Modern Language Journal, 70*(2), 125-132.

Hunter, M. (1982). *Mastery teaching: Increasing instructional effectiveness in elementary, secondary schools, colleges and universities.* Thousand Oaks, CA: Sage, Corwin.

Hycner, R. H. (1985). Some guidelines for the phenomenological analysis of interview data. *Human Studies, 8*, 279-303.

Jakubowski, A. (2013). *Using visual aids in the secondary language classroom: An action research study on the use of illustrations during TPRS instruction* (Master's thesis). Toledo, OH: The University of Toledo.

Jennings, J. (2009). *Results of a master's thesis comparing two TPRS groups and one control group of Spanish II high school students* (unpublished Master's thesis). Available for reading at Millersville University, PA, Library (special collections).

Jensen, E. (2009). *Super teaching: Over 1000 practical strategies.* Thousand Oaks, CA: Sage, Corwin.

Jensen, E., & Snider, C. (2013). *Turnaround tools for the teenage brain: Helping underperforming students become lifelong learners.* San Francisco, CA: Jossey-Bass.

Johnson, B., & Christensen, L. (2012). *Educational research: Quantitative, qualitative, and mixed methods* (4th ed.). Thousand Oaks, CA: Sage.

Johnson, K. (1982). *Communicative syllabus design and methodology.* Language teaching methodology series. Oxford, UK: Pergamon.

Kaufmann, E. (2005). *Teaching proficiency through reading and storytelling (TPRS): A communicative approach to teaching foreign language* (unpublished Master's thesis). Great Valley, PA: Pennsylvania State University.

Kariuki, P. K., & Bush, E. D. (2008, Nov. 5-7). *The effects of Total Physical Response by Storytelling and the traditional teaching styles of a foreign language in a selected high school.* Paper presented at the Annual Conference of the Mid. South Educational Research Association in Knoxville, TN.

King, K., & Gurian, M. (2006, Sep.). The brain: His and hers. *Educational Leadership, 64*(1), p. 59.

Kirby, P. S. (2012). *Research into the utility of standards in foreign language instruction: A case study of methods used in the high school setting* (Doctoral dissertation). Available from ProQuest Dissertations and Theses database. (UMI No. 3507473)

Kramsch, C. (1987). The proficiency movement: SLA perspectives. *Studies in Second Language Acquisition, 9,* 355-362.

Krashen, S. (1978). The monitor model for second-language acquisition and foreign language teaching. Washington, DC: Center for Applied Linguistics, 1-26.

Krashen, S. (1981). *Second language acquisition and second language learning* (1st ed.). Oxford, UK: Pergamon Press. Out of print. Available at www.sdkrashen.com

Krashen, S. (1982). *Principles and practice in second language acquisition.* Oxford, UK: Pergamon Press. Out of print. Available at www.sdkrashen.com

Krashen, S. (1985). *The input hypothesis: Issues and implications.* Torrance, CA: Laredo.

Krashen, S. (1989). We acquire vocabulary and spelling by reading: Additional evidence for the input hypothesis. *The Modern Language Journal, 73,* 440-464.

Krashen, S. (1992). Under what circumstances, if any, should formal grammar instruction take place? *TESOL Quarterly, 26,* 409-411.

Krashen, S. (1993). The effect of formal grammar teaching: Still peripheral. *TESOL Quarterly, 27,* 722-725.

Krashen, S. (1994). The pleasure hypothesis. In Alatis (Ed.), *Georgetown University roundtable on languages and linguistics* (pp. 299-322). Washington, DC: Georgetown University Press.

Krashen, S. (2002). *Second language acquisition and second language learning* (1st internet ed.). First published in 1981 by Pergamon. Available at sdkrashen.com

Krashen, S. (2003). *Explorations in language acquisition and use: The Taipei lectures*. Portsmouth, NH: Heinemann, Houghton Mifflin Harcourt.

Krashen, S. (2004). *The power of reading* (2nd ed.). Englewood, CO: Libraries Unlimited.

Krashen, S. (2006). Is first language use in the foreign language classroom good or bad? It depends. *The International Journal of Foreign Language Teaching, 2*(1), 9.

Krashen, S. (2007). Extensive reading in English as a foreign language by adolescents and young adults: A meta-analysis. *The International Journal of Foreign Language Teaching, 3*(2), 23-29.

Krashen, S. (2009). *Principles and practice in second language acquisition* (1st internet ed.). Retrieved at http: sdkrashen.com/Principles_and_Practice/Intro.html

Krashen, S. (2011a). *Free voluntary reading*. Santa Barbara, CA: Libraries Unlimited.

Krashen, S. (2011b). The compelling (not just interesting) input hypothesis. *The English Connection* (KOTESOL), *15*(3).

Krashen, S. (2013). *Second language acquisition: Theory, applications, and some conjectures*. New York, NY: Cambridge University Press.

Krashen, S. (2015). Introduction to TPRS theory. In T. Waltz, *TPRS with Chinese characteristics* (pp. 168-171). Albany, NY: Squid for Brains Educational Publishing.

Krashen, S., & Terrell, T. (1983). *The natural approach: Language acquisition in the classroom*. Hayward, CA: Alemany Press and Tappan, NJ: Prentice Hall Regents.

Lantolf, J. (2007). Sociocultural source of thinking and its relevance for second language acquisition. *Bilingualism: Language & Cognition, 10*(1), 31-33.

Lantolf, J. (2009). Knowledge of language in foreign language teacher education. *The Modern Language Journal, 93*(2), 270-274.

Larson, J., Smith, K., & Bach, C. (1998, 2004). Spanish WebCAPE Computer-Adaptive Placement Exam (the CAPE Test). Department of Humanities: Technology and Research Support Center. Provo, UT: Brigham Young University.

Latin Best Practices. (n.d.). https://groups.yahoo.com/neo/groups/latin-bestpractices/info

Lichtman, K. (2012a). Research on TPR Storytelling. In B. Ray & C. Seely, *Fluency through TPR storytelling* (6th ed., pp. 304-311). Berkeley, CA: Command Performance Language Institute.

Lichtman, K. (2012b). *Child-adult differences in implicit and explicit second language learning* (Doctoral dissertation). Available from ProQuest Dissertations and Theses database. (UMI No. 3600697)

Lichtman, K. (2014, Oct.-Nov.). Teaching language through storytelling. *The Language Educator*, 46-47.

Lichtman, K. (2015). Research on TPR Storytelling. In B. Ray & C. Seely, *Fluency through TPR storytelling* (7th ed., pp. 364-379). Berkeley, CA: Command Performance Language Institute.

Lichtman, K. (2016, July 28). TPRS research, presentation, and handout. NTPRS 2016 (National TPR Storytelling conference), in Reno, NV.

Lichtman, K., & Krashen, S. (2013, July 25). Show me the data: Research on TPRS. Presentation at the National Teaching through TPR Storytelling (NTPRS) Conference, in Dallas, TX.

Lightbown and Spada. (2013). *How languages are learned* (4th ed.). Oxford, UK: Oxford University Press.

Liskin-Gasparro, J. (2000). The proficiency movement: Current trends and a view to the future. In O. Kagan & B. Rifkin (Eds.), *The learning and teaching of Slavic languages and cultures* (pp. 9-28). Bloomington, IN: Slavica.

Long, M. (1991). Focus on form: A design feature in language teaching methodology. In DeBot, K., Ginsberg, R., & Kramsch, C. (Eds.), *Foreign language research in cross-cultural perspective* (pp. 39-52). Philadelphia, PA: John Benjamins.

Lunenburg, F. C., & Irby, B. J. (2008). *Writing a successful thesis or dissertation: Tips and strategies for students in the social and behavioral sciences.* Thousand Oaks, CA: Sage, Corwin Press.

MacGowan-Gilhooly, A. (1993). *Achieving fluency in English* (2nd ed.). Dubuque, IA: Kendall Hunt.

Magnan, S. S. (2005). A letter from the editor: Presenting the special issue. *The Modern Language Journal, 89*(3).

Markelz, A. (2016). *Teaching in the moment: With-it teachers use ESP (Engagement, Scanning, Praise).* Alexandria, VA: *ASCD Express, 12*(7).

Marimon Gil, V. (2015). *Is the Teaching Proficiency through Reading and Storytelling (TPRS) approach an efficient methodology for infant education students?* (Master's thesis). Universitat Jaume: UJI.

Marsh, V. (1998). Total Physical Response Storytelling: A communicative approach to language learning. *Learning Languages: The Journal of the National Network for Early Language Learning, 4*(1), 24-27.

Marzano, R. J., Pickering, D. J., & Heflebower, T. (2011). *The highly engaged classroom*. Bloomington, IN: Marzano Research Laboratory.

Maxwell, J. C. (2013). *The 5 levels of leadership*. New York, NY: Hachette Book Group.

McKay, T. (2000). *TPR Storytelling: Especially for children in elementary and middle school*. Los Gatos, CA: Sky Oaks.

Merinnage De Costa, R. M. (2015). *Traditional methods versus TPRS: Effects on introductory French students at a medium-sized public university in the Midwestern United States* (Master's thesis). Available from ProQuest Dissertations and Theses database. (UMI No. 1606293)

Medina, J. (2014). *Brain rules: 12 principles for surviving and thriving at work, home, and school* (2nd ed.). Seattle, WA: Pear Press.

Merriam, S. B. (2009). *Qualitative research: A guide to design and implementation*. San Francisco, CA: Josse-Bass.

Met, M. (1991). Learning language through content: Learning content through language. *Foreign Language Annals, 24*, 281-293.

Met, M. (2004). Improving students' capacity in foreign languages. *Phi Delta Kappan, 86*, 214-219.

Miles, B. (2014). *A phenomenological study of African American middle school students with five or more days of out-of-school suspensions in one academic year* (unpublished Doctoral dissertation). Aston, PA: Neumann University.

Miles, M. B., & Huberman, A. M. (1994). *Qualitative data analysis* (2nd ed.). Thousand Oaks, CA: Sage.

Miller, M. (2011, Nov.). How well do junior high TPRS German students do on the AATG level 2 exam? Answer: Not bad! *The International Journal of Foreign Language Teaching, 7*(1), 10-12.

Mitchell, R., Myles, F., & Marsden, E. (2013). *Second language learning theories* (3rd ed.). New York, NY: Routledge, Taylor & Francis.

Moustakas, C. (1994). *Phenomenological research methods*. London, UK: Sage.

Murray, C. (2014). *Does the introduction of a TPR and a TPRS teaching method into a French 1 classroom positively affect students' language acquisition and student appreciation of the language?* (Master's thesis). Caldwell, NJ: Caldwell College.

National Standards in Foreign Language Education Project. (1999). *Standards for foreign language learning in the 21st century*. Yonkers, NY: Author.

Nguyen, K., Yonghui, W., Stanley, N., & Stanley, L. (2014). Perceptions about storytelling in teaching Chinese as a second/foreign language: Opportunities and challenges. Innovations and Good Practices in Education: Global Perspectives. Hue City, Thailand. *Proceedings of the 7th International Conference on Education Reform (ICER 2014),* 458-467.

Neubauer, D. (2015). Using second language acquisition quotes with students. *The International Journal of Foreign Language Teaching, 10*(2), 47-49.

Nijhuis, R., & Vermaning, L. (2010). *Onderzoek lesmethode TPRS* (Research on the teaching method TPRS, thesis). Tilburg, Netherlands: Fontys Hogeschool te Tilburg.

Noels, K. A., Pelletier, L. G., Clement, R., & Vallerand, R. J. (2003). Why are you learning a second language? Motivational orientations and self-determination theory. *Language Learning, 53*(33), 33-63.

Nurlaili, N., Nurani, S., & Yohana, L. (2015). The effectiveness of teaching English vocabulary through Total Physical Response Storytelling (TPRS). *Deiksis, 7*(1), 63-68.

Nuttall, C. (1996). *Teaching reading skills in a foreign language.* Oxford, England: Oxford Heinemann English Language Teaching.

Oliver, J. (2012, Feb.). Investigating storytelling methods in a beginning-level college class. *The Language Educator*, 54-56.

Oliver, J. (2013). *From novice low to advanced high: Five decades of paradigmatic shifts in foreign language pedagogy* (Doctoral dissertation). Available from ProQuest Dissertations and Theses database. (UMI No. 3567871)

Omaggio-Hadley, A. (2000). *Teaching language in context: Proficiency-oriented instruction* (3rd ed.). Boston, MA: Heinle & Heinle.

Patrick, R. (2015a, Spring). Making sense of comprehensible input in the Latin classroom. *Teaching Classical Languages, 6*(1), 108-136.

Patrick, R. (2015b, Oct.). The growth of Latin programs with comprehensible input. *The International Journal of Foreign Language Teaching, 10*(2), 50-54.

Perna, M. (2007). *Effects of total physical response storytelling versus traditional, versus initial instruction with primary-, reinforced by secondary-perceptual strengths on the vocabulary- and grammar-Italian-language achievement scores, and the attitudes of ninth and tenth graders* (Doctoral dissertation). Available from ProQuest Dissertations and Theses database. (UMI No. 3279261)

Pippins, D. (2015). The sweetest sounds: Learning names and asking personalized questions. *The International Journal of Foreign Language Teaching, 10*(2).

Pippins, D., & Krashen, S. (2016, May). How well do TPRS students do on the AP? *The International Journal of Foreign Language Teaching, 2*(1), 25-30.

Polkinghorne, D. E. (1989). Phenomenological research methods. In R. Valle & S. Halling (Eds,). *Existential-phenomenological perspectives in psychology* (pp. 41-60). New York, NY: Plenum Press.

Pufahl, I., & Rhodes, N. (2011). Foreign language instruction in U.S. schools: Results of a national survey of elementary and secondary schools. *Foreign Language Annals, 44*(2), 258-288.

Rapstine, A. (2003). *Total Physical Response Storytelling (TPRS): A practical and theoretical overview and evaluation within the framework of the national standards* (Master's thesis). Available from ProQuest Dissertations and Theses database. (UMI No. 1416100)

Ray, B. (1990). *Look, I can talk!* (Spanish version). Los Gatos, CA: Sky Oaks.

Ray, B. (1992). *Look, I can talk! Teacher's guidebook.* Los Gatos, CA: Sky Oaks.

Ray, B. (1993). *Teaching grammar communicatively.* New York, NY: Gessler.

Ray, B. (1998). *Look, I can talk! Teacher's guidebook* (3rd ed.) and *Look, I can talk! Student book in German.* Los Gatos, CA: Sky Oaks.

Ray, B. (1999, 2007). *Pobre Ana.* Bakersfield, CA: Blaine Ray Workshops.

Ray, B. (2001). *Patricia va a California.* Bakersfield, CA: Blaine Ray Workshops.

Ray, B. (2005). Teaching grammar with TPRS. *The International Journal of Foreign Language Teaching, 1*(2), 30-37.

Ray, B. (2006). *Spanish mini-stories for Look I can talk!* Bakersfield, CA: Blaine Ray Workshops.

Ray, B. (2013, May). New developments in the evolution of TPRS. *The International Journal of Foreign Language Teaching, 8*(1), 41-42.

Ray, B. (2016, Aug. 4-6). Workshop handout and 3-day TPRS workshop held near Philadelphia (in Essington), PA. *TPR Storytelling®: Teaching Proficiency through Reading and Storytelling.* Eagle Mountain, UT: Blaine Ray Workshops.

Ray, V. (2015, Oct. 22-23). Handout for 2-day TPRS workshop held in Philadelphia, PA.

Ray, B., & Gross, S. (1998). *TPRS gestures and mini-situations.* Bakersfield, CA: Blaine Ray Workshops. Out of print.

Ray, B., & Seely, C. (1997). *Fluency through TPR Storytelling: Achieving real language acquisition in school* (1st ed.). Berkeley, CA: Command Performance.

Ray, B., & Seely, C. (1998, 2000, 2001). *Fluency through TPR Storytelling: Achieving real language acquisition in school* (2nd ed.). Berkeley, CA: Command Performance Language Institute.

Ray, B., & Seely, C. (2002, 2003). (3rd ed.). *Fluency through TPR Storytelling.* Berkeley, CA: Command Performance Language Institute.

Ray, B., & Seely, C. (2004, 2005). (4th ed.). *Fluency through TPR Storytelling.* Berkeley, CA: Command Performance Language Institute.

Ray, B., & Seely, C. (2008, 2009, 2010). *Fluency through TPR Storytelling: Achieving real language acquisition in school* (5th ed.). Eagle Mountain, UT: Blaine Ray Workshops and Berkeley, CA: Command Performance Language Institute.

Ray, B., & Seely, C. (2012). *Fluency through TPR storytelling: Achieving real language acquisition in school* (6th ed.). Eagle Mountain, UT: Blaine Ray Workshops and Berkeley, CA: Command Performance Language Institute.

Ray, B., & Seely, C. (2015). *Fluency through TPR storytelling: Achieving real language acquisition in school* (7th ed.). Eagle Mountain, UT: Blaine Ray Workshops.

Richards, L. (2011). *Handling qualitative data: A practical guide* (2nd ed.). Thousand Oaks, CA: Sage.

Richards, L., & Morse, J. (2013). *READMEFIRST: For a user's guide to qualitative methods* (3rd ed.). Los Angeles, CA: Sage.

Richards, J. C., & Rodgers, T. S. (1987). *Approaches and methods in language teaching* (1st ed.). New York, NY: Cambridge University Press.

Richards, J. C., & Rodgers, T. S. (2011). *Approaches and methods in language teaching: A description and analysis* (2nd ed.). New York, NY: Cambridge.

Riemen, D. (1986). The essential structure of caring interaction: Doing phenomenology. In P. Munhall & C. Oiler (Eds.), *Nursing research: A qualitative perspective*. Norwalk, CT: Appleton-Century-Crofts.

Roberts, B., & Thomas, S. (2014, Dec.). Center for Accelerated Language Acquisition (CALA) test scores: Another look at the value of implicit language instruction through comprehensible input. *The International Journal of Foreign Language Teaching, 10*(1), 2-12.

Roberts, B., & Thomas, S. (2015, Oct.). Center for Accelerated Language Acquisition (CALA) test scores: Another look at the value of implicit language instruction through comprehensible input. *The International Journal of Foreign Language Teaching, 10*(2), 24-30. Republished with corrections to the 2014 article.

Robinson, A., Shore, B., & Enerson, D. (2007). *Best practices in gifted education: An evidence-based guide.* Waco, TX: Prufrock.

Roof, L., & Kreutter, C. (2010). An interactive storytelling puzzle: Building a positive environment in a second language classroom. Networks, C., Compton-Lilly, and Porath, WI: University of Wisconsin Digital Collections Center, *12*(1), 1-10.

Rojas, V. (2001). A view from the foxhole: Elevating foreign language classrooms. In A. L. Costa (Ed.), *Developing minds: A resource book for teaching* (3rd ed.). Alexandria, VA: Association for Supervision and Curriculum Development.

Rowan, K. (2013). Ten ideas for personalizing the language classroom every day. *The International Journal of Foreign Language Teaching,* May, p. 46.

Safdarian, Z. (2013, July). The effect of stories on young learners' proficiency and motivation in foreign language learning (Master's thesis, 2012). *The International Journal of English and Education, 2*(3), 200-248.

Sanders, J. Oswald. (2007). *Spiritual leadership.* Chicago, IL: Moody Publishers.

Savignon, S. (1998). *Communicative competence: Theory and classroom practice.* New York, NY: McGraw-Hill.

Schmitt, C., & Woodford, P. (1999, 2008). *¡Buen viaje!* New York, NY: McGraw Hill.

Schwabe, F., McElvany, N., & Trendtle, M. (2015, Jan. 5). The school age gender gap in reading achievement: Examining the influences of item format and intrinsic reading motivation. *Reading Research Quarterly, 50*(2), 219-232.

Schulz, R. (1999). Foreign language instruction and curriculum. *Education Digest, 64,* 29-38.

Seely, C., & Romijn, E. (2006). *TPR is more than commands--at all levels* (3rd ed.). Berkeley, CA. Command Performance Language Institute.

Senn, N. (2012). Effective approaches to motivate and engage reluctant boys in literacy. *Reading Teacher, 66*(3), 211-220.

Sievek, M. D. (2009). *Una evolución de TPRS* (An evolution of TPRS, Master's thesis). Salamanca, Spain: Universidad de Salamanca.

Slavic, B. (2007). *TPRS in a year!* (3rd ed.). Littleton, CO: www.benslavic.com

Slavic, B. (2008). *PQA in a wink! How to succeed with TPRS by personalizing the classroom* (3rd ed.). Littleton, CO. Available from www.benslavic.com

Slavic, B. (2014). *Stepping stones to stories! Ben's system of starting the year with comprehensible input* (2nd ed.). Littleton, CO: www.benslavic.com

Slavic, B. (2015). *The big CI book: A step by step survival guide for foreign language teachers* (1st ed.). Littleton, CO. Available from www.benslavic.com

Sousa, D. (2017). *How the brain learns* (5th ed.). Thousand Oaks, CA: Sage, Corwin.

Spangler, D. (2009). *Effects of two foreign language methodologies, communicative language teaching, and teaching proficiency through reading and storytelling, on beginning-level students' achievement, fluency, and anxiety* (Doctoral dissertation). Available from ProQuest Dissertations and Theses database. (UMI No. 3396360)

Susan, I. (2013). The use of Teaching Proficiency through Reading and Storytelling (TPRS) to improve students' listening comprehension. *Journal of English and Education, 1*(1), 104-113.

Swain, M. (1985). Communicative competence: Some roles of comprehensible input and comprehensible output in its development. In S. Gass & C. Madden, (Eds.), *Input in second language acquisition* (pp. 235-253). Rowley, MA: Newbury House.

Swain, M. (2005a). The output hypothesis: Theory and research. In Hinkel, E. (Ed.), *Handbook of research in second language teaching and learning*. Mahwah, NJ: Lawrence Erlbaum Associates.

Swain, M. (2005b). Languaging, agency, and collaboration in advanced second language learning. In H. Byrnes, (Ed.), *Advanced language learning: The contributions of Halliday and Vygotsky*. London, UK: Continuum.

Swender, E. (2003). Oral proficiency testing in the real world: Answers to frequently asked questions. *Foreign Language Annals, 36*(4), 520-526.

Tate, M. L. (2016). *Worksheets don't grow dendrites: 20 instructional strategies that engage the brain* (3nd ed.). Thousand Oaks, CA: Corwin, Sage.

Taulbee, A. (2008). *Twenty TPRS lessons for the Spanish I classroom* (Master's thesis). Available from ProQuest Dissertations and Theses database. (UMI No. 1460842)

Tatum-Johns, D. (2010). Teaching proficiency through reading and storytelling: Workshop handout for TPRS beginners. National TPRS Conference.

Terrell, T. D. (1977). A natural approach to second language acquisition and learning. *The Modern Language Journal, 61*, 325-336.

Truscott, J. (1996). The case against grammar correction in L2 writing classes. *Language Learning, 46*(2), 327-369.

Truscott, J. (1999). What's wrong with oral grammar correction? *The Canadian Modern Language Review, 55*(4), 437-456.

Truscott, J. (2007). The effect of error correction on the learner's ability to write accurately. *Journal of Second Language Writing, 16*, 255-272.

van Manen, M. (1990). *Researching lived experience: Human science for an active sensitive pedagogy.* Albany, NY: State University of New York Press.

VanPatten, B. (1996). *Input processing and grammar instruction.* Norwood, NJ: Ablex.

VanPatten, B. (2002). Processing instruction: An update. *Language Learning, 52*(2), 755-803.

VanPatten, B. (2004). (Ed.). *Processing instruction: Theory, research, and commentary.* Mahwah, NJ: Erlbaum.

VanPatten, B. (2014, Oct.-Nov.). Creating comprehensible input and output. *The Language Educator,* 24-26.

VanPatten, B. (2015). Film and language acquisition. *Hispania, 98*(3), 391-393.

VanPatten, B. (2016). Why explicit knowledge cannot become implicit knowledge. *Foreign Language Annals.* doi: 10.1111/flan.12226.

VanPatten, B. (in preparation, 2017). *While we're on the topic: Principles for contemporary language teaching.* Accepted for publication by the American Council on the Teaching of Foreign Languages. Alexandria, VA: ACTFL.

Cited with written permission from the author obtained Dec. 24, 2016.

VanPatten, B., & Williams, J. (2015). (Eds.). *Theories in second language acquisition* (2nd ed.). New York, NY: Routledge.

Varguez, K. C. (2009, Summer). Traditional and TPR Storytelling instruction in the beginning high school classroom. *The International Journal of Foreign Language Teaching, 5*(1), 2-11.

Vogt, W. P., Gardner, D. C., & Haeffele, L. M. (2012). *When to use what research design*. New York, NY: The Guilford Press.

Waltz, T. (2011). *Anna Méi Bànfǎ!* A short novel in simple Chinese based on the novel *Pobre Ana* by Blaine Ray. Albany, NY: Albany Language Learning.

Waltz, T. (2013). *The three pandas*. A PandaRiffic™ book for early Chinese-as-a-foreign language (CFL) readers, vol. 1 (Chinese ed.). Albany, NY: Squid for Brains.

Waltz, T. T. (2014). *Zhongwen Bu Máfán! Chinese through comprehensible input for Western students*. Albany, NY: Squid for Brains Educational Publishing.

Waltz, T. T. (2015). *TPRS with Chinese characteristics: Making students fluent and literate through comprehensible input*. Introduction to TPRS theory by Stephen Krashen. Albany, NY: Squid for Brains Educational Publishing.

Watson, B. J. (2008). *Communicative language instructional approach for teaching foreign language: A comparative study* (unpublished Master's thesis). Lisle, IL: Benedictine University.

Watson, B. (2009, Summer). A comparison of TPRS and traditional foreign language instruction at the high school level. *The International Journal of Foreign Language Teaching, 5*(1), 21-24.

Webster, M. (2003). *Research for developing an in-service for world language curriculum within the tenets of second language acquisition and total physical response storytelling* (unpublished Master's thesis). Holland, MI: Grand Valley State University.

Welch, B. (2014). *Más allá del TPRS: Lecciones para la clase de literatura* (Master's thesis). Available from ProQuest Dissertations and Theses database. (UMI No. 1561887)

Wenck, T. M. (2010). *Using language acquisition strategies in the secondary German classroom* (Master's thesis). Bethlehem, PA: Moravian College.

Whaley, M. (2009). Retirement. *Letter: Newsletter of the American Council of Teachers of Russian, division of American Councils for International Education, 35*(3), 1-4.

Whitehead, J. M. (2006). Starting school: Why girls are already ahead of boys. *Teacher Development, 10*(2), 249-270.

Wong, W., & VanPatten, B. (2003). The evidence is IN: Drills are OUT. *Foreign Language Annals, 36*(3), 132-149.

Wooldridge, J. (2016). About Señor Wooly. DVDs. Skokie, IL: www.senorwooly.com.

Yalden, J. (1983). *The communicative syllabus: Evolution, design, and implementation.* Oxford, UK: Pergamon.

Zadina, J. N. (2014). *Multiple pathways to the student brain: Energizing and enhancing instruction.* San Francisco, CA: Jossey-Bass.

LIST OF TABLES

Table 4.A.1. Common Lived TPRS Teacher Experiences, part 1 203

Table 4.A.2. Common Lived TPRS Teacher Experiences, part 2 206

Table 4.B.1. Obstacles, part 1 216

Table 4.B.2. Obstacles, part 2 217

Table 4.B.3. Obstacles, part 3 217

Table 4.B.4. Obstacles, part 4 218

Table 4.B.5. Obstacles, part 5 221

Table 4.AB.1. Comparing Groups A and B, part 1. 224

Table 4.AB.2. Comparing Groups A and B, part 2. 225

Table 4.AB.3. Comparing Groups A and B, part 3. 225

LIST OF APPENDICES

APPENDIX A – Interview Questions for Group A - Current TPRS Teachers

APPENDIX B – Interview Questions for Group B - Rejected Using the Method

APPENDIX C – Interview Questions for Group C - No Experience with TPRS

APPENDIX A – Interview Questions for Group A -- Current TPRS Teachers

What languages do you teach, what levels, and how many years have you been teaching?

How did you first hear about the TPRS method? How long have you been using TPRS?

Tell me about your first workshop experience. Have you been to others? NTPRS?

What differences did you experience in your teaching before and after using TPRS?

Have you encountered difficulties, challenges, or resistance from students, colleagues, parents, or administrators when using TPRS? What was the result?

Do you, or why do you believe that your students become more fluent through TPRS?

What evidence do you have of improved student achievement?
What formative and summative assessments do you use?

Could you give an example of a student success story?

Were you ever reluctant to try out the method? If so, why? Why do you use TPRS?

Could you relate a personal, specific, rewarding experience you had using TPRS?

Describe an ideal TPRS class. What does the teacher do and what do the students do?

Is mastery learning part of TPRS? If so, how? How do you check for mastery?

What language-learning theory, or theories inform the TPRS method?

In your opinion, is there a difference between learning and acquisition?

How does TPRS include what is known about brain research?
How does the brain acquire language?

In what ways does TPRS address multi-sensory learning and long-term memory?

Are gestures and movement part of the method? If so, how?

What obstacles or problems have you encountered using TPRS? What was the result?

Was it difficult to learn TPRS? What are the challenging aspects?

What else can you tell me about your experiences with TPRS? Any closing remarks?

APPENDIX B – Interview Questions for Group B -- Rejected Using the Method

What languages do you teach, what levels, and how many years have you been teaching?

What did your TPRS teacher do that helped you learn during the workshop?

What were the classroom procedures? How was the class conducted?

What did the teacher do to help students, teachers-in-training, understand the story?

How did the teacher incorporate the repetition of vocabulary words?

What types of questions did the teacher ask? How was the questioning done?

How did the teacher assess whether students understood the story, during and after class?

What did the teacher do that helped you learn the most?

What do you think is helpful (or not) about using stories to learn another language?

Was learning grammar part of the lesson? If so, how was it included?

How did the teacher try to make the class interesting or enjoyable for students?

How is the TPRS method different from other methods?

Why did you choose not to continue using TPRS in your classroom teaching?

What changes would you recommend for the TPRS method?

What techniques, strategies, or activities are missing from the method?

How would you describe an ideal TPRS class? What would it look like?
In a TPRS class, what does the teacher do? What do the students do?

What language-learning theory, or other theories inform the TPRS method?

Is mastery learning part of TPRS? If so, how? Tell me what TPRS is, and is not.

Did you try out the method? How did it go? Tell me your TPRS story. What happened?

How should the method be changed? Improved? Why don't you use it all the time?

What did you not get a chance to tell me? Anything to add? Any closing comments?

APPENDIX C – Interview Questions for Group C -- No Experience with TPRS

What languages do you teach, what levels, and how many years have you been teaching?

Have you ever been to a Blaine Ray workshop or been trained in TPRS?

Could you relate a personal, specific, rewarding experience you've had in teaching?

What are your goals for student learning? Which are the most important?

What approaches, methods, and techniques do you use in your teaching?

Which techniques are the most effective for promoting student learning, in your opinion?

What techniques and classroom activities do you perceive as most effective in helping students to comprehend, speak, and write well in the target language?

Which techniques and activities best promote listening and reading?

What do you regard as the most important developments in modern world language teaching? Has language teaching improved over the years? Is it effective?

What are your goals for student learning? Which are the most important?
What does a typical day, or week, look like in your classroom?

What language-learning theory, or theories inform your teaching approach?

How do you check for mastery? Describe an ideal modern language class.

Does, or how does brain research inform your teaching?

Do you, or how do you incorporate gestures and movement into your teaching?

Do you, or how do you teach grammar? What role does grammar have in your class?

In your opinion, is there a difference between learning and acquiring a language?

Do you consider your approach to language teaching communicative? If so, how?

What does it mean to have an acquisition-rich classroom?

What recommendations or advice would you give a new teacher?

Any closing remarks? Comments? What did you want to say that I didn't ask you?

Made in the USA
Coppell, TX
15 July 2020

30600020R20175